THE
GAA
AN ORAL HISTORY

JOHN SCALLY

MAINSTREAM
PUBLISHING

EDINBURGH AND LONDON

First published in Great Britain in 2009 by
MAINSTREAM PUBLISHING COMPANY
(EDINBURGH) LTD
7 Albany Street
Edinburgh EH1 3UG

ISBN 9781845964436

A catalogue record for this book is available
from the British Library

Typeset in Caslon and Gill Sans

Printed in Great Britain by
Clays Ltd, St Ives plc

To the GAA's most prized assets:
the keepers of the flame

ACKNOWLEDGEMENTS

AT TIMES LIKE THIS, TALKING ABOUT A LABOUR OF LOVE IS almost expected. In my experience, writing a book creates an awful lot of labour but very little love. A writer friend of James Joyce was dying after a traffic accident and someone insensitively asked him what dying was like, and the writer with his final breath said, 'Oh Seánie it's terrible, but at least it's not nearly as bad as writing a book.'

There are, though, paybacks, and one of the great paybacks for me has come in the opportunity to meet many of the greats of both football and hurling. This book has been 20 years in the making and includes interviews with many who have passed on to their eternal reward, such as Mick Dunne, Jack Lynch, Seán Purcell, Enda Colleran, Eddie Boyle, Dermot O'Brien, John B. Keane, Tim Kennelly, John Wilson, Jimmy Murray and Eamonn Coleman. While this book was being written, I was greatly saddened by the deaths of the legendary Frank Stockwell and Billy Rackard.

To someone like me, whose sporting experience is defined by failure and whose only exposure to a Marathon has been to eat one, I could never have constructed a work like this without the expert guidance of Jimmy Barry-Murphy, Mick Bermingham, Seán Boylan, Nickey

Brennan, Seamus Bonner, Alan Brogan, Padraig Brogan, Francie Brolly, Mick Byrne, D.J. Carey, Martin Carney, Tom Carr, Brian Carthy, John Connolly, Matt Connor, Brian Corcoran, Anthony Daly, Declan Darcy, Jimmy Deenihan, Joe Dunphy, Dermot Earley, Paul Earley, Nicky English, Ciaran Fitzgerald, Jim Fives, Dermot Flanagan, Jimmy Flynn, Mick Galwey, Ciara Gaynor, Dr Angela Gleason, Pat Hartigan, Seamus Heaney, Nudie Hughes, Babs Keating, Eddie Keher, Aoife Kelly, Brendan Kennelly, Enda Kenny, T.J. Kilgallon, Noel Lane, Pat Lindsay, Brian Lohan, Ger Loughnane, Brendan Lynch, Máirín McAleenan, Joanne McDonagh, Joe McDonagh, Packy McGarty, Eugene McGee, Willie McGee, Peter McGinnity, Jim McKeever, John McKnight, Seánie McMahon, Tony McManus, Tom McNicholas, Enda McNulty, Kevin McStay, Jimmy Magee, Tim Maher, Pat Mangan, John Maughan, Barnes Murphy, Jamesie O'Connor, Gay O'Driscoll, Mick O'Dwyer, John O'Mahony, Mícheál Ó Muircheartaigh, Colm O'Rourke, Eddie O'Sullivan, Paddy Prendergast, Martin Quigley, Billy Quinn, Paddy Quirke, Sue Ramsbottom, Matt Ruth, Jimmy Smyth, Pat Spillane and Kevin Walsh.

As always, my writing and life are enriched by the wit and wisdom of Peter Woods. Thanks also to Liam O'Brien for encouraging my interest in Mayo football.

My gratitude to James Brennan, Iggy Clarke, Ozzie Dunne, Damien Eagers, John Murray, Seán Duggan, Ann Colleran, Dónal McAnallen, Kevin O'Neill, Mary O'Neill, Orla O'Neill, John Purcell, Teresa Scally, Niall Sloane and Brian Talty for help with photos.

Thanks to the wonderfully hospitable Kathryn Brennan of Castle Bookshop in Castlebar for her ongoing love affair with books.

Thanks to my good friend John Tiernan for his supply of amusing GAA stories.

My thanks in particular to the organiser of the Ballintubber GOAL walk, John Boyle, for his wonderful photos, and to the great and generous Liam Horan for his practical assistance.

Thanks to Joe Finnegan, Eithne Kelly, John Lynch, Mike Mulvihill and Joao Soares at Shannonside-Northern Sound for their practical support.

Thanks to Bill Campbell, Graeme Blaikie, Karyn Millar and all at Mainstream for their help.

Special thanks to the legendary Jack O'Shea for honouring me by writing the foreword.

CONTENTS

FOREWORD

NOTHING IS EVER LOST OR FORGOTTEN. IT IS IMPORTANT THAT the great players and personalities and the classic victories and thrilling contests of the last 125 years of the GAA be stored in the popular imagination.

Giants of the games like Mick O'Dwyer, Christy Ring, John Joe O'Reilly, D.J. Carey, Peter Canavan, Nicky English and the late, great Frank Stockwell, who symbolise all that is great in our games, have captivated the nation with their sublime skills and style and have made a magnificent contribution to Irish life. The GAA can never repay the debt it owes to legends such as these, as they have inspired subsequent generations to carry the torch that still burns so brightly. As a parent myself, I have witnessed the power of these heroes to inspire youngsters.

When I wore the Kerry jersey for so many years, I saw at first hand that the GAA is about more than sport: it is about identity and pride in one's place, too. I also discovered that it is bigger than just the players on the pitch; it feeds into an evolving tradition that belongs to the greats of the past, like the peerless Mick O'Connell, and to the heroes of tomorrow.

THE GAA

This book is a well-earned tribute to outstanding players of our national games down the generations. Our challenge now is to create even better memories over the next 125 years.

Happy reading!

Jack O'Shea
August 2009

THE THROW-IN

A KERRY COUNTY COUNCILLOR IS ATTENDING A JUNKET –
a fact-finding mission – in New York. He checks in at the team
hotel, where he is greeted at reception by a young African American
woman. When she asks for his name, his very strong Kerry accent
and her Bronx accent cause a cultural clash and a major 'lost in
translation' moment. He says 'Geraghty'. The young woman is
thrown by his accent and repeatedly, to the councillor's increasing
frustration, asks him to say it again. Even when he spells out G-
E-R-A-G-H-T-Y, she is none the wiser. Finally the man gets a
brainwave and says with a flourish, believing he has found the key
to making her understand: 'Geraghty – as in Graham!'

A prominent official of the Connacht Council is in Los Angeles,
and a major catastrophe ensues when he tries to check in to his hotel
and discovers that his booking details are wrong. When it looks like
he is not going to be checked in to the hotel, his exasperated wife digs
him in the ribs and whispers 'Tell them you're from the Connacht
Council!'

Two little parables that illustrate in a humorous way both the
pervasiveness and the power of the Gaelic Athletic Association

15

THE GAA

(GAA) in Irish life and the way it has indelibly inhabited our thinking process over the last 125 years.

Love it, hate it or try to be indifferent to it, Gaelic games subtly shape Irish social history and everyday life. They permeate the media, set the mood of Monday's post-match workplace and dominate pub talk. For many, life and death still come second to major GAA events. Almost every young boy, and an ever-increasing number of girls, dreams of playing in Croke Park.

Gaelic games offer us a group identity, a spiritual home to belong to, a sacred space where we can be among our people and therefore be ourselves. There is something innocent, something mysterious about Gaelic games' hold on our identity that cannot be analysed. This is its power. To shamelessly borrow from Don McLean, something touches us deep inside. We all crave it: the sense of connection, the thought that we can be better than we are, even if better only through others, our 15 representatives on the field. The surging runs of Michael Donnellan or D.J. Carey take us to a higher power, altered for a moment, alive in another's body and mind. That's the reason we need our own heroes: so that we, too, can be elevated.

The past isn't dead and buried – it isn't even dead. There is a need, to quote John McGahern, to 'rescue the past from forgetfulness'. Institutional memory is a prized asset in all walks of life today. Memory rescues experience from total disappearance. The lamp of memory holds traces of everything that has ever happened to us. Nothing is ever lost or forgotten. It is important that the great players and personalities and the classic victories and thrilling contests of the last century and a quarter of the GAA be stored in the popular imagination.

For one hundred and twenty-five years, the GAA has been the one fixed point in a fast-changing age. Those years have not been without their troubles, but even when the storm clouds have gathered, the people's organisation has not withered before their blast; and a greener, better, stronger movement lay in the sunshine when the tempest had passed.

Our economic system values measurable outcomes, but what is deepest about us transcends what can be said and outstrips what can be analysed. It is not given to us to peer into the mysteries of the future, but we can safely predict that in the coming 125 years Gaelic games will continue to reach into something profound within us. We may not always be sure what this elusive quality is, except that there are moments when we know that there is more to life – and to us – than the grim and grasping existence of seeking and striving and succeeding. There are moments of wonder, hope and grace that give us hints of ecstasy and lift us out of ourselves. They are, in Yeats's phrase, the soul's 'monuments of its own magnificence'. These moments take us to the heart of the deep mystery of being a person, the subterranean stirrings of the spirit, the rapid rhythms of the human heart. They have to do with remembering who we are, enlarging our perspective, seeing ourselves whole.

This book does not purport to be a definitive history of the GAA. I would need ten volumes, not one, to even attempt to write such a work. Rather, this is a mosaic of moments and memories over the last 125 years that hints at the texture and some of the humour of the bigger story – the story of who we are as a people in the games we love. As it is an oral history, the story is told via a series of snapshots through the memories and reflections of some of the key players and managers who made the magic happen.

This volume stretches back to Celtic times, when Gaelic games in their embryonic form developed. We begin in earnest by documenting the complex social, economic, political and cultural forces that led to the formation of the GAA. I wanted the four corners of Ireland to be fully represented, as the GAA is a truly national association. Accordingly, the football chapters are written on provincial rather than narrowly chronological lines in the interests of inclusivity. The hurling chapters pay homage to great games and peerless players. On the journey, we observe the many ways in which the GAA mirrors, and in some respects leads and defines, Irish society, and we conclude by considering some of the most pressing issues facing the Association. Our starting point is to set the scene through a game that captures the essence of the GAA, an epic encounter of guts, glory and grace.

John Scally
August 2009

THE FAMINE DAYS ARE OVER

1

'IT WAS ONE OF THE DAYS OF OUR LIVES. YOU COULD CUT THE atmosphere with a knife.'

Babs Keating glows as if he is transmitting electricity while he recalls the 1987 Munster final replay, when his Tipperary team defeated Cork in one of the most memorable matches between the two old rivals.

Michael Lowry has been one of the most controversial figures in recent Irish political life, but he was to play a significant role in the revival of Tipperary's hurling fortunes in 1986. Before Babs took over as manager of Tipperary, the county had been in the doldrums for 15 years. The call to serve would come from an unexpected quarter. Lowry's offer to Babs would change hurling history.

'When Michael became county chairman, he asked to meet me. We met in a private house, the late Seamus Maher's home, because I wanted to meet in secret, knowing the stories that would go around. To be fair to him, he could give me the power to pick my own selectors. I'll always remember he said, "You have the job, but we have no money." The county board was broke after hosting the Centenary All-Ireland in '84, and the economic situation was very bleak. I got the idea to start the Supporters Club. Then I decided we would raffle a racehorse, and Christy Roche bought an ideal horse for us. I got everyone I ever knew to buy a ticket, like Charlie Haughey and Jack Lynch. I remember being at home one morning and getting a call from Niall Quinn, when he was at Arsenal. He told me he had sold seven tickets for me and listed a who's who of Arsenal greats who had bought one.

'Having secured our finances, I was ready to turn fully to hurling matters. My back-up team [of selectors] was Donie Nealon and Theo English. They had played for the county for about 12 years in our glory days, and I don't think Cork ever beat them. They couldn't understand why there was such fear of Cork, and they transferred that attitude. Our captain, Richie Stakelum, would always say that Tipperary had such fear of Cork at that stage.

'People talk about the great team Tipperary had in the '84 Munster final, but those players brought Tipp into Division Two. We played our first league game away against Antrim and won it fairly impressively. The great thing that happened to us was that in our second league match we played Laois, who were coached by Jimmy Doyle, and they beat us by ten points in Thurles. We got rid of six or seven players and went in a different direction. If that defeat had come later in the campaign, it would have been much harder to regroup. As with everything in life, you need a bit of luck. We got it with that game in Laois.

'One thing I did every January was to take out the two selectors and their wives for a meal and tell them to pick the team they would play in the All-Ireland that year. The three of us had thirteen identical choices that night in '87, so we only had to find two players.

'We had huge confidence going into the Munster final, even though Cork were 3–1 on. We had come from nowhere in Division Two and had twelve new personnel. We had money behind us. When we travelled away for big matches, we stayed in five-star hotels. I will never forget the first game we played against Cork. Both of us got to the ground at the same time. Our bus was in the Tipperary colours. The Cork players were in their jeans and jumpers. Our lads looked like film stars in their blazers. Richie Stakelum said it was worth five points to us.'

Nicky English won six All-Stars in seven years and was hurler of the year in 1989. He is ideally placed to give an insider's guide to that game.

'When I came on the scene, Tipperary changed managers almost every year because we weren't winning Munster championships. It is a bit like what has been happening in Galway in the last decade: in a county where you have a lot of hurlers there is a massive turnover of players with each new manager, and that means there is little or no continuity, and a lot of good players are thrown out in the wash before they have the chance to develop. We came close in a high-scoring Munster final that we should have won in 1984, but Seánie O'Leary scored a late goal to win for Cork.

'Things changed when Babs came on board. He did things differently. He raised a lot of money and arranged things in what was a radically different way back then, though county players take it for granted today. He got us blazers and we stayed in hotels before matches. Things were tight economically in the 1980s. There was no money around. The Tipperary County Board were putting all their money into upgrading Semple Stadium. All their financial focus was on infrastructure, not on looking after players. Up to then, we would drive through the traffic on the day and be stuck in a jam. After Babs, anything we needed in terms of gear or hurleys was got for us. Before that, you got your own hurleys and handed in receipts, and often there was a long delay before you got your money back. Sometimes you wouldn't get your money back at all. It is hard to quantify how much all of this helped us on the field of play, but it did make an impact. Babs blazed the trail, and every football and hurling team followed to a greater or lesser extent. He brought a whole new attitude and confidence. Babs believed, and we believed because of him.

'Winning the 1987 Munster final was my greatest day in hurling. The fact that we beat Cork after extra time in a replay added to it. Tipperary hadn't won a Munster final since 1971, so that's why Richie Stakelum's comment that the "famine days are over" struck such a chord. The emotion our victory unleashed was unreal. Nothing has ever matched that feeling.'

Hurling is the ultimate virtual reality because it can take you anywhere you want to go. The heart of all sport is the quality of experience it provides. Contrary to real life, sport offers us a state of being so rewarding that one does it for no other reason than to be a part of it. Such feelings are among the most intense, most memorable experiences one can get in this life. Nothing captures the unique magic and tribalism of the GAA more vividly than that Munster final replay in 1987. To see it at first hand is to know that the GAA is about more than sport: it is also about identity and pride in one's place. Something bigger than just the players on the pitch, it feeds into an evolving tradition that belongs to the greats of the past and to the heroes of tomorrow.

A special day in a special history.

2

IN THE SHADOW OF CÚCHULAINN

NO NEW NATIONAL MOVEMENT DEVELOPS IN A VACUUM.
Invariably, it is a response to a complex web of economic, social,
political and cultural forces. The GAA is no exception. To understand
the origins of the Association, we must reach further back into time
and try to weave together the threads of the rich, though often dark,
tapestry of Irish history.

The Ireland of the 1840s was a vision of hell; the years of a tragedy
beyond belief, when over a million people on this tiny island died in
the Great Famine. Nothing prepared people for it. Nothing could
prepare anyone for the sight and smell of death on a massive scale
– bundles of corpses where once there had been life.

The mid-1840s saw the plagues of Ireland – hunger, disease and
government neglect – compound each other like a battleground of
contending dooms. Fragile lifelines of aid reached only a minority of
the population. In the first year, there were barely enough potatoes
for poor families; in the next, only a trickle. Then nothing. Potato
stalks withered and died. There was nothing for seed. Many people
had nothing to live on and nothing to live for.

THE GAA

The death toll was seemingly unending in many districts. Everything had to be rationed. It would have taken too much land to bury the corpses individually, so their relatives normally buried them in a mass grave. There were so many people dying it was impossible to make coffins for them all, or even have a coffin for each family. Timber was very scarce. Sometimes villagers decided to build one proper coffin with a sliding bottom. They solemnly put the corpses into the coffin, carried them up to the grave and slid back the bottom of the coffin so that the body tumbled into the grave. The coffin was then brought back to the village and passed on to the family of the next casualty.

Fear was the only real sign of life as people died slowly in agony. To the embattled, emotionally bankrupt and hopelessly disorganised, life's ordinary joys and sorrows were an irrelevance. The chances of survival were slim. For many, death was a welcome escape from pain and heartache. The afterlife was the only dream they could still cherish. For the strong, life was a victory over death. Where possible, the corpses were buried under hawthorn trees, because of their alleged special favour in the eyes of God. These trees were long palls in a parched place. They sang a lament to the angel of death. The memories were too sad ever to be healed.

Ireland was a country of extremes, from the beginning to the end. It seemed simultaneously connected to the Garden of Eden in the landlords' palaces and to some foretaste of doomsday destruction where the peasants lived to die. Nowhere were the gardens more luxuriant or a people more miserable. The tragedy was a moral test, which those with power failed.

Deep in their psychic memory, the famine was still a painful experience for Irish people right through the nineteenth century and beyond. They used the words 'I'm famished' whenever they were cold or hungry. The frequent usage of these words was just one symptom of the lasting effect of the famine. Often Irish people buried thoughts of it deep in their subconscious. The story of the famine years was so horrific that they just wanted to erase it from their memory. There was great shame attached to failing to feed one's family. Parents always blamed themselves for their children's deaths. Successive generations inherited their shame. Even in the twentieth century, some people in rural Ireland would not travel anywhere without taking a piece of bread in their pocket because the fear of hunger was so strong.

The term 'Great Famine' is itself a misnomer. It is more accurate to say there was a 'Great Starvation'. Although the people's suffering was exacerbated by the natural disaster that was the potato crop failure, in fact there was plenty of food produced in Ireland in those years – and famines should not occur when there are large quantities of food in a country. That food was exported while Irish people starved in the country's greatest human tragedy is an enduring monument to inhumanity, ineffectiveness and indifference.

There were two main options open to these people: emigration if they could afford it or the workhouse. In many respects, people thought they were safer in their own place. There was so much disease in those coffin ships that their chances of surviving the long journey in such a weak state were remote. People by and large did not trust the sea. They had all heard the stories of the American sailing ship *Stephen Whitney*: on a foggy night in 1847, the ship sailing on a voyage from America to Liverpool was wrecked off the Irish coast on Western Calf Island. Within days, 94 bodies were washed up on the beaches. Some people were desperate enough to try anything, but the majority preferred to meet their maker on their own land rather than risk death on the Atlantic Ocean.

Nobody knows how many people went on the coffin ships, but one reliable statistic comes from a group who went to Canada, where many died of typhoid fever in a place called Grosse Isle, just outside Quebec City. Twelve thousand Irish people were buried in mass graves in Canada. They set out to make their mark in the world, but the only mark they made was in a grave – a people with no name. It was their final indignity.

The workhouses had a huge stigma attached to them. Like the infamous coffin ships, there was so much disease in the workhouses that to sign into them was often to sign one's death warrant. Generally, the workhouses postponed death for a short while but no more. In the workhouses and soup kitchens, families were separated from each other. All the men were housed in one section, the women in another. There were separate places for babies and young girls and boys. Once a family went in, they might never see each other again. There were strict rules about communication with another section. If one person broke the rules, the whole family might be thrown out. In many ways, the workhouse was worse than jail. At least in jail you could get news from your family. It has often been claimed these places should have been called deathhouses.

POWER TO ALL OUR FRIENDS

Ireland had been governed from Westminster since the Act of Union in 1800. In the House of Commons, there were about a hundred members who represented Irish constituencies. The Viceregal Lodge in Phoenix Park was home to the Queen's representatives. The Chief Secretary and his staff administered the daily routine of government from Dublin Castle.

One of the main problems faced by administrators in Ireland in the nineteenth century was reconciling the democratic principle with the continuation of Protestant Ascendancy privilege. Local government was in the hands of the grand juries, which were non-elected bodies dominated by the largest landowners in the country. The British army had an important and visible presence throughout the country. The Royal Irish Constabulary was an armed body, though the Dublin Metropolitan Police was not.

The close connection between Britain and Ireland made it natural to judge by British standards, and in comparison with Britain, Ireland was still a poor country. In the conventional portrait, the most familiar figures are the greedy and tyrannical landlords squeezing every last penny of rent out of hungry peasants to finance their lives of debauchery. While there were a number of such landlords, they were not all like that. The evil was not all on one side. Southern Protestants were slow to forget the stories they had been told of the fanatical fury waged against Protestants during the 1798 Wexford Rising and the social intimidation of Protestants that had persisted for years afterwards. Until 1869, the Church of Ireland was the State Church. Its disestablishment under an Act of Parliament made a major dent in the exclusiveness of Protestant Ascendancy.

The second half of the nineteenth century saw the gradual extension of voting rights in both Britain and Ireland. For the first time, the demand for votes for women was being made with conviction. In the Irish context, an important milestone was the introduction of the secret ballot after 1872, since it relieved voters from pressure to vote according to their landlords' dictates.

The education system was imperialist rather than Irish, with the prescribed reading books filled with Victorian values and designed to inculcate British loyalties. However, there were a number of counterbalancing forces at work, particularly the press. By 1860, national papers were available cheaply, following the repeal of heavy taxes on the newspapers. *The Nation*, founded by Thomas Davis, carried on its national tradition in the 1860s. Songs also formed an important agent of political evangelisation – notably 'God Save Ireland', which became virtually a national anthem in 1867.

The Irish national pulse was strengthening perceptibly. The demand for self-government was being made with more vigour. Political structures were not as secure as they had been. The old Establishment was being challenged in various ways. In the countryside, the stirrings could be seen among the tenant farmers.

Throughout rural Ireland, agrarian unrest accelerated with increasing demands for tenant right reforms. Landlords were seen as a privileged minority, alienated from the majority of their tenants by differences in both religion and politics. Tenants normally held their holdings from year to year, thus having no security. In times of bad harvests, many could not afford to pay the rent. A high number of landlords were absentees living outside the country and leaving the management of their estates to agents. The great disaster of the famine was followed by mass evictions of tenants. The need for reform of the system became more obvious in the years that followed.

In 1870, a formal demand for Home Rule began when Isaac Butt, a lawyer and Member of Parliament, founded an association to campaign for a separate Irish parliament. However, the movement really only began in earnest when Butt was replaced as leader by Charles Stewart Parnell, a charismatic figure whose tactics brought increasing success to nationalist members of the House of Commons and eventually succeeded in making the 'Irish question' one of the central issues in British politics.

THE BARREL OF A GUN?

For a long time, people who talked about the origins of the Irish state did so in very simple terms. Nationhood was to be won through a barrel of a gun in a David and Goliath struggle. From this perspective, there was only one problem in Ireland – the British presence. The way to get rid of this presence was through violence. The 1919–21 War of Independence was the final episode in a whole series of attempts, including Grattan's volunteers in 1782, the bold Robert Emmet ('the darling of Eireann') in 1803, the Young Ireland rising in 1848, the militant revolution of the Fenians in 1867 and the 1916 Easter Rising (in Yeats's phrase, 'A terrible beauty is born').

However, as Brian Farrell incisively demonstrates in his groundbreaking work *The Irish Parliamentary Tradition* (1977), the reality is much more complex than the illusion. As demonstrated by the experience of many countries established in the wake of the collapse of the great colonial empires after the Second World War, to start a nation state from scratch is very difficult. A number of things need to be in place before nationhood can be sustained, such as literacy, a civil service, roads, schools and so on. Farrell identifies three essential prerequisites for nationhood: religious freedom, ownership of wealth and participation in the electoral process. Ireland had achieved these conditions in advance of the War of Independence.

Under the Penal Laws, Irish Catholics were denied religious freedom because of the prevalent belief at the time throughout Europe that in Church–State relations you proved your loyalty to the king by being part of the established religion. In 1829, following Daniel O'Connell's triumph in a by-election in Clare, Catholic Emancipation was won.

The Great Reform Bill of 1832 was a very minor bill in itself. It increased the number of people who could vote to 2.5 per cent of the adult male population, but its importance was more for what it promised in the future than what it delivered in the present. Although it was to take almost a hundred years for women to get the vote, the Act began a process that eventually brought universal adult suffrage. The 1918 British Representation of the People Act was a crucial milestone along the way, as it removed the property qualification on the right to vote.

As John B. Keane's wonderfully evocative play *The Field* demonstrates, land is crucial to Irish people not just in economic terms but in terms of identity, too. Irish people waited for centuries to own their land. The Land Acts of 1870 and 1881 began the process by which Ireland was transformed from a nation of peasants to a nation of landowners.

By a supreme irony, the Act of Union – which so many Irish people considered anathema and fought so long and hard to abolish – was step by step turning Ireland into a modern state. Each of these important advances – religious freedom, ownership of wealth and participation in the electoral process – was achieved by an Act of Parliament. Thus in the second half of the nineteenth century, on many different levels, change was driving Irish life like a great engine. All aspects of Irish culture could not but be affected by this dramatic transformation, including the national games. These games are steeped in Irish history.

THE WHIRR OF THE SLIOTAR

Apart from the Irish language, nothing is more central and unique to Irish heritage than the game of hurling. In the popular imagination, it can be traced back to folklore and stories of Cúchulainn. However, we also have tangible historical proof that hurling has been an integral part of Irish life for over a thousand years.

In recent years, there has been a major debate in the GAA about the 'sin bin'. But while top intercounty managers today might fume about their players having to cool their heels on the sidelines after serious fouls, seventh-century players who committed transgressions faced far more onerous punishments, such as two days' fasting or handing over a prize heifer.

THE GAA

These unusual punishments have been discovered by Dr Angela Gleason, a young American academic based for a time at Trinity College Dublin, who has been researching the rules of the ancient stick-and-ball games that were precursors to the modern hurling and shinty.

'I have found a number of ancient texts that go into some detail about the penalty system associated with these ancient games. From their inception, Gaelic games were seen as "manly activities". However, there have always been sanctions when players stepped over the mark. There were penalties for injuries that resulted from play, and as is the norm in Brehon law, they were financial and could be paid in cattle.

'The texts are more vague on the precise nature and rules of the games, but it is believed that they involved teams several dozen strong and were violent affairs.

'These games are seen by many people as the predecessors of hurling, but in some texts they could be referring to hoop-and-ball games as well as stick-and-ball. These games should not be considered as in any way resembling the modern sport.

'Law texts dating from as early as the seventh century state that, while partaking in games, players had a degree of legal immunity from the Brehon laws. But they could be punished with special game-related fines. Penalties were graded according to the age of the player and the severity of the injury inflicted on an opponent.

'Adults who committed a foul during the play were judged on whether they had set out to injure the other party intentionally. If the offence was deemed intentional, the player was expected to pay full sick maintenance to his victim. In the case of death, not uncommon in these violent sports, the full "honour price" of the victim had to be paid to his family.

'If the injury was unintentional and resulted from "fair play", the penalty was half sick maintenance or one quarter of honour price. The financial levy, usually a payment in cattle, was calculated according to the status of the injured person and whether they were "profitable or idle".

'Children were immune from paying penalties until they reached a culpable age, usually about seven. But if their offence was deemed to be deliberate, they could expect to be punished according to the rules applicable to an older age bracket.'

So what did Angela uncover about the genesis of the game?

'In popular historical texts, the first references to hurling seem to have been written in approximately 1272 BC at the Battle of Moytura, near Cong in County Mayo. The Firbolgs were rulers of Ireland and were protecting their position in a battle against the Tuatha Dé Dannan. While they prepared for battle, the Firbolgs challenged the invaders to a hurling contest in which teams of 27 a side took part. The Firbolgs won the contest, but lost the battle.

'There is no historical reference to Gaelic football until 1670, in 'Iomàn na Boinne', a poem by Seamus MacCuarta. The poem described a game in Fennor – in which wrestling was allowed!'

THE HURLING GENESIS

In 1841, Samuel Hall and Anna Maria Hall published their book *Ireland*. They begin their section on sport by surprisingly claiming that the great game in Kerry, considered today as the home of football, and throughout the south, is hurling. The following lengthy extract is instructive on many levels, capturing the social history of the period and both the similarities with and differences from the game we know and love today:

> It is a fine manly exercise, with sufficient of danger to produce excitement; and is indeed, par excellence, the game of the peasantry of Ireland. To be an expert hurler, a man must possess athletic powers of no ordinary character; he must have a quick eye, a ready hand, and a strong arm; he must be a good runner, a skilful wrestler, and, withal, patient as well as resolute. In some respects it resembles cricket; but the rules, and the form of the bats, are altogether different; the bat of the cricketer being straight, and that of the hurler crooked.
>
> The forms of the games are these: the players, sometimes to the number of fifty or sixty, being chosen for each side, they are arranged (usually barefoot) in two opposing ranks, with

their hurleys crossed, to await the tossing up of the ball, the wickets or goals being previously fixed at the extremities of the hurling green, which, from the nature of the play, is required to be a level extensive plain.

Then there are two picked men chosen to keep the goal on each side, over whom the opposing party places equally tried men as a counterpoise; the duty of these goalkeepers being to arrest the ball in case of its near approach to that station, and return it back towards that of the opposite party, while those placed over them exert all their energies to drive it through the wicket.

All preliminaries being adjusted, the leaders take their places in the centre. A person is chosen to throw up the ball, which is done as straight as possible, when the whole party, withdrawing their hurleys, stand with them elevated, to receive and strike it in its descent. Now comes the crash of mimic war, hurleys rattle against hurleys – the ball is struck and re-struck, often for several minutes, without advancing much nearer to either goal; and when someone is lucky enough to get a clear 'puck' at it, it is sent flying over the field. It is now followed by the entire party at their utmost speed; the men grapple, wrestle, and toss each other with amazing agility, neither victor nor vanquished waiting to take breath, but following the course of the rolling and flying prize.

The best runners watch each other, and keep almost shoulder to shoulder through the play, and the best wrestlers keep as close on them as possible, to arrest or impede their progress. The ball must not be taken from the ground by the hand; and the tact and skill shown in taking it to the point of the hurley, and running with it half the length of the field, and (when too closely pressed) striking it towards the goal, is a matter of astonishment to those who are but slightly acquainted with the play.

At the goal is the chief brunt of the battle. The goal-keepers receive the prize, and are opposed by those set over them; the struggle is tremendous – every power of full speed to support their men engaged in the conflict; then tossing and straining is at its height; the men often lying in dozens side by side on the grass, while the ball is returned by some strong arm again, flying above their heads, towards the other goal. Thus for hours has the contention been carried on, and frequently the darkness of night arrests the game without giving victory to either side. It is often attended with dangerous, and sometimes with fateful results.

Matches are made, sometimes, between different townlands or parishes, sometimes by barony against barony, and not infrequently county against county; when the 'crack men' from the most distant parts are selected, and the interest excited is proportionately great.

The Halls then go on to describe the most famous match of them all – the clash between Munster and Leinster in the Phoenix Park in 1790:

It was got up by the Lord Lieutenant and other sporting noblemen, and was attended by all the nobility and gentry belonging to the Vice-Regal Court, and the beauty and fashion of the Irish capital and its vicinity.

The victory was contended for a long time with varied success; and at last it was decided in favour of the Munster men, by one of that party [Matt Healy] running with the ball on the point of his hurley, and striking it through the open windows of the Vice-Regal carriage and by that manoeuvre baffling the vigilance of the Leinster goals-men, and driving it in triumph through the goal.

However, by the late nineteenth century, Gaelic games were in crisis. Remedial action was needed. One man stood up to the plate.

THE MAGNIFICENT SEVEN

For a considerable time in the 1880s, Michael Cusack, a native of Clare, teacher, Fenian, editor of *United Ireland* and later immortalised as 'The Citizen' in James Joyce's *Ulysses,* had been perturbed about the decline of native Irish games in the face of growing competition from British sports, like the 'garrison game' (soccer) and rugby. In keeping with the heated political temperature and nationalist fervour developing under the 'uncrowned king of Ireland', Charles Stewart Parnell, Cusack advocated that the Irish people take control of their own games in the same way Parnell had led them to win back ownership of their own land. Initially Cusack sought to wrestle control not only over field games but also athletics, and to introduce a more egalitarian dimension to Irish sport, publishing these words in his own newspaper, the *Celtic Times*:

> No movement having for its object the social and political advancement of a nation from the tyranny of imported and enforced customs and manners, can be regarded as perfect, if it has not made adequate provision for the preservation and cultivation of the national pastimes of the people. Voluntary neglect of such times is a sure sign of National decay and of approaching dissolution . . .
>
> A so-called revival of athletics was inaugurated in Ireland. The new movement did not originate with those who have ever had any sympathy with Ireland or the Irish people. Accordingly, labourers, tradesmen, artisans, and even policemen and soldiers were excluded from the few competitions which constituted the lame and halting programme of the promoters . . .
>
> We tell the Irish people to take the management of their games into their own hands, to encourage and promote in every way, every form of athletics that is peculiarly Irish and to remove with one sweep everything that is foreign and iniquitous in the present system. The vast majority of the best athletes in Ireland are Nationalists. These gentlemen should take the matter in hand at once, and draft laws for the guidance of promoters of meetings in Ireland next year . . .
>
> It is only by such an arrangement that pure Irish athletics will be revived, and that the incomparable strength and physique of our race will be preserved.

In the billiards room of Hayes's hotel in Thurles on 1 November 1884 were gathered schoolteacher Michael Cusack, athlete Maurice Davin (a world-record holder in the hammer), stonemason John K. Bracken, District Inspector Thomas St George McCarthy, journalists John McKay and John Wyse Power, and solicitor P.J. O'Ryan. Two days later, the *Cork Examiner* reported:

> A meeting of athletes and friends of athletics was held on Saturday at three o'clock in Miss Hayes's Commercial Hotel Thurles for the purpose of forming an association for the preservation and cultivation of our national pastimes.
>
> Mr Michael Cusack of Dublin and Mr Maurice Davin of Carrick-on-Suir had the meeting convened by the following circular: 'You are earnestly requested to attend a meeting, which will be held in Thurles on 1 November, to take steps for the formation of a Gaelic Association for the preservation and cultivation of our national pastimes, and for providing rational amusements for the Irish people during their leisure hours.'
>
> Mr Davin was called to the chair and Mr Cusack read the circular convening the meeting . . . Mr Cusack then proposed that Mr Maurice Davin – an athlete who had distinguished himself much both in Ireland and in England – should be the president of the association.

PATRONS

The two most important political figures of nationalist Ireland – the leader of the Irish Parliamentary Party, Charles Stewart Parnell, and the founder of the Land League, Michael Davitt – were quickly persuaded to act as patrons. Crucially, so too was the Archbishop of Cashel, Thomas William Croke, to give an ecclesiastical imprimatur to the fledgling body – beginning the patronage of the Archbishop of Cashel at a national level that continues to this day.

Stereotypes have done a great disservice to Irish history – none more so than those that depict Ireland as a priest-run society. The clergy have never had it all their own way in Ireland. Towards the end of the eighteenth century, for example, a bishop in the west of Ireland was afraid to disclose the fact that Rome had suppressed a number of festivals in honour of Our Lady lest the news should provoke a riot. The Irish have always been delighted to follow their clergy – provided they are leading where the Irish want to go!

As Patrick Corish has impressively documented in his study *The Irish Catholic Experience* (1982), the seventeenth century was a profoundly unhappy one for the majority of Irish people because many Catholics lost all their property and were subjected to great cruelty at the hands of the English forces in Ireland. Protestants suffered from many atrocities as their Catholic neighbours sought to exact revenge. The legacy of this century lingers maddeningly to this very day, particularly in Northern Ireland. Another damaging stereotype – perhaps the most damaging of all – emerged: 'Popery' meant treason and the killing of Protestants; 'Protestant' meant loyalty and hatred of Popery. Each took their identity from their opposition to the other.

In the late nineteenth century, thanks in no small part to the work of Cardinal Paul Cullen, the Catholic Church exerted a massive cultural influence in Irish society. To have its blessing and, above all, to be seen to have its blessing was important for the GAA. Archbishop Croke was a shrewd choice. He was one of Parnell's most outspoken supporters among the Catholic hierarchy. In fact, he was summoned to Rome by Pope Leo XIII to explain his support for nationalist politicians. Croke's biases and prejudices were very clear in his letter of acceptance as patron:

> We are daily importing from England, not only her manufactured goods . . . but together with her fashions, her accents, her vicious literature, her music, her dances and her manifold mannerisms, her games also and her pastimes, to the utter discredit of our own grand national sports, and to the sore humiliation, as I believe, of every genuine son and daughter of the old land.

Ball-playing, hurling, football, kicking, according to Irish rules, 'casting', leaping in various ways, wrestling, handy-grips, top-pegging, leap-frog, rounders, tip-in-the-hat, and all such favourite exercises and amusements among men and boys, may now be said not only dead and buried, but in several localities to be entirely forgotten and unknown. And what have we got in their stead? We have got such foreign and fantastic field sports as lawn-tennis, croquet, cricket and the like – very excellent, I believe, and health-giving exercises in their way, still not racy of the soil, but rather alien, on the contrary, to it, as are indeed, for the most part, the men and women who first imported and still continue to patronise them . . .

Indeed if we continue travelling for the next score of years in the same direction that we have been going in for some time past . . . we had better at once, and publicly, abjure our nationality, clap hands for joy at the sight of the Union Jack, and place 'England's bloody red' exultingly above 'the green'.

We Irish are always happy to blame somebody else. Flann O'Brien claimed that he wrote *At Swim-Two-Birds* in order to become a millionaire; and he liked to complain that Hitler started a war a few weeks after publication just to frustrate this noble enterprise. Croke's fervent anti-English prejudices resonated strongly with Cusack and the other founders, who saw themselves as actors in the age-old battle of good and evil. Accordingly, from its inception the GAA had a two-fold objective of promoting Irish games and reducing the perceived malign influence of 'foreign games'.

Two further patrons came on board within months: the founder of the Irish Republican Brotherhood (IRB), John O'Leary, and the Nationalist MP William O'Brien.

From the outset, the GAA took on the parish organisation that had been so effectively deployed by Daniel O'Connell in the campaign to win Catholic Emancipation in 1829. The sense of parish identity was further copper-fastened by the use of local patron saints or historical figures in the names taken by parish clubs. Davin drew up rules for four sports: football, hurling, athletics and handball. In reality, however, no serious attempt was made to regulate handball until the birth of a new organisation, the Irish Amateur Handball Union, in 1912.

Representations of handball survive from the eighteenth century. Championships tended to be organised along the lines of boxing championships, where the title-holder remained champion until he was successfully challenged and beaten. However, it was not until the Irish Amateur Handball Association was founded that the GAA made a concerted effort to organise handball on a larger scale. In 1973, RTÉ television began its Top Ace tournament, and televised handball immediately catapulted handballers like Pat Kirby and Joey Maher to national celebrity status. The work of the Irish Amateur Handball Association can be seen in corners of rural Ireland in the old handball alleys that populate many villages and small towns, many of which have fallen into disuse.

ARE YOU RIGHT THERE, MICHAEL?

Like so many Irish organisations since, almost the first thing the GAA did was to have a split. From the beginning, the GAA has had a history of abrasive personalities with the gift of rubbing people up the wrong way. Michael Cusack will always be remembered for his role in founding the GAA in 1884. Yet, having given birth to the Association, Cusack almost strangled it in its infancy because of his acerbic character. People often miss out on the historical significance of the 'Athletic' in the title of the GAA. In the early years, it was envisaged that athletics would play a much greater role in the life of the GAA. One of the people trying to ensure this was the influential athletics administrator John L. Dunbar. He wrote to Cusack in December 1885 suggesting that the GAA and the athletics organisation should meet 'with a view to a possible merger'. Cusack, an enthusiastic hurler, did not mince or waste his words in his response. The letter read as follows:

```
GAA
4 Gardiners Place
Dublin

Dear Sir,

I received your letter this morning and burned
it.

Yours faithfully,
Michael Cusack
```

Cusack suffered from 'Irish bad memory' – which forgets everything but a grudge. He also alienated Archbishop Croke, who threatened to resign as patron 'if Mr Michael Cusack is allowed to play the dictator in the GAA's counsels, to run a reckless tilt with impunity and without rebuke'.

AMONGST WOMEN?

Cusack claimed that the new organisation spread like a 'prairie fire'. In the 20 months Cusack acted as secretary of the GAA, it did indeed grow dramatically, as the hurling and football records prove conclusively. Without his passion and commitment, the Association would not have flourished in the same way. After Cusack's departure, the growth rate was less spectacular, but the rank-and-file membership grew steadily as the popularity of the games proved an effective recruitment tool.

However, women did not play a central role in the early years of the GAA. Although the tide of social change sweeping Ireland at the time impacted on women as much as men, much of the Establishment in Ireland continued to marginalise them. It is instructive to consider the Church's attitude towards the newly established Ladies' Land League as an indication of its views on women at the time. The organisation was set up in January 1881 and by May had 321 branches. The women became responsible for a detailed register known as the 'Book of the Kells'. This was a record of every estate, the number of tenants, the rent paid, the official valuations, the name of the landlord or agent, the number of evictions that had taken place and the number that were still pending. The register was compiled from weekly reports sent in by the county branches. The Ladies' Land League, which had grown out of Parnell's Land League, was also active in relief work – when notice of a pending eviction was received, a member travelled to the area with money for assistance.

The league quickly fell foul of the Church. This was not perhaps surprising given that involvement of women in such a political group was entirely new. Archbishop McCabe of Dublin denounced the organisation and in the same breath recalled the traditional modesty of Irish women and the splendid purity of St Brigid. He went on to state that the proper place for women was 'the seclusion of the home'. In a letter read at all Masses in the archdiocese of Dublin in March 1881, he continued:

> But all this is to be laid aside and the daughters of our Catholic people are called forth, under the flimsy pretext of charity, to take their stand in the noisy arena of public life. They are asked to forget the modesty of their sex and the high dignity of their womanhood by leaders who seem utterly reckless of consequences.

The GAA's attitude to women was more benign in theory because there were no explicit measures to exclude women, but the few involved were very much on the periphery.

THE BROADER CANVAS

One of Ireland's leading academics, Declan Kiberd, draws attention to the need to situate the founding of the GAA in a wider context in which cultural nationalism was flourishing.

'At the start of the last century, our people experienced a national revival epitomised by the self-help philosophies of various movements from the Gaelic League to the Co-ops, from the Abbey Theatre to Sinn Fein. In the previous two generations, the Irish had achieved such mastery of English as the lingua franca of the modern world that they went on to produce one of the great experimental literatures in that tongue. A few years later, the process of global decolonisation was headed by men like Collins and de Valera, who managed to dislodge the greatest empire that the world until then had known . . . It might have been expected that the native elite that took over in 1922 would end old attitudes and rapidly develop a productive middle class; but no such thing happened.'

So why, then, did the country not make similar progress in successive decades? Kiberd advances three reasons.

'The sheer energy expended in removing British forces may be one reason. The civil war is another. Both left people with very little energy with which to reimagine a society. Instead, exhausted revolutionaries lapsed back into the inherited English forms. The civil war induced a profound caution, making many distrustful of innovation. Fancy theories about a republic had, after all, cost hundreds of Irish lives.

'Many of those republicans who lost the civil war could not bear to live on in a land which was a sore disappointment to their dreams. A number went to a real republic, the United States, where they made fortunes in business – and bootlegging. Even today, if you walk the streets of New York, you see vans plying up and down with names like "P.J. Brennan, Est. 1926" inscribed on their doors. The republican idea has always been linked to entrepreneurship: after all, the French revolutionaries of 1789 were the first politically organised businessmen of the modern world, keen to replace a parasitic upper class with a society of "careers open to talents".

'The loss of such flair to Ireland in the mid-1920s was something that the fragile young state could ill afford. It became a mantra among commentators that the Irish were successful in the US in ways they never could be at home. One reason for this was that Irish-Americans continued to believe in their own culture, long after their "sophisticated" stay-at-home cousins seemed to have given it up. It is surely significant that the recent revivals of Irish dancing and fiddle-playing have been led by Irish-Americans like Michael Flatley and Eileen Ivers. For there is a demonstrable link between cultural self-belief and economic achievement.'

Shortly after she was elected president of Ireland in 1990, Mary Robinson coined the phrase the 'Irish diaspora' to describe the intrinsic link between Irish emigrants abroad and 'their native sod'. From the outset, Gaelic games have been one of the most formidable imaginative batteries that allow Irish exiles in the four corners of the earth to feel they continue to belong to 'home'. Nationalism and the GAA often went hand in hand. In the early days, many IRB members were involved in the GAA, using it as a recruiting ground for new members. Archbishop Croke, though, had influenced the young organisation from falling under the control of the Fenians. The tensions between the nationalist elements within the GAA and their opponents would endure for most of the Association's history.

The GAA was the product of a unique set of historical circumstances. After the tragedy of the Great Famine, more and more Irish people were turning their backs on the native Irish culture and language in favour of the English language and culture. If this trend was left unchallenged, Ireland risked becoming no more than an outpost of England and all cultural identity would be lost. The GAA was to prove the most influential of a number of organisations set up to preserve Ireland's cultural heritage. Over the next 125 years, it would extend its reach to every parish in Ireland.

3

THY KINGDOM COME

WHAT MATTERS IS WHAT WORKS. AS THE MOST SUCCESSFUL COUNTY in Gaelic football, nobody knows more about what works in Gaelic football than Kerry footballers. In turn, nobody knows more about Kerry football than Mícheál Ó Muircheartaigh.

Mícheál has carved out a unique place in the affections of Irish sport lovers over the last 50 years. The most mundane of matches come alive in his commentaries, which are famous for the richness of their texture, abounding with references that delight and surprise. Everything he says into his microphone is informed by a passion that is as fundamental to him as breathing. He was born in Dún Síon, near Dingle in Kerry. He paints a picture of an idyllic childhood growing up on his parents' dairy farm. The fourth of eight children, the young Mícheál loved riding horses, bringing the milk to the creamery and being by the sea.

'I was pretty old when I went to school, nearly six. I remember putting up a huge fight to be allowed to go to school. I am sure I couldn't actually read then, but I actually liked going to school.'

At the age of 15, he left Dingle for the first time to attend a college in West Cork, which was the first step towards a career in teaching.

'It wasn't a conscious decision for teaching then. As far as I was concerned, the preparatory exam could just as well have been fishing. I had never been to Tralee, let alone Cork, and had never travelled on a bus or a train.'

Was it a huge cultural shock for him?

'I would say it was more exciting, really. I've never forgotten when we got into Cork City to hear the young people selling newspapers and shouting out "*Echo*". We didn't know what they were saying and it was coming from all corners; it was something new.'

His story is the broadcasting equivalent of *Roy of the Rovers*. The sad reality is that he would probably not get a job in RTÉ if he were to apply now because of his lack of experience. He was only 18, training to be a teacher and still adjusting to life in Dublin when a friend saw an advert on the college noticeboard for part-time Irish-speaking commentators. The auditions were at Croke Park, where a club game was in progress, and each applicant was given a five-minute slot – an opportunity to sort out the real thing from the pretenders.

'A group of us went – we went with the idea that it would be great fun, we'd be in Croke Park, a place we revered, and most importantly, we knew we would get in for free. It was an adventure.

'They had to pick somebody, and they picked me. It is still a very vivid memory. Naturally, none of us knew any of the players, except me: I knew one who managed to go to school in Dingle – Teddy Hurley – and another player in midfield. I just talked away at random and people I knew featured very prominently, even though they were not on the scene of the action at all! I then moved into the big-money league and was offered a massive contract – all of £6! The important thing, though, is that I still enjoy it as much now as I did then.'

DESIGNER GENES?

Mícheál is perfectly placed to answer the question of whether Kerry's elite status in Gaelic football over the last hundred years is because of some kind of genetic aberration.

'You have to remember that Gaelic football is completely different now from how it was back then. If it was possible to watch the great games of the 1920s, I'm sure we'd be dazzled by their spectacular high-fielding and kicking, but now football is a passing game – five passes for every kick. The other change is now the scores in games are much higher. If you look back at the scores in All-Ireland finals back in the 1930s, you might find a score like five points to four. Of course, the answer that old-timers would give is that the backs were good in those times as well. I'll let you work out the implication for yourself!

'Players are much fitter and more mobile now. You could never imagine a player like Pat Spillane staying in the one position in his glory days. The famous Dr Eamonn O'Sullivan trained Kerry on and off from the 1920s to the 1960s. He was a firm believer in all players keeping their positions. He actually wrote a book about his ideas. I think the name of it was *The Art and Science of Gaelic Football*. He pointed out that for Gaelic football to be seen at its very best, all players should keep to their positions and that every tussle for the ball should be just between two players. He also said that good kicking and fielding would win out in the end. In the book, you'll find sentences like: "There is no justification for finding a right-handed midfielder over on the left." He took it to an extreme, but he did win a lot of All-Irelands with Kerry. His theory would be perfect if every player was the ideal and perfect player, but of course they're not. It's now a running and supporting game, as they say.

'Certainly Kerry have a great tradition. As a result of that, almost every young boy in Kerry dreams of playing for the county in Croke Park. I suppose it would be fair to say that a lot of Kerry people believe that winning All-Irelands is their birthright. It is hard to quantify how much that tradition means in concrete terms, but it is fair to say it contributes to the assembly line of talented players that have emerged from Kerry.'

HEALING HANDS

Although Limerick won the first All-Ireland in 1887, Gaelic football really came of age in 1903, when Kerry won their first All-Ireland. They beat Kildare in a three-game saga that grabbed the public imagination. Kerry won the first game, but the match was replayed because Kerry had been awarded a controversial goal. So intense was the second game, which finished in a draw, that the referee collapsed at the end. On the third occasion, Kerry were comprehensive winners by 0–8 to 0–2.

The following year saw the first taster of what would become one of the great rivalries in the GAA, when Kerry beat Dublin to claim their second All-Ireland. By then, the first true star of Gaelic football, Dick Fitzgerald, had emerged. He won five All-Ireland medals, captaining the team to All-Irelands in 1913 and 1914. Like many men of the time, Fitzgerald was active in the IRA, as the movement for Irish independence gathered momentum. After the 1916 Easter Rising, he found himself interned with Michael Collins in Wales.

Political turmoil cast a dark shadow on the world of Gaelic games at the height of the War of Independence on Sunday, 21 November – Bloody Sunday – when the reviled Black and Tans shot dead 13 people at a football match between Tipperary and Dublin in Croke Park. The Tipperary player Michael Hogan was shot, and the biggest stand in Croke Park was subsequently named in his honour.

History's roots go deep in Kerry. Memories of the civil war lasted a very long time. This was most tellingly revealed in a conversation between an Eamon de Valera and a Michael Collins fan in the 1960s. The de Valera fan said: 'De Valera was as straight as Christ and as spiritually strong.' The Collins fan replied: 'Wasn't it a great pity the hoor wasn't crucified as young.'

Gaelic football and hurling were always about more than sport in rural Ireland, and in Kerry in particular. Professor Liam Ryan has pointed out that throughout Irish history in the last century, the GAA played a greater part than the Catholic Church in healing the many rifts that have threatened to rupture families and communities: 'Neighbours, for example, who had shot at one another in the civil war, displayed a greater desire to forgive and forget when gathered around the goalposts than when gathered around the altar. Nowhere was that more apparent than in Kerry.'

However, Kerry's All-Ireland triumph in 1924 not only deprived Dublin of a three-in-a-row but also brought both sides of the political conflict together behind the county colours. The late John B. Keane also saw at first hand the power of the GAA to heal the wounds of the past.

'Football has also been part of our identity here. In Kerry, football was called *caid*, as it referred to the type of ball used. The ball was made from dried farm-animal skins with an inflated natural animal bladder inside. We take our football very seriously in Kerry, but we also take politics very seriously. Sometimes our twin passions collide. This was probably most clearly illustrated in 1935, when Kerry refused to take part in the football championship because of the ongoing detention of prisoners in the Curragh.

'The civil war not only cost many lives; it also split families down the middle and left intense bitterness. During one particularly bitter election campaign, I decided to put up a mock candidate who went by the name of Tom Doodle. The plan was to inject laughter and reduce the bitterness. Doodle was the pseudonym given to a local labourer. My slogan depicted on posters all over the town was "Vote the Noodle and Give the Whole Caboodle to Doodle". I organised a brass band and a large crowd to accompany the candidate to my election meeting. We travelled to the square standing on the back of a donkey-drawn cart. It was a tumultuous affair. In a speech that poked fun at the clientelist, promise-all politics of the time, Doodle declared his fundamental principle: "Every man should have more than the next."

'The one place in Kerry where the civil war was put aside was on the GAA fields, and it did bring old enemies together.'

HOLY WRIT

The long relationship between the GAA and the Catholic Church is rich and complex. Although culturally, and in many respects spiritually, they were very close, and the Catholic Church was to the forefront in promoting the GAA, the Church banned its priests and seminarians from actually playing intercounty football for years. Seminarians and priests had to assume pseudonyms to allow their footballing careers to continue at the highest level, despite the curious irony of men who so often preached the importance of telling the truth practising deception. Everybody knew who they were, including the bishop, and a blind eye was turned. It was a Jesuitical solution to a uniquely clerical problem.

Kerry is the only county that has produced a bishop who was the holder of an All-Ireland medal. In 1924, Kerry faced Dublin in the All-Ireland final. Kerry's Mundy Prendiville was a student priest in All Hallows College in Dublin at the time and sprinted the short journey down the road just in time to play, helping Kerry to win. Christianity is all about forgiveness, but they took football seriously back then and Mundy was refused readmission to the college after that! He had to find a new seminary to continue his studies and subsequently became Archbishop of Perth.

In 1955, the late Father Michael Cleary was in line for a place on the Dublin team to play Kerry in the All-Ireland football final. The problem was that he was also attending the diocesan seminary in Clonliffe at the time. Under college regulations there was no way he would be freed to play the match. It was a straightforward choice: which was the more important to him – to play in the final or to become a priest? He chose to become a priest, but as the final was being played, he could practically see the ball down the road from the college. After his ordination, he played for Dublin under the name of Mick Casey.

POETRY IN MOTION

Football is to Kerry what films are to Hollywood: a countywide obsession that sets a pecking order, discussed endlessly and by everyone, complete with its own arcane laws and rituals. Pubs are the churches of this strange sporting religion, its gurus are anyone who can hold an audience and its bible is *The Kerryman* newspaper. In the kingdom, you are the number of your All-Ireland medals.

Football-talk is no idle form of idle gossip here, but a crucial element in the county's psyche to which business, romance, the land and the weather regularly take second place. One of the art's greatest princes is Brendan Kennelly, perhaps Ireland's best-loved poet. He was born in 1936 in Ballylongford. Although it has been a long time since he lived in Kerry, there is one part of his native county that has never left him. His All-Ireland memories are not those of the standard Kerry footballer.

'Football is a lovely game: it's personal and it's intelligent, and it uses all your faculties from your roguery to your sense of opportunism. In football you only get one moment.

'It has a great history. I remember hearing stories going back to the origins of the GAA, when Ballylongford were playing Tarbert. There was great rivalry between them then, as there is now. The football began on the first bell of the angelus at noon, and they kicked the ball between the two parishes until six o'clock in the evening, when the second bell rang for the second angelus. Whatever parish the ball was in, that parish lost the game. I think it was wonderfully ironic because now whoever gets acquisition of the ball is the team that has the advantage.

'What I liked most about football in my playing days was the sense of intimacy. You could meet a fella on a football field and never see him again, but you would know him better than someone you knew for four or five years in an office. There's something about the intensity of a football match and actually what they call "marking" somebody. Marking somebody is just studying him and his ways, his body, his mind. Is he open to conversation? Can he fool you? It was always like a battle. I always loved the way the old players used their heads – Eddie Dowling, Gus Crimmins, Paddy Walsh and all the great Kerry footballers used their heads. To my mind, they were real intellectuals. John B. Keane was a good footballer, and he would tell you that he learned a lot from football.

'Mind games have long been part and parcel of football in Kerry, as I discovered to my cost. As a boy in one of my first matches, I found myself marking Pata Spring. I knew he was good, and as he lined up at the halfway line before the throw-in, I was really psyched up. Just before the ref threw in the ball, Pata said, "Do you know anything about sex?"

'I replied, "I don't, Pata."

'"Well, I'll tell you about it now. It's like Kelly's bull and Sullivan's cow, and that's how it happens, and that's how you were born. Would you ever think about that now?"

THE GAA

'The ball was thrown in and I was left standing looking at Pata with my mouth open, pondering on the mysteries of the origins of life. It was a deliberate ploy to throw me. Pata was gone up the field with the ball while I was rooted to the spot burdened with the big questions of life.

'My late brother Colm played right half-back for Kerry in their 1953 All-Ireland victory over Armagh. I met a man from Cork recently who told me that Colm had a great "tan" for a ball. What he meant was that at the time, once you got the ball you hoofed it up the pitch as far as possible, but Colm, like one of the Kerry greats, Seán Murphy, would kick the ball more diagonally to place it into the hands of a teammate.

'I, on the other hand, had the dubious privilege of losing an All-Ireland minor final for Kerry! I didn't really lose it because the referee, Bill Jackson from Roscommon, pulled me up for a foul on the left half-forward of the Dublin team – and I swear to God I never fouled him. They got a goal from it, and then another goal from the kick-out. We had been five points up with three minutes to go, but they got two goals and I was the cause of the first one. I can assure you that's been the cause of many a nightmare for me down the years!'

Brendan was a close friend of John B. Keane.

'John B. had some reservations about my career in academic life. He pointed out that at the time teachers were very respected but had very little money. John B. used to say that I would be better off if I had a job with a little less respect and a little more money!

'As a child, John B. was enthralled by the thought of lifting the Sam Maguire Cup and captaining the Kerry team to win the All-Ireland. So much was he exercised by this that when his mother brought him to Mass one Sunday, as the priest lifted the chalice during the consecration, John B. turned to her and whispered, "Why does he get to win the cup every Sunday?"

'As a young man, John B. was very serious about football – so much so that he decided to give up the drink for Lent as a sign of his commitment to the game. One Ash Wednesday, John B. met his neighbour, Micky Joe. In local parlance, John B. was "fond of a sup". So Micky Joe was shocked when John B. told him that he was giving up drink for Lent. He then qualified his answer by saying "except in emergencies".

'"What does that mean exactly?" asked Micky Joe.

'With a twinkle in his eye, Master Keane replied, "Well, someone might say, 'What are you having, John B?'"'

BLESS ME, FATHER

As Brendan recalls, 'Kerry football has produced many other great characters, such as Jackie Lyne. Jackie was a great player himself and produced three fine sons, who all played for the local club team: Dinny, Jackie and another son who had been ordained to the priesthood. Jackie referred to him as "His Reverence". Jackie always, always wore his hat. The only time the hat came off his head was during the consecration at Mass. After a club match, Jackie was holding court in the pub, reliving the crucial moment in the game: "Dinny kicked the ball out. Jackie caught it and kicked it in to His Reverence," – he paused his dramatic narrative to lift his hat at the mention of "His Reverence"; the religious aura, though, was quickly dissipated as he came to the climax – "and he kicked it into the f***ing goal."'

THE MAN FROM VALENTIA

The most obvious reason for Kerry's success has been a phenomenal array of fantastic footballers, from Dick Fitzgerald to Paddy Kennedy to Gooch Cooper.

At the top of the footballing hierarchy in Kerry for John B. Keane was Mick O'Connell, who left the dressing-room immediately after captaining Kerry to victory in the All-Ireland in 1959 and headed straight home for Kerry. Asked why he had to forego the celebrations, he is said to have replied, 'I had to go home to milk the cows.'

In emphasising O'Connell's ability to strike a ball, John B. Keane told a story that showed how ecumenical his appeal was for both the sacred and the profane.

'Mick was rowing from Valentia to the mainland and decided to practise his striking by taking a free from the boat. He hit it so hard that the ball burst on its journey. The cover of the ball landed outside the presbytery in Lisdoonvarna. The bladder landed outside a hoor house in Buenos Aires.'

Ireland's finest sports writer, Peter Woods, has produced the most elegiac assessment of the man from Valentia.

'I always remember seeing a television programme about the great Kerry footballer, Mick O'Connell. O'Connell used to run the roads of Valentia on his own. It was easy to tell he was well within himself: the camera showing him leaping upwards and touching the branches of trees with his fingertips. Those branches were, I was well aware, far beyond the leap of any mortal. It would have been impossible not to have been impressed with the grace of O'Connell. To watch him as a player rise upwards, field the ball and place a kick in a single fluid motion, like the half-seen dart of a deadly snake, so quickly that it might never have happened, was a unique thrill.'

Mick O'Connell is probably the most iconic name in Gaelic football, in the same way Jack Kyle is in Irish rugby. Perhaps the best way to offer a measured assessment of him is to canvas the views of some of the players who played against him. Ace Kildare midfielder Pat Mangan's view of O'Connell is unreservedly positive.

'Mick was a tremendous player. He played football as I liked to play it. He concentrated on the ball, and it was never a man-to-man situation when you were playing on him. He went for a ball and he caught it in the clouds, and I think one of the great thrills is seeing a high ball floating in the sky and someone grabbing it. He also kicked superbly and was a tremendous man to lay off the ball. His accuracy was tremendous. He had a very sharp brain, and in my opinion, he was one of the all-time greats.'

Packy McGarty's senior intercounty career began in 1949 and finished in 1971, when he was 39. In 1984, McGarty was selected on the Team of the Century, for players who never won an All-Ireland senior medal, and 15 years later was the only Leitrim player chosen on the Connacht Team of the Millennium. McGarty prefaced his assessment of O'Connell with a relevant story from his own career.

'George Geraghty of Roscommon was an All-Ireland Colleges champion high jumper. I vividly remember the first time I ever saw him play. He was selected for my club, Seán McDermotts, at midfield. Although I wasn't a big man, I loved running for the ball and jumping, and could reach a fair height. I was on the 40 that day, and I went up for the ball once and had my hand on it, but somebody soared in like a bird and took it off me. It was my own teammate, George. I knew we were playing Roscommon the following Sunday in the Connacht Championship and we would be in big trouble because they had both Gerry O'Malley and George at midfield.

'That whole week I spent thinking about how we would stop George because I knew we wouldn't be able to stop O'Malley no matter what plan we came up with. At half-time, we were leading Roscommon by eight points to three and we had been playing with a bit of a breeze. Twenty minutes into the second half it was 8–8, and George and O'Malley were lording it at midfield. I decided to go to centre-field because we weren't in the game. I switched out on George because Gerry was like an octopus. I had a plan in my mind. As the ball was cleared out, George was winning everything by running up and catching it, so I would back into him and stop him running, but when the ball was about to drop, I'd sprint out and catch it. We won by eleven points to nine. The next morning, the headline in the paper was, "Super Switch by Leitrim Wins Game". The thing was, Leitrim didn't know a thing about it! I told George later that the biggest mistake he ever made was playing for Seán McDermotts the week before because I knew his form.

'I saw Pat Donnellan of Galway doing the same to Mick O'Connell once in an All-Ireland final, and Mick didn't like it! It was effective, but it wasn't dirty. O'Connell, for all his skills, couldn't handle that tactic.'

Midfielder Jimmy Flynn was literally at the centre of the most successful period of Longford's history, in the 1960s. There is no equivocation or qualification when he is asked who was the best player he ever saw.

'Definitely Seán Purcell was the best natural footballer I ever watched playing the game.'

When quizzed about Mick O'Connell, he offers a much more nuanced answer.

THE GAA

'I played on Mick O'Connell twice. I especially recall a match down in Killarney. We both caught the ball together, and whatever way it happened, I kind of dragged him down and landed on his backside. The next time we clashed, I was picking up the ball off the ground and he came in and pulled on me. I said, "Now listen Mick. That's not the way the game is played." But because of the previous incident he said, "Well, it's better than pulling and hauling." I remember that remark well, and I kind of laughed. He took football very seriously. I thought he was a purist. He was a complete footballer in that he had all the skills: he could strike the ball off the ground, had a great catch, was a great athlete and could kick with both feet. But I don't regard him though as a match-winner in the same way as I would have seen Jack O'Shea or Eoin Liston. I had huge time for the Bomber. I would have a question mark about O'Connell's temperament: it wasn't as strong as other parts of his game. It was possible to psyche him out of a match, and the Offaly boys were pretty adept at that.'

Kerry's dominance down the years has been threatened at various intervals in Munster by Cork. Kerry has been the benchmark all counties have tried to emulate, none more so than in Leinster. No rivalry has lit up the wonderful world of Gaelic games like that between Kerry and Dublin.

4

LEINSTER LEGENDS

IN A TIME WHEN MARRIAGE WAS FOR RICHER OR POORER – OR FOR the land – Wexford became the first county to win the All-Ireland Senior Championship for a fourth successive year, in 1918. In 1925, the National League was introduced, with Cork winning the hurling title and Laois winning the football title. Kildare became the first winners of the Sam Maguire Cup in 1928. The new trophy was presented by friends of a Cork man, Sam Maguire, a prominent figure in both the GAA and the Irish Republican Brotherhood, who had died the previous year.

In the 1930s, the GAA entered a new era with the emergence of the greatest evangelist since St Paul. In 1938, Michael O'Hehir made his first GAA commentary at the Galway–Monaghan All-Ireland football semi-final in Mullingar.

Someone who is ideally placed to comment on O'Hehir's effect on the GAA's profile is Dermot O'Brien, one of Gaelic football's great gentlemen and characters, who captained Louth to their third senior All-Ireland title in 1957. Of course, he was equally famous for his powers on the accordion and his singing and as one of Ireland's best-loved showbusiness personalities he was responsible for hits like 'The Merry Ploughboy'.

THE GAA

'Growing up, there were few distractions, apart from the wireless with the wet batteries and dry batteries, and of course we listened to O'Hehir's commentaries religiously. Listening to the radio we never saw those great players, but Michael, who really made the GAA, turned them into superheroes.

'Michael O'Hehir was the man who brought Gaelic games in vivid form to the people of Ireland at a time when television was unknown and transistors unheard of. He showed that hurling, football and other Gaelic sports were an art apart, their extent and depth perhaps not fully realised, rather merely accepting them as just games. He was a national institution. As we march, not always successfully, to the relentless demands of a faster, more superficial age, just to hear his voice was to know that all was well with the world. He painted pictures with words like a master craftsman. Young boys listening to him immediately decided they wanted to join the ranks of the football and hurling immortals. Irish sport is not the same without him. He was irreplaceable. Nobody ever did more for the GAA than him.'

Seven years after Louth's All-Ireland win, Bob Dylan would sum up the spirit of the 1960s in his song 'The Times They Are A-Changin''. Yet even in Louth's All-Ireland victory in 1957, there were portents of things to come. One of the Wee County's midfielders was the former Mayo star Dan O'Neill. As Liam Horan brilliantly documents in his book *Divided Loyalties*, player power was already an issue in the 1950s when O'Neill left Mayo in a row over expenses.

THE WICKLOW WAY

Jimmy Magee lives up to his nickname, 'the Memory Man', as he trawls through the history of the GAA in the corridors of his mind.

'Wicklow have always produced great footballers (though never enough at the one time), like the county's first All-Star, Kevin O'Brien, in the 1980s and '90s. In the 1950s, Andy Merrigan was very strong and a real slogger. It was like hitting a brick wall clashing with him. He was an iron man. They talk about Paddy McCormack, who was very tough all right, but I doubt if he was as tough as Andy Merrigan.

'Among Wicklow's finest and Ireland's greatest was Gerry O'Reilly in the 1950s. He was right half-back on the Team of the Century for players who'd never won All-Ireland medals, and he was one of the nominees for the Team of the Millennium. He was a sensational wing-back, but the only time you'd see him play was on St Patrick's Day in Croke Park, playing for Leinster. That evening, people would be saying what a marvellous player Gerry O'Reilly was and how they'd have to wait for another year to see him perform again. He was tenacious, a good kicker, worked hard and never seemed to play badly. In more recent times, the player who reminded me most of Gerry was Kerry's Páidí Ó Sé. They even looked a bit like each other. They both knew that the first job of a back is to stop a forward from scoring.'

Mícheál Ó Muircheartaigh shares Jimmy's high opinion of O'Reilly.

'You know the difference straight away between the casual fan and the real thing. The casual fan will ask: who will win on Sunday? The serious fan will ask: who was the greatest player you ever saw? Or, even more tellingly: who was the greatest player never to win an All-Ireland?

'In hurling, generations of great Wexford players went without winning an All-Ireland. A lot of great Galway hurlers, like Josie Gallagher and Seánie Duggan, never won one, and if you like they laid the foundations for modern-day hurling in Galway. They won a National League medal and a Railway Cup in 1947. Josie Gallagher was as good a hurler as I ever saw. Harry Gray of Laois was a great hurler. He did win an All-Ireland medal with Dublin in 1938. He went back to Laois and spent many fruitless years there.

'God, you could make a team of the footballers who never won All-Ireland medals. There's Gerry O'Reilly, Jim Rogers and Andy Phillips of Wicklow, and if you moved north you would have Iggy Jones of Tyrone and P.P. Treacy of Fermanagh, and if you go west you have the great Gerry O'Malley of Roscommon and, of course, Dermot Earley, who played so well for Roscommon for so long.'

On a visit home from his residence in Wales, Gerry O'Reilly told me that the 1940s and '50s were a vintage era for Gaelic football, and he is not too impressed by the changes that have taken place in the game.

'The standard is nowhere near as high now as it was in our time. In fact, it's a different game now, with so much hand-passing. The other huge change is that positional play means nothing. Players now can turn up anywhere. A right half-back can pop up to score a goal.'

JEEPERS KEEPERS

It was a case of so near yet so far for Willie Nolan when he captained Offaly to a place in the 1961 All-Ireland final. In front of a record crowd that exceeded 90,000, his team lost by a solitary point to the reigning champions, Down.

Willie's football career began in the National School in Clara, and he won a stack of underage medals. In 1957, he played minor for the Offaly side that were beaten by a Meath that went on to win the All-Ireland. The following year, he made his senior debut for Offaly when he came on as a sub for Larry Fox against Laois, and he retained his place from then on. Offaly made a breakthrough of sorts in 1959, when they reached the National League semi-final, although Kerry beat them easily. Laois beat Offaly in a replay in the first round of the Leinster Championship that year and went on to the Leinster final, where they lost to Dublin. Offaly were taking shape the following year, but the team needed a catalyst to pull the threads together. Willie Nolan has no doubt that the decisive influence was a 'blow-in' from Dublin.

'There was no such thing as a manager then, but Peter O'Reilly had trained the Dublin team to win the All-Ireland in 1958, although he fell out with them. Some of our boys knew him from playing club football in Dublin and knew he was at a loose end and asked him to take us on. He loved the idea of the chance to get back at Dublin.

'Carlow were leading us by six points at half-time in our first match in the championship, but we beat them by three points at the finish. That meant we would be playing in the Leinster semi-final against Dublin. I had seen them play in the previous round against Longford and Dublin beat them by seven goals. I thought to myself, "We're rightly bunched." We beat them by 3–9 to 0–9. It was one of the biggest thrills of my life. Peter [who died in 1998] was the figurehead and was a lovely man, so we were really fired up to win the match for him.'

In the Leinster final, Offaly were unable to raise their game to quite the same standard but scraped a one-point victory over Laois. It was a historic occasion as it was the county's first Leinster senior title in either football or hurling. Their opponents in the All-Ireland semi-final were Down, who had the advantage in terms of experience, having contested the All-Ireland semi-final the previous year. The match turned on a controversial incident, as Nolan recalls in a face that is a map of concentration.

'We were leading by two points with a couple of minutes to go. Jim McCartan got the ball and charged with it towards the goal, and some of our fellas went towards him, and the referee gave them a penalty, which Paddy Doherty scored. We got a point to equalise. Mick Dunne was writing for the *Irish Press* at the time, and in his report the next day he wrote that it shouldn't have been a penalty. It should have been a free out for charging.'

The final score was Down 1–10, Offaly 2–7. Down won the replay by two points, and comfortably beat Kerry in the All-Ireland final.

In 1961, Carlow were accounted for again in the Leinster Championship, paving the way for a Leinster semi-final clash with Kildare.

'The match was played in Portlaoise. Kildare were supposed to be the coming team that year. Mind you, they've been saying that nearly every year since, and they still haven't come! There was a lot of hype about them, with the result that the game attracted a massive crowd. Too many people were let into the ground, and the crowd had to be let in on the sideline. The referee wouldn't start the match because of the crowds, so he got the two captains to speak to them and get them back a bit more. We got going eventually and beat Kildare to qualify for another Leinster final against Dublin.

'A lot of people in Offaly and elsewhere felt that Dublin should not always have home advantage in Leinster finals and that the match should be taken from Croke Park. The powers that be agreed, but where did they hold it? Portlaoise. Sure they couldn't get in or get out with the chaos. All hell broke out after the match. It wasn't too easy during the game, either! There wasn't a final played outside Croke Park since, and there won't be one, either.'

Having accounted for Dublin in the Leinster final, Offaly brushed aside the challenge of Roscommon in the All-Ireland semi-final. Was Willie nervous captaining the team in an All-Ireland final?

'If you were not nervous before an All-Ireland, there was something wrong with you. It was the thrill of my life, but I was as nervous as a kitten. Basically all I had to do was keep the backs from roaming up the field.

'I was lucky I had a great full-back line: Greg Hughes, Johnny Egan and Paddy McCormack. Paddy went on to win two All-Irelands in 1971 and 1972. He was a hard man and a great footballer. He ended his career at full-back, but he was a better corner-back. You have to remember it was much harder to be a goalie then. If you went for the ball, then you got five or six lads on top of you in the square. Nowadays goalies get so much protection from referees that no one can even get near them.

'We also had great players up the field. Phil Reilly was a great right half-back. Our centre-back was Mick Brady. He was too classy for that position. He was a much better natural footballer than Jim McCartan, but McCartan was a tough man who could push him out of the way.'

At twenty-one, Willie did not foresee that his one chance of winning an All-Ireland had passed him by. Although in 1962 he had the consolation of winning his second consecutive Railway Cup medal, Offaly surrendered their Leinster title to Dublin in the final. It was to be Nolan's last game with the county.

'Losing that match was effectively the end for that Offaly team. My great hero Mick Casey had been playing for years, and Seán Foran likewise, and we didn't have replacements for them. Offaly won the minor All-Ireland in 1964, and it wasn't until some of those lads came through that Offaly achieved success in the seniors.

'We were invited to America a while after losing the 1962 Leinster final. We played New York twice. My brother Peter was playing for them. I stayed on for a few weeks after the tour was over because I had two brothers over there. I came back in November. Offaly had played two matches in the league at that stage. Tommy Furlong, an older brother of Martin, was in goal. The Reverend Chairman of Offaly at the time was very annoyed with me for staying on in America. Although Peter O'Reilly was supposed to be in charge, the Reverend Chairman had the final say and there was no way he was going to let me play again. My heart was broken because I wasn't playing football, so I went back to America to stay. I started playing in New York.

'At the time, every county who won the league came out to play New York. In 1963, Dublin came over and we beat them. That was one of the biggest thrills of my life. Four years later, we beat the great Galway three-in-a-row side, which was another great thrill.'

Nolan's recollections are affectionate, vivid and entertaining. Asked about the greatest player he ever saw, he answers with lightning speed.

'Mick O'Connell was the best natural footballer I ever saw because of his sheer ability, class and fitness, although he played on some average enough Kerry teams. In 1972, he had great tussles with Offaly's Willie Bryan. In the second half of the replay Willie pulled ahead, and in the last 20 minutes he was something special, but I'd have loved to have seen them clash when they were both at their peak.'

THE LONGFORD LEADER

Jimmy Flynn was pivotal to the most successful period of Longford's history. His towering performances at midfield helped Offaly to beat the mighty Galway in the National League final in 1966. Longford's only previous success at the national level had been the All-Ireland Junior Championship of 1937. In 1968, Flynn helped Longford to take their only Leinster senior title.

As Flynn recalls his early days, in the distance the yellow sun glimmers on the trees and a creamy haze wraps itself around the peaks of the Dublin mountains. He first made his mark with his native Clonguish. The most formative influence on his career was one of the most famous characters in the history of Longford football, Bertie Allen.

'He was the greatest character I ever came across in football. I remember playing a nine-a-side juvenile match in Longford. Eamon Barden and I were in the half-back line and were pretty strong, so we were winning a lot of ball and sending it in to the forwards, but they couldn't score. At half-time, Bertie said that the four forwards were like Khrushchev, Eisenhower, Macmillan and de Gaulle, they were so far apart. He had a great turn of phrase and all kinds of comments were attributed to him, though I'm not sure if all of them were true!'

Success quickly came at schoolboys, juvenile and minor levels with his club. That trend accelerated when he went to the famous footballing nursery, St Mel's College. In 1961, Flynn helped them reach the All-Ireland Colleges final.

'I was playing at midfield on John Morley. We lost by a point in front of 15,000 in Athlone. Apart from the best from Longford, we had up-and-coming talent from other counties, like Mick Ryan from Offaly and Dermot Gannon, who went on to play for Leitrim and Connacht. His father had been the last man to captain Leitrim to win a Connacht final, back in 1927.'

Flynn made his senior debut for Offaly in 1963, as a 19 year old marking Larry Coughlan. A turning point in Longford's fortunes came when three-times All-Ireland winner Mick Higgins of Cavan agreed to become county trainer in 1965. Longford had reached their first Leinster final earlier that year, losing out to Dublin by 3–6 to 0–9 after missing a penalty at a crucial stage. That September they won their first senior tournament of note, when they defeated Kildare to take the O'Byrne Cup.

'To win the League was a great achievement for a small county like Longford, and although there was a lot of dedication on the part of the players, I think Mick Higgins has to take a lot of the credit for it. He was never a hard taskmaster in training or anything, but he grew into the job with us. There was always great local rivalry between ourselves and Cavan, but Longford people up to then had never had much to shout about in comparison with our northern neighbours. But we changed that. He gave us the confidence to do it.

'We should have won the Leinster final in 1965. We were a far better team than Dublin on the day, but we hadn't the experience or the confidence. We didn't drive home our advantage. I was marking Des Foley that day, and I remember talking to him about it later and he pointed out that they had got two very soft goals from speculative balls that went into the square.'

Flynn, though, points out that Higgins was not the only one responsible for the upturn in Longford's fortunes.

'We had a great county chairman in Jimmy Flynn (no relation). He had a very cool head and was a very astute man. Another key figure was our manager, Father Phil McGee (brother of Eugene). He had a great love for the game. It was much more a passion than an interest for him, and you need people like that behind you. In 1966, we were invited to go to America. I well remember Father Phil making a statement that I think he regretted afterwards. He said, "We'll go to America when we're All-Ireland champions." We never got there because we never became champions! There was no such thing as foreign holidays then. You were lucky if you got to stay in a good hotel before a big match.'

Surprisingly, Flynn does not see the victory over Galway as the defining moment in Longford's changing fortunes.

'One of the great memories I have of that league campaign was of playing Sligo, who had a very strong team that year. They were a bit like ourselves in that they could have made the breakthrough, especially as they had Mickey Kearins, who was a fantastic footballer. When Sligo wanted to beat you, they dragged you into Ballymote, which was a fairly remote part of the country. Our sub goalie was the late Michael "Smiler" Fay, but on that day he was doing the sideline. At one stage, John Donlon got the ball towards the end of the game and ballooned it over the line. It was as clear as the nose on your face it was a line ball to Sligo, but Smiler gave it to us. Afterwards, we got a point and stole the match. The Sligo crowd was incensed by that, and rightly so. When the game was over, the crowd was baying for Smiler's blood. Smiler saved a fair few goals for Longford in his playing career, but he saved that match for us, and I believe that was the day we won the league.'

THE GAA

In the build-up to the league final, Galway looked invincible, but an indication that they did not regard Longford as pushovers came when they flew their outstanding half-back Martin Newell back from Frankfurt, where he was attending university. Longford, though, won by 0–9 to 0–8. Eight of Longford's points came from Bobby Burns, while Seán Murray got the remaining score. Jimmy Flynn's high-fielding and work rate earned him the man-of-the-match accolade.

'There were hardly 5,000 people left in the county the day of the final. When we got home on the Monday evening, we hopped on a truck. I'll always remember Larry Cunningham, who was at the height of his fame, got up with us and sang a song. Particularly as it was the first time we won a national title, there were ecstatic celebrations in the county. Although we didn't become Longford's answer to the Beatles, at least when any of us went to a dance in Rooskey after that we were recognised!

'The final was one of those days when you are up for it, and the game went well for me. The one incident I remember most from the game was Martin Newell coming up the field with the ball and hitting a diagonal pass to Cyril Dunne. I intercepted it, and there was nobody between me and the goal – which was about 70 yards away. We were two points up at the time, and there were about ten minutes to go, and I was very tired. I soloed through and had nobody to beat but the goalie, but I shaved the post and put it wide. I fell on the ground with exhaustion, and I can still hear Jackie Devine saying to me, "Why didn't you f***ing pass the ball to me?" It made for an agonising finish because Galway were throwing everything at us, but our backs held out well.

'The memory, though, that stays with me to this day is of the joy on the faces of the Longford crowd. We had a hell of a night in Power's Hotel afterwards and a hell of a day the following day. The party finished on Tuesday – but I'm not saying which Tuesday! We came down to earth with a bang, though, when we lost in the first round of the Leinster Championship against Louth. I thought though it was unfair to us to have to play a championship match just two weeks after winning the league final.'

Having reached the dizzy heights of success, Longford football soon found itself shrouded in controversy.

'After we won the League, we had to play a two-header with New York: one in Croke Park and the second game a week later in Longford. The Croke Park match was a fiasco and ended in an absolute shambles. The Longford fans were livid with the referee because they felt that he let the New York lads away with murder. Murder is too strong to describe what they were up to, but they were very, very physical. I talked to journalists after the match, and they told me we should refuse to play them in the second game. A lot of the Longford crowd came onto the pitch to try and get at the New York fellas afterwards. When we played them in Longford, it was the first time they had to put barbed wire around the pitch.'

Success, though, helped to tighten the bonds within the team.

'We would be training in Longford once a week. There were a number of us based in Dublin at the time, and sometimes we'd have two carloads of us travelling down to training. There were stories told about fellas coming out of various towns at night with maybe too many on board. I remember a situation one night where a few of the lads, who shall remain nameless, headed off to the Fleadh Cheoil in Clones but made a detour into a bog!'

Happy days returned to Longford in 1968, particularly after they beat the reigning All-Ireland champions in the Leinster semi-final in Mullingar.

'Winning the Leinster title against Laois was a big thrill, though I got a knee injury. I was injured and missed out on the All-Ireland semi-final against Kerry. It was a big disappointment to have to miss out, but what really killed me was losing out on the opportunity to mark Mick O'Connell. I was on the sideline, and we lost by two points. One of the problems of Longford and weaker counties generally was that we didn't have strength in depth and that told against us in the Kerry game. We had good players when we were all free from injury, but couldn't afford to be short of anyone.

'We won the Grounds Tournament later that year. After that, the team began to break up. Fellas like Bobby Burns, Seán Murray, Brendan Barden and Seán Donnelly were stepping down.'

Flynn retired from intercounty football in 1972.

'I was only 28, but at that stage you were becoming a veteran when you reached the age. It's hard to motivate yourself when you know your team is on the way down.'

He feels that Gaelic football is in a healthy state, but that it could benefit from minor surgery.

'I think something the GAA has to work on is to have the rules applied consistently. Another thing I would like to see is to allow players to pick the ball off the ground. This is where injuries happen, and from a refereeing point of view it would help. I can't see what the current rule adds to the game as a spectacle.

'The fitness levels are fantastic now, and the dedication is incredible. I don't think training was anything like as intensive then as it is now. Maybe we did a bit more ball play, though, which produced a different type of team.

'The best team I saw in terms of excitement was the Down team of the early '60s.

'My father worshipped the ground Seán Purcell walked on. When I was young, my father often brought me to see him play and he was a colossus. His Galway team of the '50s were a great team. I'd be doing Longford a disservice if I didn't say the Galway three-in-a-row side weren't a great team also! The great thing about all Galway teams was that they were always very clean and fair. Mind you, they had a couple of hard men, but I'm not going to mention any names! After I retired, the great Kerry team were of course something special.

'If you're talking about great footballers, one of the lads I would have to mention is Willie Bryan. We had some great tussles. I met him a few years after we retired and he said, "I've a great photograph of you and me up in the air catching the ball, and we both have our hands around the ball – but I have mine on the inside!" I thought it was a great remark. He had a great sense of humour and was a lovely footballer.'

Who was Flynn's most difficult opponent?

'Football at the time was very tough. When you played teams like Laois and Offaly, you always knew it was going to be a physical battle. There was no quarter given. There was quite a lot of tough stuff and quite a bit off the ball. You nearly had to protect yourself. I remember Jimmy Magee asked me one evening in Power's Hotel to pick my dirtiest team of all time. Any time I mentioned a player for consideration, he would come back with three lads that he reckoned were twice as tough.'

Apart from his career with Longford, Jimmy Flynn can also look back on a representative appearance with Ireland.

'I played for Ireland against Australia in Croke Park – the first time Ireland went up against Australia. I was marking a famous Australian player called Ron Barassi. We put together a team with the likes of Jimmy Keaveney, Tony Hanahoe and Paddy Cullen. We were a motley crew! In fairness, I think it was more a question of who was available than who was the best. My only specific memory of the game was Jim Eivers getting the oval ball and trying to solo it at one stage. The Australians wore sleeveless black singlets, and all of them were tanned and bronzed. We were wearing white vests and were all as white as sheets. I reckon there was about seven or eight thousand in the crowd that day, and when we trotted out they started laughing at us because we looked so anaemic in comparison!'

Leinster counties have made an indelible imprint on the GAA, and that living tradition keeps driving the Association forwards. Across the Shannon, Connacht counties, too, have been making a distinctive mark.

5

WHEN ALL BESIDE
A VIGIL KEEP

THE DECISION OF A THIRD OF THE BALLYDUFF HURLING TEAM TO
emigrate in 1958 inspired John B. Keane to write the play *Many Young
Men of Twenty*. The shadow of emigration loomed over Ireland like a
vulture hovering over its prey. It was the traditional Irish solution to
economic problems. It churned out an assembly line of bodies for the
boats to England and America.

Emigration was central to the culture of the west of Ireland.
Communities were stripped of their young people in the same way a
flock of sheep would demolish a field of fresh grass. It shaped the way
people thought and felt, conditioning them to accept the grotesquely
abnormal as normal. That was the way it was and that was the way
it would always be. Although there were no industries, there was one
highly developed export: people.

There were many scenes of families travelling en bloc to the train
station. Everyone wore their Sunday best. The mother was blind with
tears. The father's eyes were dry, but his heart was breaking. Men did
not betray emotion. It would have been seen as a sign of weakness.

THE GAA

The young people leaving leaned out of the window choking with sadness as they saw their parents for perhaps the last time. Younger brothers and sisters raced after the train shouting words of parting. Sometimes white handkerchiefs were produced and waved until the train went out of sight. Those handkerchiefs gave a ritual, almost sacramental, solemnity to the goodbyes. Their presence was a symbol of defeat, a damning indictment of an economy unable to provide for its brightest and most talented.

Hundreds of young and not-so-young people left every year. The collective tale of woe concealed thousands of individual nightmares. Young people wanted to stay in the country they loved, but had no way of making a living. They wanted to be close to family and friends, but they had no other choice than to leave. Many had good skills. Some had excellent examination results. Yet the piece of paper that was most important was the ticket to America. Former Donegal and Mayo footballer and *Sunday Game* analyst Martin Carney feels that emigration has been a major impediment to the development of football.

'Connacht counties were hit disproportionately by emigration. It is hard to quantify exactly how big an impact it has had, but I have no doubt it has held back the endless stream of young footballers who left home to find a better life. What is particularly tragic is that we thought we had put all that darkness behind us, but in the current recession, the spectre of emigration is back to haunt us again.'

THE GREEN AND RED OF MAYO

The first Connacht team to win an All-Ireland was Galway in 1934. Two years later, Mayo won their first All-Ireland. The star of the Mayo team was Henry Kenny, father of Fine Gael leader, Enda Kenny. Enda knew his father's story well.

'A mythology developed in the county about the '36 team, not least because they went 53 games without defeat. People thought they could jump over telegraph poles.

'My father went to teacher-training college at De La Salle Waterford. Times were very tough and the food was so scarce there that he said you needed to have the plates nailed to the tables! After he qualified he went to teach in Connemara and cycled 16 miles to train for the club team and 60 miles to Castlebar to play for Mayo. One of his teammates was Paddy Moclair, who was the first bank official to play county football, and he cycled from Clare. I've seen telegrams from the time from the Mayo County Board, and they said, "Train yourself, you've been selected to play."

'My father was particularly famous for his fielding of the ball. He grew up on the same street as Patsy Flannelly, another of the stars of the '36 team. They had no footballs as kids, so they went to the butcher's shop and got pigs' bladders from him to use instead. Dad always said, "If you could catch those, you could catch anything."

'The other thing he was noted for was his ability after he caught the ball in the air to turn before his feet touched the ground. When my brothers and I started playing, his advice to us was always, "Be moving before the ball comes." He found a big change in the way the game was played, especially when they started wearing lighter boots like the soccer players. When he saw a pair of them he said, "These boots are like slippers." He didn't have much time for the solo runs and that's why he called it "the tippy toe". He said he would "beat the solo runner with his cap".

'Dad had great admiration for athletes. That's probably why the player he admired most was Kildare's Larry Stanley, who, of course, holds the unique distinction of winning All-Irelands with Kildare (in 1919) and Dublin (in 1923) and of representing Ireland in the Olympics (in the high jump at the 1924 games in Paris).

'In 1936, Seamus O'Malley captained the Mayo team to the All-Ireland. He travelled to Dublin by train the evening before the match. The next day, he announced that he could not stay for the celebrations and got a lift back to Mayo after the match. The Sam Maguire Cup was put in the boot of the car. He had to go to his work as a teacher the next morning. He left for work by bicycle with the Sam Maguire Cup strapped on his back! The times have changed!'

Tom McNicholas is the only survivor of the 1936 Mayo team. At 95 years of age, he is still driving his car and his former career as a teacher is evident in the clarity of his directions to his home. Bureaucracy deprived him of the chance to play in the All-Ireland.

THE GAA

'I played in every match except the final. I was a teacher and neither the school nor the Department of Education would release me to go on collective training with the Mayo team. As a result of that, I was only a sub, and as we beat Laois by 4–11 to 0–5, my services were not needed. The great perk of winning the final was that we got a trip for six weeks, courtesy of a building firm in New York, to America. Again, I was not given leave, so I resigned my job to travel. We played in Madison Square Garden in New York, and in Philadelphia and Boston. It was an incredible adventure.'

He retains vivid memories of that team.

'It was a very different time then, on the field and off it. We used a leather ball rather than the pigskin they use now. It was as heavy as lead when it was wet and you can kick the ball 50 per cent further today. Our trainer was Dick Hearns, who was European cruiserweight boxing champion. He had a different approach to trainers today. We were driving to a match, and I had a sore throat and was losing my voice. When I told him the problem, he handed me a small bottle of vodka!

'There was none of the hype you have today. We had some great players like Patsy Flannelly, who died tragically in a shooting accident, and Purty Kelly, who was a rock in defence. He had a jaw like granite. There wasn't the same cult of personality back then, but there was no question that the star of our team was Henry Kenny. He was wonderful at catching balls in the air. He had great duels with the mighty Kerry midfielder Paddy Kennedy, and was probably one of the very few players, if not the only footballer, who could hold his own with Kennedy. This was particularly the case in the All-Ireland semi-final in Roscommon when we beat Kerry 1–5 to 0–6 in 1936, when Kennedy was the new star in the game. Henry had big hands and he could hold the ball in one hand.

'Jackie Carney was a smart forward. He had a lovely manner and was good with people, and that is why he was such a success training Mayo to the All-Ireland winning team in 1950 and 1951.

'I don't think any of our team would believe the way the game has changed, especially the emphasis on stopping teams from playing and above all the number of times people pass the ball backwards. We believed in positive football and playing your own game rather than the opposition's.'

THE ROSSIES

Charlie Finneran's award-winning Derryglad Folk Museum in Curraghboy in south Roscommon is a repository of secrets and dreams. It is a unique theatre of Irish social history, evoking reminiscences of a different time and stirring abiding memories in its visitors, who recall bygone days of horse-drawn machinery and homemade butter-making. It shows how our destiny as a nation was crossed, matted as fibres long inwrought into the fabric of other stories, like our national games. The museum's sports section holds the ultimate in memorabilia for any Roscommon fan: a copy of the 1944 All-Ireland programme.

The 1940s saw the most glorious era in the history of Roscommon football with the county's only All-Ireland successes in 1943 and 1944, both under the captaincy of the late, much-loved Jimmy Murray, who never tired of talking about Roscommon's greatest days.

'The first time I lined out in an All-Ireland final in 1943 and an hour before we got to Dublin, I was nearly standing up just to get my first glimpse of Croke Park. That was my dream come true.

'One of my most vivid memories of my playing career is my brother Phelim telling me that the prince of midfielders, Paddy Kennedy, came over to him in the 1946 All-Ireland final and said, "Phelim, I think it's your All-Ireland." Phelim replied, "You never know, anything can happen, there's still over five minutes to go." Phelim's words were prophetic because Kerry got two goals in the dying minutes to draw the game, and they went on to win the replay.'

That is the magic of Croke Park. One team's disappointment opens the door to another's glory and yet another chapter in the lush tapestry of GAA lore. That game was a case in point.

Brendan Lynch was right half-back on that Roscommon team. He announced his arrival on the national stage in bold print in the All-Ireland semi-final against Louth in 1943.

'I was marking Peter Corr, who had been the player of the year up to that point. He had scored 13 points in the Leinster final. I decided it was his career or mine. I handled him roughly and kept him scoreless. Peter, who was related to the singers the Corrs, went on to play for Everton.

'My lasting memory from the game was when the county secretary, John Joe Fahy, came running up to me at the end of the game and said, "Ye'll beat them in the second half if you play like that." I turned to him and said, "We have already." He looked shocked and said, "God, did I miss it?" He was so embroiled in the whole game and the tension it created, he had lost all track of time.

'We beat Cavan in the All-Ireland final after a replay. I marked Mick Higgins, who was very quiet and a very clean and good footballer. What I remember most was the mayhem at the end. First Cavan's Joe Stafford was sent off after having a go at Owensie Hoare. We got a point, but Barney Culley didn't agree and put the umpire into the net with a box. Big Tom O'Reilly, the captain of Cavan, came in to remonstrate and T.P. O'Reilly threw the referee in the air.'

It was not the medal that mattered to Lynch.

'The euphoria of winning was incredible. I felt like jumping out of my skin. I was on top of the world. I was 20 years of age and the world seemed my oyster. I've given away all my medals to my family. I read that Christy Ring had donated one of his All-Ireland medals to the foreign missions, and I did the same. It was the sense of achievement that mattered most to me.'

Roscommon had a slice of luck before claiming a second title in 1944, as Brendan Lynch recalls with a wry smile.

'Sligo drew with us in the first round of the Connacht Championship in Boyle. They should have beaten us. We were lucky to survive. There were only 2,000 people in attendance when we played Mayo in the Connacht final because of the transport problems during the war. We were worried by Cavan at half-time in the All-Ireland semi-final, but they collapsed completely in the second half and we had an easy win. The belief then was that you hadn't really won an All-Ireland until you beat Kerry in a final, so we were all keen to do that. I was marking the famous Paddy Bawn Brosnan. He was a fisherman and fond of the women, fond of the porter and fond of the rough and tumble!

'I made the most impact on their great midfielder Paddy Kennedy when I had a head collision with him and he had to be stretchered off. He asked me, "Jaysus, what did you do to me?"'

Roscommon were not to recapture the same winning feeling again.

'We were unlucky with illness. Phelim Murray got TB and spent 12 months in a sanatorium. I would consider Phelim to be Roscommon's best-ever footballer. The nearest to him I have seen since was Dermot Earley, who was close to perfect. TB also finished Liam Gilmartin's career. We also lost John Joe Nerney, so we were never the same force again.

'Mayo beat us in the first round of the championship in 1945. We were suffering from burnout and they were hungry. It was a relief in a way because you had the chance to take holidays. I met Jimmy Murray that summer and he asked me how I was finding the summer without football. When I said I thought it was great, he told me he felt the same.'

Roscommon were to come within a whisker of taking another All-Ireland in 1946.

'It was a Mickey Mouse ruling in the GAA that cost us the title. We played Mayo in the Connacht final in Ballinasloe. They had a goal disallowed, and then we got a goal that was going to be disallowed. Jimmy Murray grabbed the green flag and waved it, and we were awarded the goal. After the game, Mayo lodged an objection. What should have happened was that the referee should have produced his report saying Roscommon won the match, and that would have been that. Instead we had to go into a replay, and on top of the heavy collective training we were doing, we didn't need another match. We lost Frank Kinlough with a leaky valve in his heart and Doc Callaghan, our full-back, was injured. By the time we faced Kerry in the All-Ireland final replay, they were getting stronger and we were getting weaker. I was never as happy as when the final whistle sounded in that game because the whole year had been absolutely exhausting with the two replays and all the collective training.

'It finished us as a team. We lost to Cavan in the All-Ireland semi-final in '47, which meant they went on to play in the Polo Grounds instead of us. I didn't begrudge them. It was only right that players like John Joe O'Reilly finally won an All-Ireland.'

BIG TOM

If the 1940s were the summit for Roscommon football, the 1950s enjoy the same status for Mayo, with the county winning back-to-back All-Irelands in 1950 and 1951. One man was key to Mayo's success.

It was the classic confrontation between Gaelic football's beauty and the beast. The late Mayo full-forward Tom Langan went shoulder to shoulder with the celebrated Paddy Bawn Brosnan in the All-Ireland semi-final replay in 1951. In conversation with this writer, the great John B. Keane explained the legend of Paddy Bawn.

'His commitment to football was evident at an early age. Attending the local Christian Brothers school he was asked to conjugate the Latin verb *venio*. Paddy Bawn simply shrugged his shoulders and said, "Ah sure Brother, I'm only here for the football."

'Once Paddy Bawn suffered a nose injury in a club championship match. To stop the blood that was flowing with the ferocity of the Niagara Falls, a piece from *The Kerryman* was stopped up his nose, but true to form, Paddy played on. A week later, he felt a stinging pain and went to the doctor. The poor medic had much more difficulty in extracting the paper than healing the fractured nose.

'The Bawn loved to play up his image of a hard man. Stories abounded about his ability to stand up to a hard tackle. "How hard was he hit?"

'"Hit hard is it? If he was a stone wall, he'd be in rubble."

'"And he still played on?"

'"He played better than ever. Sure the blows only straightened him."

'The Bawn is one of the giants of Kerry football. The only player I ever saw make him look like a dwarf was Tom Langan in Croke Park in 1951. If he wasn't it before, that was the day Langan became one of the all-time immortals of Gaelic football.'

Mayo's full-back on that team was Paddy Prendergast. His conversation draws you to him like a warm fire in a blizzard. He recalls Tom Langan with undisguised affection.

'Tom was one of the best footballers I've ever seen. Above all he was one of the original thinking footballers. He won many games for us, but he was very badly done-by by the Mayo selectors in the early years. Our whole history is peppered with stories like that. I could think of a litany of them. Our centre half-back, Henry Dixon, was the same. He was nearly over the hill when he was brought on to the team.

'Tom was all knees and bones and was very shy at times. He was from Ballycastle and there we are not allowed to be too forward! As a Garda, he was more inclined to give people a warning than apply the full rigour of the law. He was very special. One of my clearest memories of him was when we played Kerry in the drawn game in the 1951 All-Ireland semi-final. We were four points down, but Eamonn Mongey gave Tom the ball and he flashed it into the net.

'My abiding memory of him, though, was the night for the 1951 All-Ireland final. He was in the lobby of the hotel and he had one of the lads pretending to be the Meath full-back Paddy O'Brien, who, of course, was chosen as full-back on the Team of the Century and was as tough a marker as you could get. Tom would do a sidestep to the left and a sidestep to the right with the ball, and I remember one stage he went crashing into a chair. When the game began, the first ball that came into him, he sidestepped Paddy O'Brien and stuck the ball into the net.

'We would like to think that we brought something new to the game, and we had some very thoughtful people, especially Seán Flanagan and Eamonn Mongey. Crucial to our game plan was to get the opposition full-back line on the back foot by the way we employed Tom Langan. Only Seán Purcell was ever able to handle him. That's a big tribute to Tom and an even bigger one to Seán. Once Tom got going, you could sense the fear in the opposition.'

As the son of the man who captained Mayo to their two All-Irelands in 1950 and '51, Dermot Flanagan learned almost from the cradle the merits of his late father's teammate.

THE GAA

'Tom Langan was a lethal forward, the prototype of a goal-poacher. One of his trademarks was his ability to kick the ball with the outside of his boot to give it a swerve that made it a nightmare for backs to defend against. It was the type of curved ball that the legendary baseball pitchers use. The night before an All-Ireland final, he would be practising that skill in his hotel room.'

Mícheál Ó Muircheartaigh believes that one of the reasons why that Mayo team were so successful is that they had very strong characters.

'Characters are good for sport. There were a lot of characters in the old days in Gaelic games, when there were no managers and players were individuals. Nowadays, with managers controlling players and not allowing them to talk to the media, characters are not as plentiful as they once were. If you think of the great Dublin team who arrived on the scene in 1974, you would have to say that there were a lot of characters on that team, none more so than Jimmy Keaveney and also people like Paddy Cullen and Tony Hanahoe.

'Dinny Allen was also a great character. He captained the Cork team to win the All-Ireland in 1989. I always thought he contributed very well, but a lot of people said he did very little. As a result, Dinny christened himself the non-playing captain!

'Joe Brolly is a wonderful character. He is a person that never really surrendered to managers. Joe is himself. I often heard managers giving out about him. They said, "He's down there now letting people know how well he is playing." That didn't worry Joe. Racing, football and hurling are all about entertainment, and Joe is an entertainer. He gives the impression at times that he doesn't take things too seriously, but he also performed on the field.

'In the olden days, there were great characters, like Gunner Brady of the Cavan team that won the Polo Grounds All-Ireland in 1947. I think even his name was one of the reasons that he had this aura that surrounded him, and also from that side Bill Doonan was as interesting a character as I ever met. Another character was Paddy Prendergast from the great Mayo side of 1950 and '51. Paddy Carney, also from that side, was a wonderful character. Sometimes he would even hold up the ball to show to the crowd and usually it went over the bar. He had a little bit of arrogance, but he also had the skill to match.'

THE MASTER

Mícheál Ó Muircheartaigh is a prime candidate to ask: who was the greatest player of them all?

'That's too hard a question. I will say, though, that the best display I ever saw was by Galway's Seán Purcell. Most people remember him as a great Galway forward and for his association with Frankie Stockwell. Mayo had the best full-forward of the time – some would say of all time – Tom Langan; and Galway pulled off a shock move by bringing Seán back to mark him, and he gave the finest performance I ever saw. I saw him later that year in the All-Ireland semi-final against Kerry, and he was outstanding. Kerry were winning well, and late in the game, Galway moved him to midfield and he almost swung it for them. He had such skill and style that you could play him anywhere.'

The 1956 All-Ireland final was the apex of Purcell's achievement when Galway beat Cork by 2–13 to 3–7, as he recalled to me before his death in 2005.

'We had a great lead at half-time and Cork came back to us in a big way. They really put it up to us and they got back within a point or so. We were lucky enough to get back one or two points at the end.

'We got a wonderful reception at home. I remember that quite well, coming from Dublin into Tuam. By present-day standards the crowd was not huge, but it was a great night. The match was broadcast around the town that day and there was a great spirit of victory around the place. When we arrived in Tuam, I think the crowd met us and we were carried shoulder-high or on the lorry down to the town.'

That 1956 final turned Frank Stockwell into one of the GAA immortals. The late RTÉ Gaelic games correspondent Mick Dunne coined the phrase 'the terrible twins' to describe Seán Purcell's unique partnership with Frank Stockwell. He explained the origin of the phrase to me.

'Galway's Seán Purcell was the best player I ever saw. It could be said that there were better players in different positions, but as far as I'm concerned, he was the best all-round footballer. I remember him at full-back in the Connacht semi-final in 1954 against Mayo. It was one of the finest individual displays I've ever seen. He played on the great Tom Langan, then Danny Neill and then John Nallen, but it was all the same: Purcell was superb. He was also a magnificent midfielder, and he was the brains of the Galway team that won the All-Ireland in 1956 at centre-forward. He had such a wonderful combination with the other Galway maestro, Frankie Stockwell, and they performed as such a lethal duo that I described them as the terrible twins, and to my pleasant surprise, the phrase entered the GAA vernacular about them.'

In conversation, Seán Purcell reserved a special place for Stockwell.

'We were known as the terrible twins because we had such a great understanding and because we did a lot of damage to opposing defences. Frank was a fabulous footballer. The fact that he scored 2–5 in the 1956 All-Ireland final speaks for itself. They were all off his foot, no frees. He destroyed the Cork defence on his own. It was just a matter of getting the ball in to him the best way we could. We tried the old tricks we had worked on over the years. Things were much less scientific, I suppose, than they are now. We all contributed to each other, but we all knew Frank was the man to give the ball to and he'd do the rest. You have to remember that was a 60-minute final. I'm great friends with Jimmy Keaveney, but when he broke Frank's record by scoring 2–6 in the 1977 All-Ireland final, he had a 70-minute game to do it in.'

PRIMROSE AND BLUE

Gerry O'Malley was the star of the Roscommon team that caused a sensation in 1952 when they beat the great Mayo team that was led by Seán Flanagan, which famously won All-Irelands in 1950 and '51. Because of a national newspaper strike, many people around the country only heard the result on the Tuesday after the game, and when they did, most thought it was a mistake.

Given his stature in the game, all neutrals wanted the 1962 All-Ireland final to be 'Gerry O'Malley's All-Ireland', only for Roscommon's star player to be injured in the game and Kerry to beat the men in primrose and blue by 1–6 to 1–12. The passage of time has allowed O'Malley to see the black humour in the occasion.

'I had to be taken to hospital after the All-Ireland, and I was put in a bed beside a man I had never met before. My "neighbour" knew who I was and we got to talking, the way you do. The next day a fella came in with the newspapers who didn't recognise me from Adam, and my new friend asked him, "How did the papers say O'Malley played?"

'"Brutal," came the instant reply, and it certainly left me feeling even more brutal!'

O'Malley was also a wonderful hurler. At one stage he played for Connacht against Munster in a Railway Cup match. At the time, the balance of power in hurling was heavily weighted towards Munster, but Connacht ran them close enough. On the way home, O'Malley stopped off for a drink with the legendary Galway hurler Inky Flaherty. Given the interest in hurling in the Banner County, the barman recognised Inky straight away and said, 'Ye did very well'.

'Not too bad,' replied Inky.

'I suppose if it wasn't for O'Malley you would have won,' speculated the barman.

Flaherty answered back, 'Here he is beside me. Ask him yourself.'

GALWAY GIRL

Mattie McDonagh continues to occupy a unique place in the annals of the GAA as the only Connacht player to win four senior All-Ireland football medals in 1956 and then as part of the three-in-a-row team from 1964–66. Mattie scored the only goals against Meath in those three successive finals. He also had the distinction of playing minor hurling for Roscommon and minor football for Galway in the same year. The big Ballygar man exploded onto the national stage when as a 19 year old he formed a potent midfield partnership with Frank Evers as Galway beat Cork in the 1956 All-Ireland final. In 1966, he won the ultimate personal award when he was chosen as Texaco Footballer of the Year. Mattie managed Galway to a National League title in 1981 and took them to an All-Ireland semi-final in 1982 and an All-Ireland final in 1983.

His daughter, Joanne McDonagh, recalls not just her father but the man who was also her teacher for five years.

'As a family we were probably more the Simpsons than the Waltons! Daddy invented the first remote control and called it Shane – well, Shane was the youngest at the time and he needed the exercise. Daddy couldn't watch just one programme. We got a video recorder as soon as they came on the market, and Mammy duly became an expert at taping one sports event while we watched another.

'Daddy had a great interest in poetry. One day, when he was training with Galway and one of his teammates was not passing the ball, to describe him Dad changed Patrick Pearse's line from the "beauty that will pass" to the "beauty that will not pass"!'

'Grace is but glory begun, and glory is grace perfected.' Mattie made each game he played in Croke Park a day of grace and glory. Mattie died on 10 April 2005, the same day as Enda Colleran's first anniversary Mass. Enda had furnished me with some revealing insights into Mattie's character.

'From the dawn of time, identification with heroes has been an integral part of the human condition. Great sporting performances have always grabbed the imagination of the young of all ages as they fantasise about emulating the glorious feats of their heroes. The most casual of Galway fans took vicarious pride in the style, craft, courage and character that fired our imaginations when Galway won the All-Ireland in 1956, and because Mattie was so young, I think young fellas like me had a special identification with him.

'When we played Kerry in the All-Ireland final in 1965, they had a very physical side and hit us with everything. Mattie was concussed during the game, but played on. That's the sort of man he was. He was going to put the team before his own health.

'He was a real father figure to that team. When I became captain, I felt at first that he really should have been captain because he had won an All-Ireland medal eight years before the rest of us. Thinking he should have been captain raised my performance because I knew if I didn't I would feel terrible about it, as I would have been letting Mattie down. Then I grew into the captain's role and became confident in it.'

Enda had no hesitation when I asked him his outstanding personal memory from the three-in-a-row triumph.

'It was the All-Ireland semi-final against Down in 1965, my best-ever game. The ironic thing was that I had a terrible start to the match. I was marking Brian Johnson, and he scored two points off me in the first few minutes. I felt that if I didn't get my act together he would end up as man of the match, so I decided to change my tactics. Down were storming our goal for most of the second half, and I found that no matter where I went, the ball seemed to land into my hands. I seemed to be in the right place all the time and made all the right decisions. Often I took terrible decisions and went forward and left my man and still the ball came to me. I was so thankful that a thing like that happened to me in an All-Ireland semi-final rather than in a challenge game with two men and a dog watching.

'At one stage, Seán O'Neill had the ball around the midfield and Paddy Doherty, completely unmarked, came at speed to the full-forward position. The field was open for Seán to pass the ball to Paddy. I had two options: one was to stay on my own man and the other was to run and mark Paddy. I took the chance and ran for him, and Seán passed the ball to him. I actually remember coming behind Paddy trying not to make any noise, so that he wouldn't hear me coming towards him, and at the last second I nipped in front of him and got possession. I felt he had a certain goal, only for that. It's amazing with 60,000 people present that I still thought my approach had to be as quiet as possible.'

THE BAN

In 1887, Maurice Davin had called for a ban on rugby and soccer. The political leanings of the GAA had been clearly manifested in 1902, when Rule 27 – 'The Ban' – was introduced. It prohibited members of the GAA from playing, attending or promoting 'foreign games' like soccer, rugby, hockey and cricket. In 1938, the GAA controversially expelled its patron, Ireland's first president, Douglas Hyde, for attending an international soccer match.

THE GAA

The Ban was clearly shown to be out of step with the times in 1963 when Waterford hurler Tom Cheasty was banned for attending a dance sponsored by his local soccer club. The Ban cost him a National League medal.

Mayo great of the 1960s Willie McGee had reason to be worried about being reported on another occasion.

'When I first started playing championship football, the Ban was still in operation, so you daren't be seen at a soccer or rugby match, or play them, either. I vividly remember attending a soccer match in Dalymount Park one day when I heard this chant, "Burrishoole, Burrishoole!" coming from behind the goal. I'm from Burrishoole and knew the chant meant someone had been identified, so I lifted my collar up to hide my face because I was scared stiff of being reported, but it was a Roscommon man and good friend of mine, Noel Carthy. I was glad to know it was him! But the Ban did create that kind of climate of fear. It was as if the GAA was saying to the world, "We are not confident enough to trust our own members." Thankfully that situation has changed.'

Thanks in large measure to a persistent campaign of Dublin's Tom Woulfe, the ban on GAA players playing or even watching 'foreign' games was revoked in 1971. Political issues, though, continued to trouble the GAA, particularly in Ulster.

6

OBSERVE THE SONS OF ULSTER MARCHING ON

THE GAA HAS ALWAYS ATTRACTED ABRASIVE PERSONALITIES SUCH as Patrick Kavanagh, who was one of Ireland's greatest poets of the twentieth century. Kavanagh took time off from his career as a poet to have a very undistinguished career as a goalkeeper. His career as a sporting administrator fuelled even more venom. As club treasurer he kept club funds under his bed, which prompted some nasty rumours. Kavanagh's own response to the innuendo was, 'It is possible that every so often I visited it for the price of a packet of cigarettes, but nothing serious.'

Asked to predict the outcome of the county final, after a dramatic pause, Kavanagh responded, 'The first half will be even. The second half will be even worse.'

CAVAN'S GLORY DAYS

In 1933, Cavan became the first Ulster team to win the All-Ireland. Further titles followed in '35, '47, '48 and '52. The most famous of them all was the 'Polo Grounds Final' in 1947, when they were captained by 'the Gallant' John Joe O'Reilly. Right half-back on that team was the late John Wilson, who went on to become Tánaiste in the Irish government.

'The final was held in New York as a gesture by the GAA of goodwill to the Irish people in America. Once it was announced, it aroused great interest in every county. To get there was a great prize in itself. The teams left Cobh together for a six-day trip on the SS *Mauritania* to New York, after getting our vaccinations against smallpox, which were compulsory at the time. The fact that we were playing the aristocrats of football, Kerry, added to the occasion for us, but the fact that it was the first final played abroad gave it a much more exotic quality, so it really grabbed the public imagination.

'The pitch was usually used for baseball and was much smaller than the usual Gaelic pitch. The grass was scorched and even bald in a few places, and there was a mound in the playing area. The ground was rock hard and the weather was scorching hot. Kerry got off to a great start, but Peter Donohoe was on fire for us that day. The American press described him as the Babe Ruth of Gaelic football, after the greatest baseball star of the era. We had a great leader and one of the all-time greats in Gaelic football in John Joe O'Reilly – the young army officer who died so tragically after a short illness in 1952 at the tender age of thirty-four. We won by 2–11 to 2–7. By coincidence, one of the biggest stars of our team, Mick Higgins, who scored a goal and two points in that match, was born in New York.

'Mick captained Cavan to an All-Ireland final victory in 1952. The first match against Meath ended in a draw. It was the first time the GAA brought the two teams together for a meal after the game. When Mick and some of the Cavan boys got to the hotel, they ordered drinks – just bottles of ale and a mineral. Mick went to pay for them, but the barman said they were on the GAA. Mick double-checked if he had heard correctly. Quick as a flash once this was confirmed, one of his colleagues said, "Forget about the ales and get us brandies." For the replay, though, there was no free drink!

'Mick later took up coaching and found that management was a more frustrating experience than playing. He often told the story of taking charge of Cavan for a championship match against Armagh. As the match reached its climax, Armagh took control over midfield and Cavan's dominance was threatened. Corrective action was required urgently, and Higgins decided to send on a sub, big Jim O'Donnell, whose high-fielding prowess was just what Cavan needed. Jim, though, didn't seem to realise the urgency of the situation. After going onto the pitch, he strolled back to the sideline seeking a slip of paper with his name on it for the referee. Moments later, O'Donnell was back again seeking a pair of gloves. Higgins forcefully told him to get back to his position immediately and not to mind about the gloves. A minute or two later, he was back a third time to ask, "Mick, would you ever mind my false teeth?" As he calmly handed the manager his molars, Mick's blood pressure hit record levels.'

THE BOYS FROM ARMAGH

Armagh were the next Ulster county to make a claim for All-Ireland glory. As a player with Armagh, John McKnight had few peers, and this was reflected in his selection at left full-back on the Centenary Team of the greatest players never to have won an All-Ireland medal. His football career began with street and altar-boy leagues in Newry and at school in the local CBS.

'The Cavan team was the one to be feared at the time, although Armagh were the only county then who would always give them a good match. When we were in secondary school, all of us were packed into the library to hear the commentary of the All-Ireland final from the Polo Grounds in 1947, which made a big impression on me at the age of 14 or 15. All my heroes as a youngster were Cavan players.'

McKnight made the breakthrough with the Armagh junior team in 1951 and won an Ulster Junior Championship medal in the same year. Inevitably, opportunities to play for the senior team quickly followed.

'I started getting games with the senior team. I was a permanent fixture by 1953, and in my first year we got to the All-Ireland final! We beat Roscommon in the semi-final.

'I suppose the county went wild. We were the first team from the six counties to get to the final, and that, by our standards, was a great achievement. I think that was probably the wrong attitude in a sense because we thought, "It's great to be here," and if we won it – even better. We should have gone in there thinking, "This is our title and let's go out and claim it." Nonetheless defeat (by four points) was hard to take, especially because we missed a penalty.

'The ball had been kicked in by Brian Sealey, and our fellas maintained that the Kerry goalie, Johnny Foley, had carried the ball over the line. The umpires didn't flag it, but Peter "The Man in the Cap" McDermott [who also refereed the final three years later, having captained Meath to win the All-Ireland in 1954, and in the process becoming the only man in history to have refereed an All-Ireland final before and after winning one as a player] gave a penalty. Billy McCorry took it. He was a great man to take a penalty and had never missed one before, but he missed that day. I think Billy's attitude was that he was going to put the goalkeeper, ball and all behind the line.

'There were some great players around in the '50s. I remember once marking Mayo's Tom Langan. For the first 20 minutes, everything was going perfect for me. Then he started doing flicks and punching the ball away from me and setting up goals and points all over the place. He really ruined that day for me!

'We lost the Ulster final in 1954 to Cavan. We thought we had a better team in 1954 because we had an experienced team. Meath beat Cavan in the All-Ireland semi-final and walloped Kerry in the final, so maybe if we had beaten Cavan we could have gone all the way. We had much the same team as the previous year, but it's so difficult to come out of Ulster two years in a row. You also have to bear in mind that the GAA population in Armagh is quite restricted. There is not much support for Armagh football in certain parts of Portadown!'

KEEPING UP WITH THE JONESES

Cavan's dominance of Ulster made it hard for other counties to make their mark. Tyrone was a case in point, despite the emergence of one of the all-time greats, Iggy Jones. Iggy had mixed feelings about Cavan.

'You could say I was a half-Cavan man because my father was from there. As Tyrone weren't doing well, we supported Cavan. When an Ulster team goes to Croke Park, the neutral Ulster fans will always back the team from their province. The only problem I had with Cavan's success was that they completely dominated the Ulster team and they were a very clannish bunch, so the rest of us never got much of a look-in. I would have been happier to have played with Ulster when the great Down team came along in the '60s because my game would have been more suited to their style. The only thing was that when we finally made the breakthrough in 1956 and won the Ulster final, we beat Cavan. That really made the whole occasion for us.

'We had stepped up our preparations in the run-up to the Ulster final, doing an hour and a half's training every night for two weeks in Pomeroy. There was none of the lavish facilities that top-class players enjoy today. If we were lucky, we got a cup of tea and a sandwich. After the training session, we washed ourselves from a galvanised basin of water that was placed on the sidelines.'

Tyrone narrowly lost the All-Ireland semi-final to the eventual champions Galway in 1956. It was a match that Jones was never allowed to forget.

'I had a goal chance to win the game when we were trailing by just two points. I made a run and cut along the in-line. You don't score goals from there, so I was looking for a teammate to pass to, but there was no Tyrone forward there for me. I remember cutting in from the in-line and getting onto the edge of the small parallelogram. The Galway goalie Jack Mangan was towards the near post. I thought to myself, "I'll not get it past him, but I'll get it over him." I punched the ball in the opposite direction to which I was travelling over his head. Unfortunately, Mangan got his hand to it. Thirty years later, I went to a school to speak to the children and this boy came up to me and said, "My Dad told me you were the man that lost the All-Ireland for Tyrone!"'

THE GAA

JIM'LL FIX IT

In 1958, the GAA world witnessed a shock of seismic proportions when Derry beat Kerry by 2–6 to 2–5 in the All-Ireland semi-final. The Foylesiders were led to the promised land by a prince of midfielders, Jim McKeever. His ability to jump and catch the ball was the hallmark of his play.

A major impediment to Derry's advancement was the fact that its footballing base was so narrow, particularly without the foundation stone of a strong colleges scene, and McKeever's memories of his days in the Derry jersey are remarkably vivid.

'I believe that success in football or hurling is largely determined by population. In a county where the playing population is small, you are always struggling to fill in the last three or four places.

'You need to be a big school to have a successful colleges side. St Columb's in Derry had a great team in the 1960s, but as a boarding school, they were mainly powered by players outside the city. I myself went to school in St Malachy's in Belfast and then went to train as a teacher at St Mary's in Belfast. After that, I went for a year to do postgraduate studies in physical education in London. It was difficult to explain the intricacies of the game to some of my classmates! A few times in the year, I flew home to play for Derry and Ulster.

'Derry was a soccer stronghold, which was a big disadvantage for us. By the law of averages, given the population of the city, it should have been providing about 40 to 50 per cent of the team, but it has given us nowhere near that. The Ban worked very badly against us in Derry.'

Seamus Heaney has incisively exposed the way in which sport, religion, race and politics were inextricably twined together in the Derry of his youth, the way in which walking through a street on Ash Wednesday with a forehead badged with the mortal dust enforced a sense of caste created by the sectarian circumstances, the way in which Pioneers were referred to as the 'strawberry brigade' and the manner in which the green chestnut tree that flourished at the entrance to the GAA grounds was more abundantly green from being the eminence where the tricolour was flown illegally at Easter. For the GAA faithful, though, football was central to their identity and an essential element of the fabric of their lives.

The bonus talking to McKeever is the quiet, self-effacing warmth with which he talks matter-of-factly about a career that must always, in the end, testify to talent so magical that it is too profound to be rationally explained. At the age of 17, McKeever made his senior debut for Derry.

'I remember listening to the famous All-Ireland final in the Polo Grounds in 1947. I didn't think then that a year later I'd be playing in a challenge game for the county against Antrim. It wasn't until the following year, though, that I made my championship debut. When I was in my teens, Derry used to play in the junior championship. We didn't have a senior team then. At that stage, there was a tremendous gap between Cavan and Antrim and the other seven counties in Ulster. We played in the Lagan Cup at the time, which featured the eight counties in Ulster apart from Cavan.'

McKeever's first brush with glory came in 1950.

'We played in an All-Ireland junior football final only to be beaten by Mayo. I played against a young Mick Loftus. I think it was my first time playing in Croke Park. Croke Park was the cathedral, but travelling to Dublin and staying overnight was a big thrill and made it almost as wonderful an occasion for us as playing in a senior final.'

As McKeever's reputation soared, representative honours quickly followed.

'The Railway Cup was a big thing at the time. It attracted massive attendances. There were crowds of 25,000 to 30,000 in every game I played. The emphasis was on playing the best football. It was great for footballers in the weaker counties to play against the very best. Everybody wanted to win. I think it's a great pity that the competition went into such decline. In the first Railway Cup match I played in, I was marking the great Mayo captain Seán Flanagan. In the second year, I marked the legendary Paddy Bawn Brosnan of Kerry. The reputation of players like that tended to emphasise their toughness or hardness, but I found nothing untoward happened.'

The high point of McKeever's career came against Kerry in 1958.

'I have no recollection of great excitement when we won the Ulster final. However, when we beat Kerry in the All-Ireland semi-final, the response was sensational. I remember the great John Joe Sheehy saying to me, "That's a rattling good team you have there."'

Dublin beat Derry by 2–12 to 1–9 in the All-Ireland final despite an imperious display from McKeever in midfield.

'We were not as devastated as people might have expected when we lost the final to Dublin. We were happy just to be there. If someone had told us a few years before that we would play in an All-Ireland final, we would have been absolutely delighted.'

McKeever was chosen as footballer of the year, much to the chagrin of some Dublin supporters who felt that the honour should have gone to one of their stars, like Kevin Heffernan. There was no precedent for a player from a county who had not won the All-Ireland final to win the award.

'I felt very honoured to win the award, not just for myself but for my county, too, and I wasn't aware of any begrudgery towards me at the time.'

While he has many happy memories from his career, there is a tinge of regret.

'I enjoyed every moment of my playing career. The 1950s I always think was the wrong time to be playing football because a number of different counties won an All-Ireland in that decade. Each year there were seven or eight counties who could have won it, which naturally made it difficult for counties like Derry to make the breakthrough. If I had to do it all again, I would take it a lot more seriously. I think we could have won an All-Ireland if we had really given it everything.'

McKeever could jump so tidily that he would be almost like a gymnast in the air, toes extended and fingers outstretched as he grabbed the ball, way above the heads of anybody else, and then he would hit the ground, turn and play. In Ted Walsh parlance, he was 'a great leper', and one of his most famous feats of fielding was caught on camera and has been immortalised in all the great subsequent coaching manuals under the caption 'the catch'.

FATHER AND SON

In his role as an analyst on RTÉ, Joe Brolly defers to nobody, especially to Colm O'Rourke. Away from the cameras, the only man to whom Brolly defers is his father, Francie.

'I played half-forward for Derry in the 1960s. Anyone who saw both of us play would agree that I was always a much better player than Joe ever was! The 1958 team had crumbled at that stage, although Jim McKeever was in charge of us, and he was both a wonderful man and coach. Although we had a star player in Seán O'Connell, we would never emulate the '58 side. I think that although Derry lost the final in 1958, it was important for the county to know that we could legitimately dream of eventually winning that elusive All-Ireland. At the time, though, we didn't think we'd have to wait so long to have that dream realised.

'In the '60s, it was the Down team that stood out in Ulster, winning three All-Irelands ('60, '61 and '68). They had great individuals and a great team.'

Kildare's Pat Mangan endorses that view.

'We played Down in the League final in 1968. I was centre half-back on that team and I played on Paddy Doherty, who was a great footballer. Seán O'Neill, though, was one of the greatest players I ever saw playing, and I had the pleasure of playing with him on the All-Star trip to San Francisco. He was a tremendous two-footed player with a great kick of the ball, a very intelligent competitor; his running off the ball was second to none; his vision and his accuracy were outstanding.'

Jimmy Magee saw that Down team as pioneers.

'Like the great Kerry team of the '70s and '80s, that Down team were full of stars and had some of the greatest players ever. They were one of the great innovators of Gaelic football. They were one of the first intercounty teams to wear tracksuits, which aroused great curiosity at the time. One young boy captured the bewilderment of the fans when he turned to his father and asked, "Why did they not take off their pyjamas?"'

THE GAA

In 1988, Peter McGinnity played his last senior game for Fermanagh after a 19-year career with the county that had begun when he was 17. He played on two successive Fermanagh teams beaten in the final of the All-Ireland Under-21 Championship, in 1970 (when only sixteen) and 1971. With his brother Gerry partnering him in midfield, in 1977 he helped Fermanagh to capture the Dr McKenna Cup for the first time in 44 years. He won four Railway Cup medals. In 1982, he became the first Fermanagh player to win an All-Star, being selected at right half-forward.

'I'm not a great man for individual awards, but I dare anybody to try and take it from me!

'One of the most formative influences in my career, James Lynch, invited the legendary Cavan player Mick Higgins to come along to an under-16 training session in Roslea. He saw that I was the free-taker. He came up and showed me how to set the ball with the laces, as it was at that time, facing the goals, the idea being that the weight of the ball would draw it towards the goals. From that day on, I always did as he advised, and when the laces went, I even set the ball with the little nipple facing the goals.'

McGinnity would link up with Higgins on one of the proudest days of his career.

'I played for Ulster from 1973 to 1987, missing one year. I especially remember my first match when we came up against the Combined Universities because there were two other Fermanagh players on the team with me, Kieran Campbell and Phil Sheridan, which was our highest representation ever, as well as having Finn Sherry play for the Combined Universities. Four Fermanagh lads playing interprovincial football on the one day was big news!

'When we went into the dressing-room, first the manager said to me, "Here you are Kieran, here's the number 3 jersey," and then he turned to Kieran and said, "Here's your number 10 jersey." It pulled us down a peg or two not to be recognised by Mick Higgins!

'The highlight of my career came in the 1982 Ulster semi-final against Tyrone in Breffni Park. We went into that game as underdogs, having beaten Derry by a single point in the first round. Just before the match, our captain, Arthur McCaffrey, cried off with flu, so as vice-captain I was captain for the day. I still remember leading the Fermanagh team around in pouring rain. It was one of those dream days when you think nothing can go wrong for you. I especially recall scoring a point from 40 yards out into the wind when I had no right to be even trying to score. I couldn't believe it when it sailed over the bar. It was a dirty old day, but my handling was good.'

However, the fairy-tale result in the Ulster final he hoped for did not materialise.

'We lost to Armagh by two points. They say time heals all wounds, but the passing years haven't washed away that bitter disappointment.'

NUDIE

One test of fame is when you are known simply by one name: Bono, Gay, Jack, Hector – no further introduction required. In Gaelic football circles, the name 'Nudie' elicits instant recognition as that of Monaghan's most famous footballer, Eugene 'Nudie' Hughes, who won All-Star awards as a forward and a defender.

'I was around at a good time in Monaghan football, when we won three Ulster Senior Football Championships in 1979, 1985 and 1988, as well as a National League title in '85. The '79 win was particularly satisfying as it was our first provincial title in 41 years. Kerry hammered us in the All-Ireland semi-final, but they were lucky to snatch a replay with us in the '85 semi-final.'

Nudie was acutely aware of the keen rivalry between the Ulster counties.

'When the Ulster side in the 1980s gathered for our Railway Cup clash with Leinster, I pretended to the hotel staff that I was the team manager and in charge of the room allocation. I did a quick scout of the rooms and saw some of them had four-poster beds. At the time, relations between the Tyrone and Down players were less than amicable, so I mischievously matched a Tyrone player with a Down player in these rooms. Sometimes there are games when players come off the field with black eyes, but that game was unusual because a number of the Ulster players went onto the pitch the next day with black eyes!'

THE GAA

THE WOUND THAT WILL NEVER HEAL

At half-time during the 1981 Ulster final, the Clones playing field was filled with people carrying black flags, supporting prisoners who were on hunger strike for political status in Long Kesh prison. Ulster football could not escape the dark shadows cast by the Northern Troubles. Crossmaglen was to have its ground occupied by the British army for 37 years. In July 1972, Frank Corr, one of the GAA's most prominent personalities, was shot dead, becoming one of the first of more than forty people to die in Northern Ireland because of their involvement with the GAA.

On 21 February 1988, the Troubles reverberated around the GAA when Aidan McAnespie was shot dead by a British soldier as he went to watch his beloved Aghaloo play a football match.

On the playing fields, Aidan's main contribution to his club was with the junior team. The closest he normally came to the senior team was watching them from the subs' bench, but he made the occasional appearance in the last few minutes when the result was usually already decided. Yet football and the club dominated his life.

Aidan's sister Eilish McCabe (who sadly lost her brave battle with cancer in August 2008) subsequently became the best-known opponent of the removal of the GAA's Rule 21, which barred members of the security forces from taking part in Gaelic games. But in her early childhood, the Troubles never really affected her family.

'We were all born in a street in the middle of the town. There were six of us. I was the second-oldest and the eldest girl. We had a lot of fun, and before 1969, life was very peaceful. My mum was from County Monaghan, just a mile from Aughnacloy. Although the border was very near, we were never aware of it until the Troubles began, when the soldiers came on the street. I remember the anger at the closing of the border roads.

'Previous to the Troubles, it was the smugglers who had been mainly concerned with the border and the customs. I remember when I was a young girl, an uncle brought me to Monaghan one day and I asked him, "Could I jump the border?" That's a phrase I had heard from adult conversation, and in my innocence, I thought it sounded great craic to be literally jumping the border!

My ball: Irish rugby legend Ciaran Fitzgerald first made his mark as a hurler. (© Irish Press)

The Brendan voyage: Brendan Kennelly recalls the glory days. (© Irish Press)

Bless me father: Charlie Haughey presents Iggy Clarke with his All-Star in 1979. (Photo courtesy of John Boyle)

The old meets the new: the GAA's modern merchandising creeps into the traditional custom of saving the turf.

Dreaming of glory: Every boy dreams of playing in Croke Park on All-Ireland final day.

In the fast lane: Noel Lane is flanked by 'the terrible twins', Seán Purcell (right) and Frank Stockwell (left).

Captain Fantastic: Dermot Flanagan raises the Nestor Cup after captaining Mayo to the Connacht title in 1988. (Photo courtesy of John Boyle)

Mayo's man mountain:
T.J. Kilgallon poses with his family.

On guard: Roscommon legend Brendan
Lynch (right) receives an award from
former Garda Commissioner Pat Byrne.

Taking a breather: Derry great Anthony Tohill
(second from right) awaits developments.

A degree of success: Galway ace Brian Talty receives
his degree from Thomond College.

The icing on the cake: Galway hurling legends
(from left) Jim Fives, Seán Duggan and Jimmy Duggan
prepare for a sweet moment.

Murphy's law: Sligo star Barnes Murphy (left) greets Michael Lyster.

'The Merry Ploughboy':
The late Dermot O'Brien.
(Photo courtesy of John Murray)

The life of Brian: Brian Cody
with Down camogie star
Máirín McAleenan.

Tuam stars: The late Seán Purcell with Jarlath Fallon.
(Photo courtesy of John Purcell)

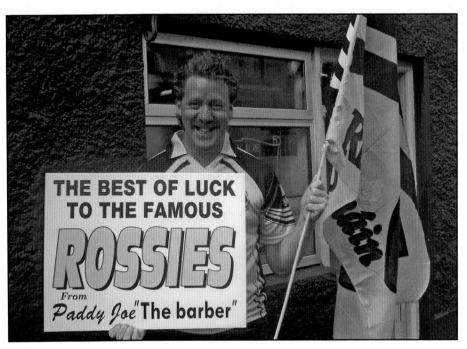

King of the Rossies: The fans are the heartbeat of the GAA,
none more so than Roscommon's greatest fan,
Paddy Joe Burke. (Photo courtesy of John Boyle)

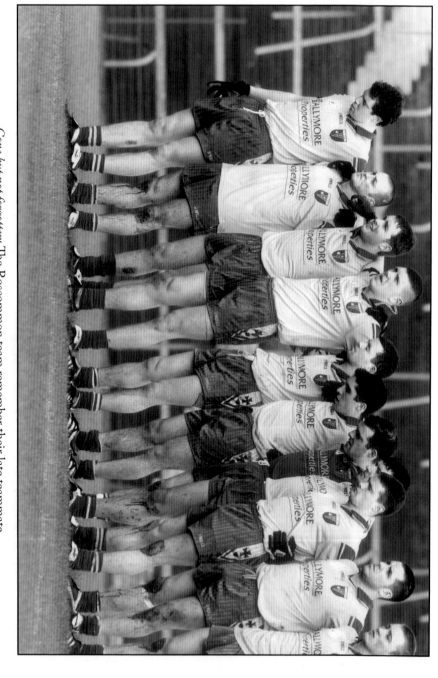

Gone but not forgotten: The Roscommon team remember their late teammate Gerard Michael Grogan, tragically killed in a car accident in 2002.

'Things changed very quickly shortly after that. We were very aware of the British army checkpoint at the bottom of the town. I remember one Saturday evening hearing bedlam outside our house, with people hooting their cars and shouting a lot. I recall asking my mum what had happened, and she told me that the crowd had opened one of the border roads and people were trucking across the border.

'As a Catholic girl in a mainly Protestant town, from an early age I was very conscious of the fact that I was different from most other girls in the town. I remember as far back as making my first Holy Communion and walking with my family to the chapel at the top of the town in my new outfit, because you didn't get an awful lot of new outfits when there were six in the family. I was dressed in the white veil and dress, and I remember the Protestant girls looking at me in bewilderment, so I was very aware of my identity.'

It was Aidan, though, who would suffer most because of his identity.

'We were a very close, tight-knit family. Aidan was always seen as a baby, and as the eldest girl, I felt I had a duty to mollycoddle him a little bit – though he sometimes rebelled against that.

'Aidan was the youngest member of the family, the only one still living at home. He had gone through a lot of harassment at the border checkpoint from the British soldiers. He had got a job in Monaghan as a poultry processor in the chicken factory, and he travelled up and down every morning and evening, and we knew that he was getting harassment every day. He had made complaints to the army, his trade union, his parish priest, to anybody who would listen, and through his own solicitor. In fact, one national newspaper had featured an article on Aidan a year before his death. The headline asked the question: "Is this the most harassed man in Ireland?" Aidan had gone to the media at the time in the hope of embarrassing the security forces for a while, and it would have worked to some extent in the short term.'

What form did this harassment take?

'It took different forms. As he drove to work, they might just pull him over to the side of the road and keep him there for five minutes, and on other occasions, they might come over and search his car, maybe take out his lunch box and search it with their bare hands and say, "Enjoy your lunch today, Mac." They sometimes called him Mac. On his way back, they might keep him for 15 or 20 minutes on the side of the road, or ask him where he was coming from or going to, or they might pull him into the big shed and take his car apart. But I think the biggest problem was the fear of the unknown – he was never sure of what was coming next. The only thing he was certain of was that they were going to hassle him. He was never going to be in a car that was waved through.'

Was he physically assaulted?

'On some occasions he was. The most recent one prior to his shooting came one evening as he was coming through the checkpoint on his way home from work. It was raining pretty heavily, and the soldiers told him to get out of his car and take off his jacket, which he did. Then they asked him to take off his shoes and socks, and he said, "I can't do that. It's pouring rain." They pounced on him and forcibly threw him down on the road and removed his shoes and socks. He came up to me that night and there were marks around his face and neck. I said we were going to have to make a formal complaint. He didn't want to go down to the police station on his own, so my husband went down with him. About six months later, he received a letter that said that no disciplinary action would be taken against any member of the security forces.'

Dealing with death is always difficult, but the suddenness of a violent death is almost impossible to accept.

'That weekend we had a death in the family: my mum's sister's husband had died from a long-term illness, and we all had been helping my aunt with the wake. He was buried on the Sunday morning and all the family were together. We all went back to my aunt's house for a meal, and afterwards, Aidan got up from the table and said to me, "I'm away to see the football match." He had gone back to the family home and lit the solid-fuel cooker so the house would be warm when my Mum and Dad returned home. He walked 269 yards through the checkpoint, when a single shot rang out. Aidan died instantly.

'We were still at my aunt's house, and I was chatting away with cousins I hadn't seen for a long time. Then my husband came inside and said to me, "Eilish, I need to speak to you immediately." I knew from the tone of his voice that it was quite serious, but to be honest, I thought it was just that our kids had been misbehaving. When I went out, he said, "There's been an accident at the checkpoint, and I think Aidan's been involved and it's serious."

'We got into the car and drove down, and just as we were driving through, a Garda car had arrived and was blocking the road to stop people driving on, but we got through. As we approached the football field, I could also see an ambulance in the background, and I thought to myself, "I'm on time and I'm going to make it with Aidan to the hospital." I still wasn't sure what had taken place, but I could see a body lying on the ground with a blanket over it. I didn't believe it was Aidan because the body looked small, but I went over towards it. I pulled back the blanket and it was Aidan and he was dead. I immediately held his hand, and his hands were very, very warm, and I hugged him and embraced him. The crowd all stood in complete silence, and I heard my parents coming through. An anger went through my body, but it had gone again as the grief came back. When I saw my parents going to witness Aidan on the roadside, that was just unbearable. I couldn't even bear to look at them with Aidan in that situation.

'The ambulance came into where the body was, and they said they were going to take him to the morgue. He was put in a body-bag and put sitting up in the ambulance, so my Dad and I said we were going with him because we couldn't let Aidan go on his own. We sat in the ambulance in total shock down to the morgue in Craigavon, and that's probably one of the longest journeys I'll ever have in my life. As we were travelling in the ambulance, we went through Armagh. Children were out playing and people were going on with living, and it was a sunny day even though it was February, so people were out walking, others kicking footballs, and you just said to yourself, "This can't be happening."

'My husband drove behind in his car, and at the morgue, my dad formally identified Aidan, and then we had to make arrangements for an undertaker and everything else. When we had everything sorted out, we went back to the house, which was packed with relatives, and even my poor aunt was there who had just buried her husband, helping my Mum, who was in a bad way. Then people were coming to me saying that they had heard it on the news that there had been an accidental discharge. An SDLP councillor told me that he had rung up the Northern Ireland Office just immediately after the shooting because he was down at the football field and he was absolutely furious that they would claim it was an accident without having the opportunity to question the soldier or to involve forensics.

'It was a long evening. We were told around ten o'clock that Aidan's body was going to be returned that night. The doctor had decided that mum, who had stayed up the previous two nights with my aunt, should be sedated. I tried desperately to get her to wake up when I realised that Aidan's remains were going to be brought back to the house, but to no avail. I looked out just before he was being brought in at around 12.30 a.m. I couldn't believe the crowds that were there at the time. There were footballers, old people, very young people and people who had come long distances. At that point I had never felt so lonely because everyone else in the family, except my mother knocked out in the bed, were in cars behind the coffin. In times like that you clasp on to the smallest things. You wouldn't believe this, but it was a comfort to know that Aidan was going to be home in his bedroom and not in the morgue.

'That night we all sat up, and around six o'clock I was making tea for all the people who'd stayed up with me. Suddenly I heard terrible crying and howling. I looked out in the hall and it was my mum, who had woken up from her sleep in a daze, and she was standing in the hall looking in at Aidan's room. Aidan was laid out in his new suit in the coffin, with the candles all lit. My mum had woken up in a nightmare. I suppose she had thought it was a nightmare, but the reality of the situation had hit her. It is hard when you are going through a situation like that, but when you see your parents going through it – it is unbearable.'

The emotional trauma for the family was compounded by further rumours about the circumstances of Aidan's death and the growing realisation that if they were to extract answers to all their questions, drastic measures would be needed.

'On the Monday, we heard that the soldier who had shot him had claimed he was cleaning his gun and his finger slipped. That evening we decided we weren't happy with the explanation, and nobody from the security forces had come to our door with any comment, so I contacted our solicitor.

'I also contacted our doctor to see if he could carry out an autopsy on Aidan's body. He thought it would be inconclusive if he did that because it was outside his area, and that we would be better off getting a pathologist who would be qualified in that field. The Irish government made a statement on the Monday evening that they were going to carry out an investigation. We decided then that we would go ahead with the funeral on the Tuesday morning, knowing that there would probably have to be an exhumation of Aidan's body.'

A family funeral is always difficult, but how difficult was the burial when there was a strong possibility Aidan would be exhumed shortly afterwards?

'It was very tough. It was very tough to see Aidan's body leaving the house on a cold February morning. It was hard to believe the amount of people who were there at the funeral from all parts of Ireland, and I mean all parts. When we walked in, we didn't realise that the cardinal was going to be there saying the Mass, or that Mick Loftus, president of the GAA, was going to be there and many representatives from the Ulster Council. All the support helped us in a small bit to carry our cross.

'The sensation of it was almost unbearable, knowing that we were going to exhume him. We didn't know how soon, but we hoped it would be sooner rather than later. When Aidan's body was being lowered into the ground, they lowered the supports that would normally be raised with his coffin, to make it easier to take the coffin out again.

'On the following Saturday, we got a phone call from the Irish government saying that we had permission to have the body exhumed the following morning and brought to Monaghan hospital, with the state pathologist, Dr Harbison, in attendance. To me, hearing the news was a relief because I knew an injustice had been done to our family and I had no confidence in British justice, so I believed that the autopsy was an opportunity for us to get to the truth.

'For my mother in particular it was unbearable. I remember breaking the news to her that Aidan's body was being exhumed, and I could see in her eyes that it was taking a lot out of her, but I knew she too wanted to get to the bottom of it. Indeed, on the Wednesday of that week, there was a soldier who was charged with the unlawful killing of Aidan, but we had no confidence that he was going to be convicted so we knew that the onus was on us to get an investigation.

The family's pain was exacerbated by the portrayal of Aidan by the British media.

'In the British media, the phrase they consistently used to describe Aidan was a "Sinn Fein activist". That to our family was very hurtful as well. Aidan was a member of the GAA, but had never been involved in any political party or political activity. I myself had stood for Sinn Fein at a local government election in 1985. Aidan had gone out and put up posters for me, as a brother would do for a sister, but neither of us had been involved in any political activity since then. It was like the British media were using this as a stick to beat us. I don't think it's right to treat any person the way Aidan was treated, regardless of their political view, but it hurt more to see him portrayed in this way, to justify what the soldier had done, to people in England.'

Did the fact that Eilish had stood for Sinn Fein contribute to Aidan's problems with the security forces?

'Aidan had been getting the harassment before I stood for election, and he had come in here to me one evening and said, "If you get elected as a councillor, they won't be able to harass me any more."'

Aidan's name lives on in the GAA club called after him in Boston. Powered by players from Tyrone, Meath, Mayo, Donegal and Cork, the Aidan McAnespie club had its finest hour in 1998 when it won the All-American Cup, having previously won the New England Cup. A major contributory factor to the club's successes that year was the presence and tactical nous on the pitch of the great Peter Canavan. Every Christmas, the returned players get together to play a challenge match. Fittingly in 1999, it was against Aghaloo.

For Eilish, the tyranny of the past could be broken for herself and her family only by putting 21 years of abandonment at the hands of the Establishment in the perspective of a future when they could finally be free from their anguish. Before her death, she told me, 'We can't lay our loved ones to rest until we know the truth and we get answers. We want to know why this happened. We want to know why there wasn't more done. When Aidan was killed, we were handed a life sentence. It's something we have to live with every day of our lives.

'The soldier who was charged with Aidan's unlawful killing was never convicted. We never had him in the witness box to give us the opportunity to have our lawyers cross-examine him.'

I asked Eilish if, in such circumstances, she felt angry.

'I'm not sure if I'm still angry. I do feel a great injustice was done to Aidan and until we get at the truth, I don't think Aidan will ever be able to rest in peace. I'd love to be able to say we can close the file. There's an anger that a British soldier can shoot somebody and not be held accountable for it.'

The first thing I noticed when I visited Eilish's home in Aughnacloy was the photo of a smiling Aidan. Aidan was the ghost that was always with her. The passing of over 20 years had done little to heal her pain.

'It's been very difficult. After Aidan's death, my husband and I and our two children moved to stay with Mum and Dad for a few weeks. We ended up staying from February until the end of July. Their lives were totally devastated because their lives had revolved around Aidan. When we moved back to our home, I was still expecting Aidan to drop in every evening, the way he always used to. He has been an absent figure from all the happy family events we've had since, like my brother's wedding. You don't ever forget him. You wonder, would he be married now and have children? We all are getting older, but Aidan will always be 23 to us.'

Sadly Eilish passed away before the publication in October 2008 of a report from the PSNI's Historical Enquiries Team, which concluded that although there were 'no legal grounds or new evidence' that would justify further investigation into Aidan's death, the soldier's 'version of events, however, can be considered to be the least likely'.

7

FROM A JACK TO A RING

THE FOUNDER OF THE GAA, MICHAEL CUSACK, SAID OF HURLING:

> When I reflect on the sublime simplicity of the game, the
> strength, the swiftness, of the players, their apparently angelic
> impetuosity, the apparent recklessness of life and limb, their
> magic skill, their marvellous escapes and the overwhelming
> pleasure they give their friends, I have no hesitation in saying
> that the game of hurling is in the front rank of the Fine Arts.

Hurling is a parable of life at its innocent best, the world as it ought to
be, the ideal for a moment realised. Our national sport is an expression
of optimism, endowing sports lovers with a redemptive feeling,
melting away depression, pain and bitter disappointment, hinting at a
bygone age of innocence and values that no longer exists.

Hurling is drama's first cousin. It is theatre without the script. At
its best, it is the beautiful game – played with strength and speed, with
courage and skill, with honesty and humour. It has the capacity to
stop your heart and leave the indelible memory of a magic moment.
A hurling artist like D.J. Carey in full flight is something unbelievable

on the pitch, a miracle of speed, balance and intense athleticism, a thoroughbred leaving a trail of mesmerised opponents in his slipstream as transfixed in wonder as the crowd by his silken skills.

In the words of Justin McCarthy, 'Hurling identifies my Irishness. I'm not an Irish speaker, so the game portrays my national spirit, it's so Irish, so unique.'

Despite its vast history and our radically different cultural, social and economic context, hurling has in many ways changed very little over the years – the changelessness is what it's been about since the beginning. Hurling takes us, at heart, into a mythic place, an ageless space alight with Celtic warriors – not men but giants – who know who they were, are and will be. It is not just part of who we are – it could be argued it *is* who we are.

GIVE IT A LASH, JACK

Jack Lynch was first elected to the Dáil in 1948, having initially been approached to contest the election by Clann na Poblachta. He was appointed Parliamentary Secretary to the government in 1951 with responsibility for the Gaeltacht. In 1957, he became Minister for Education, and two years later, he replaced Seán Lemass as Minister for Industry and Commerce. He was appointed Minister for Finance in 1965, and the following year, he reluctantly allowed his name to go forward for the leadership of Fianna Fáil when Lemass announced his retirement. He won and became the first Taoiseach of the post-civil war generation. His finest hour came in 1977, when he led Fianna Fáil to a general election victory with a 20-seat majority.

When you ask someone who held the unique distinction of winning six senior All-Ireland medals in consecutive years (1941–6) what his favourite personal sporting memory is, the last thing you expect to be told about is an All-Ireland final he lost! Yet such was the case with Jack Lynch.

'It may be paradoxical, but the games of which I have the most vivid memories are the ones we lost. Of these, I remember best the first All-Ireland hurling final in which I played. It was Cork versus Kilkenny on 3 September 1939. I was captain of the team and hopeful of leading Cork out of a comparatively long barren spell. Cork had not won a final since 1931, when they beat Kilkenny in the second replay of the final.

'The match I refer to has since been known as the "Thunder and Lightning Final". We had all kinds of weather, including sunshine and hailstones. It was played on the day that the Second World War commenced. I missed at least two scorable chances – of a goal and a point. I was marking one of the greatest half-backs of all time, Paddy Phelan, and we were beaten by a point scored literally with the last puck of the game. I can remember more facets of that game than almost any other in which I played.

'Although I was lucky enough to play in many All-Ireland finals, all the Munster finals were special. It was always about more than sport. It was a social occasion where men drank in manly moderation, but probably more than any other moment in the calendar, it defined our identity. Looking back, there were a lot of hardships in those days, with rationing and so on. To take one example, both Tipperary and Kilkenny were excluded from the 1941 hurling championship because of an outbreak of foot-and-mouth disease. Yet no matter how bad things were, the Munster final, like Christmas, was always guaranteed to put a smile on people's faces.'

THE WIZARD OF CLOYNE

Following his retirement, Jack Lynch noted a minor revolution in the game of hurling: 'Hurling certainly has changed over the past 50 years, in some respects for the better, but overall it has not improved as a spectacle. There is not the flow in the game as there was in my day; similarly with pulling on ground balls. There is now a tendency to catch an overhead ball, which admittedly can look so spectacular, but like overindulging in trying to pick every ball into the hand from the ground instead of pulling on it, it slows up the game and leads to crowding and scrambling.'

When asked his opinion of himself as a hurler, Lynch was understandably reticent: 'I would prefer to leave this assessment to people I played with or against, or who saw me play.'

However, he was much more forthcoming with his opinion of other great players. Inevitably, the analysis began with Christy Ring.

'Christy Ring was the greatest hurler that I knew. I know there are some who will contend that others were better – Mick Mackey, for example. I think Mick Mackey was the most effective hurler that I played against. Mackey was great, but in my opinion, Ring's hurling repertoire was greater. He was totally committed to hurling, perhaps more so than any player I have ever met. He analysed games in prospect and in retrospect. In essence, he thought and lived hurling.

'I conclude with the observation that Christy Ring wrote in *The Spirit of the Glen*, which depicts his club, Glen Rovers: "My hurling days are over – let no one say the best hurlers belong to the past. They are with us now and better yet to come." Typical of Ring's brilliant mind.'

THE RING OF FIRE

Nobody did more to transform our national game into our national soap opera than Christy Ring. Such was his legend that it was said he could shoot the eye out of your head from two fields away. His epic deeds were evocatively conveyed in a poem in his honour:

> Now Cork is bate,
> The hay is saved,
> The thousands wildly sing.
> They speak too soon,
> My sweet garsun,
> Cos here comes Christy Ring.

One of Ireland's national treasures, Bill O'Herlihy, often saw Ring at close quarters growing up in Cork in the 1940s and '50s.

'My generation was very lucky because we grew up at a time when sport in Cork was terrific. Cork hurling was the best hurling in the country at the time by a distance. In Cork City, you had Glen Rovers, Sarsfields, Blackrock and St Finbarr's, which was in my parish. They had unbelievable teams and there was unbelievable tribalism involved.

Ring was the greatest hurler I've ever seen, and I saw a lot of him because my father, God rest his soul, loved hurling and brought me to a lot of games. But you would have an extraordinary attitude to Ring. When he was playing for Glen Rovers, you hated him because you were from the Barrs, but if he was playing for Cork, you thought he was a god. He was a very nice man, but he had this aura about him and he wasn't the easiest man I've ever talked to. He was difficult because he was shy, not because he was rude.'

Jim Fives, who played for both Waterford and Galway, was chosen at right full-back on the Centenary Team of the greatest players never to have won an All-Ireland medal. He had the unenviable task of marking Ring on a number of occasions.

'My favourite character in the game was Kilkenny's "Diamond" Hayden. He was a great believer in psychological warfare. He would do everything and anything to put you off your game. He was always talking himself up, always trying to get you to think that you would be much better off trying to find someone else to mark. I believe Christy Ring played those sorts of mind games as well, though he never did on me. He probably felt that he didn't need to.

'Ring was the best player I ever saw. I marked him in Railway Cup matches. It was a very trying experience as a back because not alone did you ever know what he was going to do; a lot of the time you never knew where he was! He just ghosted into positions. One minute you were right beside him – the next he was gone and you were left for dead!'

Dublin's 1971 All-Star Mick Bermingham got up close and personal with Ring.

'I first got to know him when he was working in Dublin and he used go training in Islandbridge. I was 15 and he was in the autumn of his career. My uncle played against him in the Railway Cup final in 1947, so that gave me the courage to go up and speak to him. We pucked a few balls together.

'I got to know him better when I played with him later in the Cardinal Cushing Games in America. He was very intense. There were no short cuts with him. It was a great education to watch him. He had great anticipation and was a master of judging the flight of the sliotar. I learned a lot about how to play corner-forward from him. If he got a score, he'd dance a little jig to annoy his opponent and straight away won the psychological battle. I always tried to out-think my opponent and as a result, I never stood still in a match.'

Clare legend Jimmy Smyth came up against Ring often.

'Nicky Rackard was the third-best hurler of all time behind Mick Mackey, but the greatest of all was Christy Ring. Forward play has deteriorated since my time, but back play has come on a lot. They mark forwards so tightly now you can hardly do anything. I just wonder how Ring would cope now. He would still get a lot of scores, but I think he wouldn't have got quite so many.

'Ring was like Muhammad Ali. Ring once said "modesty is knowing where you stand". He always knew. If he thought he had played below his own high standards, he would be the first to say so. He was well aware of his own ability and didn't believe in concealing the fact that he knew. I remember we were playing in a Railway Cup match once, and he said to me, "When I get the ball you run in for the pass. And remember: I don't miss."'

DUNNE DEAL

Few people were better equipped to give an independent assessment of Ring's place among the pantheon of hurling greats than the late Mick Dunne – one of the unsung heroes of the GAA, having served twenty-one years as the GAA anchorman with the *Irish Press* and an equal number of years as Gaelic games correspondent with RTÉ. Yet growing up at the foot of the Slieve Bloom Mountains in Clonaslee in County Laois, a freak accident almost denied him the opportunity.

'When I was four my parents were away for the day and I slipped the attentions of my minders. A river tumbling down from the mountain flowed by at the foot of our garden. It was the Brosna and it was in full flood and I fell in! Thankfully, my little jumper got tangled in some overhanging branches at the turning of the river and this halted my progress all the way to the River Shannon. A neighbour heard my shouts and rescued me.'

Some years later, sports journalism almost lost out again as Dunne, like so many of his contemporaries at the time, decided to enter the priesthood. After a year and a half in All Hallows, he decided that the clerical life was not for him. This was a time when there was a considerable stigma attached to being a 'spoiled priest', but his family, unlike many others in that situation, supported his decision fully.

Mick was born into a very political family known as the 'Tailor Dunnes', so called because of the number in the extended family who took up the tailoring profession. The name also distinguished them from the many other Dunnes in the area. Mick's father, Frank, went to America at an early age, but during our War of Independence he was sent back by Liam Mellowes with an important message for the Big Fella, Michael Collins. He stayed on to fight in the war and became second-in-command of the Fourth Battalion. He spent time in several prisons and took part in a number of daring escapes. He was also very musical and enjoyed a great reputation as a pipe major. During the civil war, he spent 44 days on hunger strike in Mountjoy with Seán Lemass, who would go on to succeed Eamon de Valera as Taoiseach, and Sean Coughlan, who subsequently became the GAA columnist with the *Irish Press*, writing under the pen-name 'Green Flag'.

Before his death, Mick Dunne recalled some of his hurling memories for me.

'I have seen some great players in my time, like Eddie Keher and more recently D.J. Carey, though I would have loved the opportunity to have seen Kilkenny's Lory Meagher, perhaps the first true star of hurling, in his prime. He won three All-Irelands in the 1930s, and entered the club of GAA immortals on the basis of his towering performance in dreadful weather in midfield when Kilkenny beat the hot favourites and reigning champions Limerick in the 1935 All-Ireland.

'Nicky Rackard was one of the most colourful characters I ever met. He changed the whole sporting and social structure of Wexford. He went to St Kieran's College in Kilkenny and developed a love for hurling, which he brought home to his brothers and to his club, Rathnure. Wexford had traditionally been a football power going back to their famous four-in-a-row side. But Nicky Rackard turned Wexford almost overnight into a recognised hurling bastion. He was crucial to Wexford's two All-Irelands in 1955 and '56. It was a tragedy that he died so young. As people know, he had his problems with the drink, but I spoke to his brother Bobby at his funeral, who told me it was a great shame he died because he had been doing great work for AA at the time.

'Limerick's Mick Mackey was both an extraordinary hurler and a great character. When Limerick played Kilkenny in the 1940 final, Mick Mackey fired in his first shot, which was saved by Jimmy O'Connell, but Mackey kept running in, and as he turned at the edge of the square, he shouted, "You're in good form, but you won't smell the next one."

'Mick had a great physical and social presence. Few people could match him for charisma. He was sometimes described as "The Playboy of the Southern World". He always seemed to have a smile on his face – both on and off the field. He was one of those exceptional talents who made the crowd come alive because of his swashbuckling style, and the higher the stakes, the better he performed, which is a sure sign of greatness.

'He was very cute as well. One of his finest performances came in the 1936 Munster final against Tipperary. He had suffered a bad knee injury before the game, and knowing he was likely to "have it tested" by his opponents, wore a massive bandage – on his healthy knee. He scored five goals and three points that day. He captained Limerick to the All-Ireland title that year and again in 1940.

'Without question, though, the greatest player I ever saw was Christy Ring. He was probably the greatest player that ever laced a boot. He was the one I admired most, the man I was most happy to report upon and the man I was always pleased to talk with.

'He was involved in a few controversies in his time. In 1953, the Galway hurlers, powered by the great Josie Gallagher, had beaten Kilkenny in the semi-final and qualified to play against the Christy Ring-led Cork side in the All-Ireland final. Galway had the game for the winning, but Mick Burke had been struck a blow during the game and they failed to take him off despite his obvious concussion.

What made their inaction all the more inexplicable was that Burke was marking the great Christy Ring. The controversy ensued from the fact that a large section of the Galway crowd had booed Ring throughout the game and that Galway appeared to have targeted the Cork legend for "special treatment". The post-match celebration was affected by events on the field. So incensed were five or six of the Galway players by Burke's injury that they had an altercation with Ring that evening at the official reception and returned to the Cork hotel at breakfast the next morning to again vent their displeasure, albeit only using verbal means on that occasion.

'Everyone has their favourite memory of Michael O'Hehir. If he could only be remembered for one broadcast, I would like to suggest the 1956 final between Cork and Wexford, one of the greatest hurling finals of them all – which will always be remembered above all for Art Foley's save from Christy Ring. Listening to O'Hehir, anyone who'd ever seen either Christy Ring or Art Foley play would have had a very clear mental picture of the handshake that passed between them after the save.

'It was a match that captured the attention like few others, with no less than 83,000 people in attendance. Such was the interest in Wexford that two funerals scheduled for the day of the final had to be postponed until the following day because the hearses were needed to transport people to the match! The match had to be delayed until 23 September because of a polio scare in Cork. The authorities did not want a huge crowd assembling in any one place. Tradition favoured Cork. Going into the game, they had won twenty-two titles against Wexford's two.

'The crucial contest was that between Christy Ring, playing at left corner-forward, and Bobby Rackard. Ring went into the match in search of a record nine All-Ireland senior medals, having won his first in 1941. Outside of Munster, Wexford were one of Cork's greatest rivals at the time. It was the Wexford man who would win out in every sense.

'Wexford had the advantage of a whirlwind start, with a goal from Padge Keogh after only three minutes. Two minutes later, Ring registered Cork's first score with a point from a twenty-one-yards free. Wexford went on to win by 2–14 to 2–8.'

Wexford had a special place in Ring's affections.

'We in Cork treated Tipperary as our greatest rivals, but I always loved our clashes with Wexford in Croke Park. It was a different climate in Croke Park because you didn't have the pressure of the Munster Championship on your back. It was the same for Wexford; they didn't have the pressure of beating Kilkenny on them. Both of us could relax a bit,' as the Wizard of Cloyne explained before his death.

Perhaps the definitive epithet to Ring's exploits came from Mícheál Ó Muircheartaigh: 'If a novel portrayed a fictitious character accomplishing the achievements of Christy Ring, it would lack credibility.'

Jack Lynch was amused by one aspect of Ring's impact on Cork hurling after the final.

'A few days before the 1972 Munster final between Cork and Clare, Cork dual star Denis Coughlan pulled in for petrol, and who pulled in beside him but Christy Ring. Christy started to talk to him about the match and asked Denis to show him his hurley. Christy decided to take a few swings with it, but somehow broke it. The blood drained from Christy's face, but when he recovered his composure, he told Coughlan not to worry. He pulled out a hurley from the boot of the car. It was the one he used in three of his greatest All-Ireland triumphs. It was too heavy for Denis, though, so Christy called back to him a few hours later with a hurley that was a ringer for the one that he'd broken. "That will bring you luck," said Christy. With Cork leading comfortably, Denis was sent off for the only time in his career!'

FROM A JACK TO A KING

Jack Lynch won five All-Ireland hurling medals with Cork. He also won an All-Ireland football medal. His football career left him with one enduring memory from the 1945 All-Ireland football final. Lynch took mischievous pleasure in recalling Frank O'Connor's claim that Cork had a mental age of 17. You had to leave at 17 if you were to be happy and stimulated, whereas Dublin had a mental age of 21.

'Having completed my law examinations, I was in digs on the southside of Dublin in Rathgar. I met the Cork team at what was then Kingsbridge Station on the Saturday evening and I told the selection committee I would not be at the hotel the next morning as there was a bus route near my digs that passed by Croke Park and so I would go straight to the ground. The next morning, I was waiting in a queue about 20 yards long. Bus after bus passed, each taking only a couple of people at a time. At one stage, I barged to the head of the queue. The conductor told me to go back and wait my turn. I pointed to my bag of togs and said I was playing in the All-Ireland football final in Croke Park within the hour. The conductor said sarcastically that this was the best reason for breaking a queue that he'd ever heard, but let me stay on. I alighted from the bus at the junction of Drumcondra and Conyngham roads, and ran around to the back of the Cusack Stand, where the dressing-rooms were then located. I knocked at the Cork dressing-room door to be greeted by an ominous silence, except the sound of footsteps slowly and deliberately pacing the floor, and this within only about 15 minutes of the throw-in. The door opened. It was Jim Hurley, formerly a Cork hurling midfielder, then secretary of UCC and chairman of the Cork Selection Committee. I expected to be bawled out. Instead I got, "Hello, Jack Lynch, you were great to come." I had missed the president at the time, Seán T. O'Ceallaigh, coming into the dressing-room to wish the team well. I regretted that because he had been in the GPO in the 1916 Rising. I think I escaped any nasty recriminations afterwards because I was involved in the movement that set up the winning goal.'

Lynch also made his mark in a club football match.

'The star-laden Clonakilty side were playing St Nicholas in Bandon. It was during the winter, and the river adjacent to the pitch was flooded. Mick Finn deliberately belted it into the river because Clonakilty were losing and there was only one football, so he hoped the match would have to be abandoned. I jumped into the river and swam out to retrieve the ball. The Clonakilty lads never forgave me for it!'

THE GAA

DUAL STARS

There have been 18 players who have won All-Ireland senior medals on the field of play in both hurling and football. Eleven of these are from Cork, including such luminaries as Jack Lynch, Jimmy Barry-Murphy, Brian Murphy, Ray Cummins, Denis Coughlan and, famously in 1990, Teddy McCarthy.

Folklore abounds about the first Cork player to become a dual All-Ireland medal winner, Billy Mackessy, who was also a renowned publican. An enterprising Leesider who was short of a few bob had a penchant for poaching free drink in the hostelries of the city. One day, he sauntered into Billy's pub with another chancer and in a near whisper asked Billy how many All-Ireland medals he had, to which the reply was 'two'. The quick-witted duo then went to the other end of the bar and told the bartender that they were due two drinks 'on the house'. The barman gave them a puzzled look. The resourceful drinkers then confirmed their entitlement by shouting down the pub to the owner, 'Wasn't it two you said, Mr Mackessy?'

Carlow dual star Paddy Quirke hurled for the county at senior level from 1974 to '90 and played senior football with the county from '74 to '87. Quirke played for the Leinster football team in both '79 and '81, and in four consecutive years from '78 and '81 for the Leinster hurling side.

'I preferred playing most for the hurlers because I felt more like I was on a par with them than with the footballers. I think I was just one of the lads with them, but it was a bit more difficult with the footballers. In 1979, I played in the Railway Cup final in Thurles against Connacht. I was playing in my favourite position, midfield, along with Ger Henderson. Fan Larkin was the captain. I was marking John Connolly. At that stage, I feared no one and I could mix it with the best. I was playing with the best in Leinster – Tony Doran, Frank Cummins, Noel Skehan, Martin Quigley, Pat Carroll, Marc Corrigan and Peadar Carton – and enjoying it.'

Cork's Jimmy Barry-Murphy was one of the most high-profile dual players of the 1970s and '80s.

'I played both football and hurling, but dual players have died out of the GAA, really. I managed to combine it, but with the amount of games that are being played now and the back door of the championship, it just became totally impractical.

'It's a shame because you are missing players from teams who could have something to contribute. I'd like to see some of the hurlers who are good enough to play football with Cork playing with them still, for example. It's something we all enjoyed doing, and it's just unfortunate it can't be done nowadays.'

8

THE CLASH OF THE ASH

FOR 81 YEARS, CLARE HURLING WANDERED IN THE WILDERNESS.
According to local legend, their failure to make a breakthrough was
because of 'the curse of Biddy Early' – a woman who was completely
erroneously believed to be a witch and to have put a curse on the
Clare team. The man who led Clare back to the promised land, Ger
Loughnane, is dismissive of such talk.

'Biddy Early died before the GAA was even founded. She was in
today's terms a faith healer, not a witch. She devoted all her energy
to trying to help people. So the idea of her putting a curse on anyone
doesn't ring true. All of my people would have believed that the curse
was just an excuse. There was never any curse.'

For twenty years, Jimmy Smyth was never off the Clare team, and
during that period, he was selected for twelve years on the Munster
team, winning eight Railway Cup medals. Having played five years as
an intercounty minor, he made his Clare debut in a challenge match
in Gort at the age of seventeen with the great Josie Gallagher of
Galway.

'I learned a few lessons that day, I can tell you.'

In 1953, he scored six goals and four points against Limerick in the first round of the Munster Championship. Two years later, his biggest disappointment came against the same opposition.

'We lost the Munster final to them by 2–16 to 2–6. Not only had we defeated Tipperary and Cork in qualifying, but we had also beaten Wexford in the Oireachtas final the previous October in front of 30,000 in Croke Park. Losing to Limerick was a massive blow to Clare and took us a long time to recover. If Clare had won in 1955, I believe we would have won several All-Irelands.

'We had great teams in the '40s and all the way up to the '80s, but it was always the same old story – good management and back-up, commitment in training, but no delivery on the big day. Even on the days when we did deliver, as we did, for instance, against Cork in Killarney in 1986, it was no different. You could say it was almost a fear of winning and sheer bad luck. There were so many great players in Clare who could have won several All-Ireland medals if they had been with other counties. Our predicament was that we had good hurling teams that were saddled with the sorrows of past years.

'Clare's record was poor and we had no tradition of winning. When you have a tradition, it seeps into the bones and the psyche. It breeds confidence and even makes a winner out of a loser. A fair team with a good tradition would always be confident of winning against a better Clare side.

'In the past, even the language of the supporters carried the wail and the woe of what was said and unsaid. I hated the question "Will ye win?" People knew the answer to the question when they asked you. What they were saying was, "We want you to win, we know you can, but you won't."'

Despite the many losses and heartbreaks Smyth endured as a player, he was always acutely aware of the sociological importance of Gaelic games.

'The GAA achieved three very different purposes. It encouraged local patriotism. It inculcated among its members an uncompromising hostility to foreign games, and it revived local and national pride. Its philosophy is that love of country draws its strength and vitality from love of neighbours, fellow parishioners and fellow countrymen and women, and from love of the scenes, traditions, culture and way of life associated with one's home and place of origin: that a club or county provides a sense of importance, belonging and identity, shared goals, a pride and a purpose. All the traditions are equally charged with such values and aspirations.

'The balladmakers write about hurling and the ash, the glory of Munster final day as a symbol and inspiration to the Irish nation: about hurling and football and their association with the land, the sea, the plough and the spade and the atmosphere of All-Ireland day. They write with feeling about the role of the priest, the transience of life, the belief in a God and the power of prayer. All these assumptions are woven into the complex web of understanding. They are content in the knowledge that they have great games, great heroes, great people and great places. They tell us who we are, where we come from and where we stand.'

THE MIGHTY QUINN

When he scored three goals in the 1954 National League final against Kilkenny, Tipperary's Billy Quinn, father of former soccer star Niall, was propelled into national prominence. From an early age, his career had promised much.

'When I was 14, I was brought on as a sub in the All-Ireland final against Kilkenny in 1950. Tipperary had won all their matches up to then by a cricket score, so I never got a chance to come on and get used to the thing. It was crazy to bring me on for my first match in an All-Ireland final because I had no idea where I was or what I was doing.

'I captained the minor team to an All-Ireland title in 1953. There was no real pressure on me. All I had to do was to call the toss and collect the cup! The only work I had to do was before the All-Ireland final, when our goalie got a panic attack on the way out onto the pitch. The lads called me back and I got him back up against the wall of Hill 16. He was more afraid of me than of the opposition, and he went out and played a blinder.

'We were so used to winning that I got the cup and threw it somewhere and we went home. There was no celebration as such.

THE GAA

The big thing was to win the Munster final. There were massive crowds at the Munster finals then. When you came out of the ground, your feet would hardly touch the road because there'd be so many people.

'The big thrill was to be changing around with the senior team. The Munster final in Killarney was a classic match, though I'd an awful experience when a Cork man dropped dead beside me with the excitement of the game. The crowd invaded the pitch a few times, and Christy Ring had to escort the referee off the pitch.

'This was not a new thing. A decade earlier, also, such was the intensity of one Cork–Tipperary match that a man had to be anointed on the ground. The entire crowd knelt down as a mark of respect.'

Quinn's intercounty career coincided with a barren spell in Tipperary's fortunes in the championship.

'We played Cork in 1956, and Seamus Bannon got the best goal I ever saw when he ran down the wing and lashed the ball into the net. But when one of our lads threw his hurley 20 yards in celebration, the referee disallowed the goal, and Cork beat us. It was the greatest injustice I ever saw in hurling. We got dog's abuse listening in to the All-Ireland in Thurles because everyone was saying, "Ye should be there if ye were any good."

'I think the 1950s were a golden era for hurling because you had a lot of great teams, like Cork, Tipperary and Wexford. Not only had you great players on all those teams, but to go back, you'll find that each of those counties had five or six great players competing for each position. Christy Ring was the greatest player of the time, but Jimmy Doyle would run him a close second. He would get scores from left or right.'

In 1956, Quinn moved to Dublin for work reasons, and although he played a few games for his adopted county, his commitment to their cause was not total as there was always talk of a recall to the Tipp side. This indecision cost him the opportunity to play in an All-Ireland senior final.

'Dublin had a great team then, with exceptional players like Lar Foley, Des Foley and Des Ferguson. I thought I was going to go back playing for Tipperary, but I'm half sorry I didn't pursue the

122

THE CLASH OF THE ASH

opportunity to play for Dublin more. They only lost the All-Ireland final to Tipperary by a point in 1961.'

WEXFORD'S GLORY DECADE

Hurling was to get a welcome new lease of life in the 1950s with the emergence of a new power, as Mícheál Ó Muircheartaigh recalls.

'The first hurling team to make a lasting impression on me was the great Wexford team of the 1950s. I had seen John Doyle's great Tipperary three-in-a-row side of '49 to '51, but because of Tipperary's tradition, you somehow didn't wonder at that. It was different with Wexford because they came from nowhere. Remember, this was a county that had only won an All-Ireland in 1910, and by the 1950s, they had only added a solitary Leinster title back in 1918. They showed they had promise when they reached the National League final in 1951, only to lose to Galway. They took another step forward by reaching the All-Ireland that year, even though they lost heavily to Tipperary. By the next year, they were able to run Tipp to a point in the league final, and then they swept all before them in 1955 and '56, winning two All-Irelands and coming from fifteen points down against Tipperary at half-time to win by four points in a pulsating league final. The '56 All-Ireland final against Cork was an epic, with a late surge ensuring perhaps their greatest-ever triumph.

'In the 1990s, there was a famous racehorse called Danoli, a Cheltenham winner, who was known as "The People's Champion". It may not have been fully on the scale of the reaction to Clare's triumph in 1995, but when Wexford won in '55 they became the People's Champions.

'The star of that side was Nicky Rackard, but sometimes the invaluable contribution of his brother Bobby is neglected. Bobby was probably the best right full-back I have ever seen. He started off as an elegant centre half-back, but because of an injury to their great full-back Nick O'Donnell, he had to move to plug the back there. When Nick recovered, Bobby was slotted into the corner and he produced a string of astounding performances there. He had a marvellous ability to catch the sliotar – high or low – and send it far outfield in sweeping

123

clearances. I will never forget one gesture that sums up the true spirit of hurling. After Wexford beat Cork in the 1956 All-Ireland, Bobby and Nick O'Donnell hoisted the defeated warrior Christy Ring on their shoulders. That said it all about the spirit of that Wexford team.'

THE BLACK AND AMBER

Ernest Hemingway defined courage as 'grace under pressure'. By that criterion, Eddie Keher is one of the GAA's greatest heroes. When you have won six All-Ireland medals, ten Leinster medals, ten Railway Cup medals, five All-Star awards and a Texaco award, it is more than a little difficult to isolate one great sporting moment, but Eddie Keher hesitated only briefly in making his selection.

'The honour that meant most to me was my first-ever All-Ireland senior medal in 1963. Beating Tipperary in the '67 final was also very important because we hadn't beaten them at that level for 40 years, I think. There was an attitude from the fans then that "you'll never beat Tipperary in a hard game". Although we always play a certain type of game in Kilkenny, I think we toughened up a bit for that game, and it made for a very satisfying victory particularly as we proved our critics wrong.'

Joe Dunphy has a rare distinction in Kilkenny hurling, captaining his native county to two consecutive All-Ireland minor titles in 1961 and '62. The right corner-forward from Mooncoin achieved this honour via an unusual route. A study in self-effacement, his face purples with embarrassment when he is queried about his appointment.

'The captain really had to be from Mooncoin because we won four minor county titles then. Some of us had trials for the county minor team and three of us were selected for the county side, so it was between us. Our driver was the late Richard Croke. He sorted it out by getting us to draw straws.

'It was a great honour to be captain, though I had very shaky legs! When you were captain back then you didn't have to make a speech – which was just as well!'

The biggest influence on Dunphy's career was his teacher Seán Maher, brother of the famous Father Tommy Maher. His colleagues on that successful minor side included Noel Skehan, Pat Henderson and Tom Walsh. It was winning that first All-Ireland that really brought home to Dunphy the importance of hurling in Kilkenny.

'After we won the All-Ireland minor final, there was a bonfire in the town of Mooncoin in our honour. After all the fuss had died down, I went back to my home village of Luffany, a little village with just 14 farmhouses. There was a field at the back of the house where as young fellas we had always trained and practised. We were supervised by a man called Bob Collins, who would be timing us as we made runs around the field and so on. Bob hardly ever left the village. That night though when I got back from Mooncoin, there was Bob in the field with a bonfire blazing for me. It brought tears to my eyes.'

Dunphy made his senior debut for Kilkenny in a league fixture in 1964, but he was unable to hold down a regular place. Mooncoin's victory in the county final in 1965 was the catalyst for his real breakthrough onto the senior team. How intimidating was it to walk into a dressing-room that had some of the greatest hurlers of all time?

'You walked in, togged out and kept your head down! Having said that, even the most established stars were very supportive. Eddie Keher in particular was very friendly. He would always talk to you before a game and have words of encouragement to try and help you relax. I remember well him taking a couple of us new lads for a walk down O'Connell Street the evening before a big match. I had a few other walks with him.'

Although Dunphy won a National League medal, the game's highest honour eluded him. Despite the colour and excitement outside, the dressing-room of a team that has just lost an All-Ireland final is like Hell's Kitchen without the charm. Dunphy has experienced that sinking feeling.

'In 1966, Kilkenny lost the All-Ireland to Cork although we were red-hot favourites. Cork won by 3–9 to 1–10. I scored a point, but it wasn't a happy memory for me because I had missed a goal a couple of minutes earlier! The papers the next day were full of talk about "the year of the sleeping pill". It was the first year players had taken them before an All-Ireland final. There were a lot of smart comments afterwards that we took them too late because we hadn't fully woken up until after the match!'

Although he considers Christy Ring the greatest hurler he ever saw playing the game and he lists a string of Kilkenny players as amongst the best, he has particular admiration for Eddie Keher for his skill, dedication and attention to detail.

'For a perfectionist like Keher, routine is everything. You have to get the little things right. A famous incident occurred in the 1974 Leinster hurling final with the sides tied. With seconds to go, Kilkenny's legendary corner-forward had an opponent tread on his foot, breaking his lace. Almost immediately, Kilkenny were awarded a free. As a meticulous player, Keher knew he wouldn't be able to score with the lace not attended to, so he bent down and tied it. The Wexford fans thought he was engaged in gamesmanship and running up the clock and let him know with a chorus of booing, but Keher kept his concentration and slotted the sliotar between the posts to win the match.'

Keher has mixed feelings about his greatest game.

'From a personal point of view, 1971 was very satisfying and things went well for me on the day in the All-Ireland final. I scored a then record score in an All-Ireland final of 2–11 – a record that was broken by Nicholas English in 1989. I rang him up a few days later to congratulate him. Coincidentally, it was Tipp who beat us in the final in '71, and we can't complain about that because they had so many great players, like Babs Keating, who was hurler of the year that year.'

BAREFOOT IN THE PARK

For Babs, the '71 final has special significance.

'Long before players were handed out gear for free, we were very conscious of the importance of equipment. Jimmy Doyle was one of the best hurlers I ever saw. He would always arrive in the dressing-room with five spare hurleys. I had the very best pair of football boots, but the night before the final, my bag was stolen with the boots in it. I got a spare pair, but they didn't suit the conditions, so I took them off. Michael O'Hehir famously described me in his commentary as "barefoot in the park". I was marking Fan Larkin, and guys like Fan and Ted Carroll were not the sort of fellas to be walking around without some sort of protection. But Fan never stood on my feet. He tried it a few times, but I was gone before he could make contact!

'My hero as a kid was Christy Ring. I had lunch with him years later and we were discussing 21-yard frees and penalties, and he held the view that if the ball comes up right to you, you go for a goal.

'I started out with the belief that the Tipperary team who won three-in-a-row in '49 to '51 were the greatest team of them all. The press coverage was huge. They made those guys into heroes.

'I have to say the first team to make a great impression on me was the Waterford team of '57 to '59. Waterford were a bit like the Down football team of the '60s; they stood out. They were all in white. They had two wonderful midfielders in Séamus Power and Phil Grimes. Tom Cheasty at centre-forward was unique with his power and strength. He was so effective in that position because he was such a strong man. Then you had Frankie Walsh, who was a real dandy. In '57, Johnny Kiley was completely grey even though he was only 30, but he was really class. John Barron was a flashy kind of corner-back that we weren't used to because hurling was much tougher back then. They won an All-Ireland in 1959, but, a bit like the Waterford team of recent years, could have won more.

'Coming from where I was from, in rural Tipperary, we all had the dream of wearing the jersey, walking behind the Artane Boys' band and playing in Croke Park. The one thing we had was the confidence that if we got to an All-Ireland we would win it because of the power of the Tipp jersey. Football was in my blood. My great-uncle Tommy Ryan won two All-Irelands with Tipperary. He was playing in Croke Park on Bloody Sunday and helped remove Michael Hogan from the pitch after he had been shot by the Black and Tans. I played football for ten consecutive years with Munster. The fact that I came from a football background meant it came easier to me. I could play football just by togging out because I was brought up with a football, whereas with hurling I had to work a bit harder.

'I had a huge disappointment while underage, losing four All-

Ireland finals at minor and intermediate level. Then, having won an intermediate All-Ireland in 1963, three of us arrived on the Tipp senior team for the first league game against Galway. We played in most games in the league, but of the three new boys, I was the most vulnerable because the Tipp forwards were so strong.

'The highlight for me was playing in my first All-Ireland against Kilkenny in '64. Seamus Cleere was the hurler of the year in '63, and he was an outstanding wing-back. The one thing about that Tipp team was that they had the forwards thinking like backs, and the backs like forwards. Seamus Cleere had scored a couple of points from the half-back line in the final the previous year. When you have a half-back scoring like this, he's a seventh forward. My role was to stop Seamus. Luckily enough, I got the first ball that ran on between us and scored a tricky point. I made a goal for Donie Nealon as well as doing my own job, so I ended up as Sportstar of the Week and on a high. The hype at home then was as big as it is now. The only thing was that the media coverage wasn't anything like as intense as it is now. I was back at work on the Tuesday morning. There was no such thing as banquets here, there and everywhere. Having said that, there was a better atmosphere in Croke Park then because you were closer to the ground.

'The hurling ball has created the biggest change in the game since my playing days. It allows players to drive it so much further now, and you have to cater for that because it really bypasses centre-field play.'

GALWAY BOYS HURRAH

In the early '70s, new shoots were springing up in Galway. For the Irish rugby fan, an enduring image will always be Ciaran Fitzgerald's efforts to rally the Irish team in 1985. In the wake of dazzling and stylish victories away to Scotland and Wales, against England they appeared to be letting the Triple Crown slip through their fingers. Even those who had no experience of lip-reading could clearly make out his plea from the heart, as he temporarily put aside the good habits he acquired as an altar boy with the Carmelites in Loughrea: 'Where's your pride? Where's your f***ing pride?'

His record speaks for itself – Triple Crown and championship in '82, a share of the championship in '83 and the Triple Crown again in 1985. Fitzgerald, though, was a rugby virgin until his late teens.

'As a boy growing up in Loughrea, the only social outlet available was the boxing club. I won two All-Ireland boxing championships. My heroes, though, at the time were the Galway football team, who won the three-in-a-row in 1964, '65 and '66, and I attended all three finals. At Garbally, my main game was hurling. The highlight of my hurling career was playing in an All-Ireland minor final against Cork in 1970. Our team had been together from the under-14 stage and featured people like Seán Silke and Iggy Clarke. Initially, I played at half-back, but for some reason for one match they moved me to the forwards and I scored three goals. The problem was that when I played at full-forward in that All-Ireland final, I was marked by Martin Doherty, who subsequently made it big with the Cork senior team. "Big" was the word for Martin. I would have needed a stepladder to have competed with him in the air! I was moved out to centre-forward, but who followed me? Only Martin. He destroyed me. That Galway minor team went on to win an under-21 All-Ireland and most of them formed the backbone of the senior All-Ireland winning team in 1980.'

LIMERICK, YOU'RE A LADY

In 1973, Limerick ended a barren spell by winning their first All-Ireland hurling title since 1940. One of the stars of the Limerick team was Pat Hartigan, ranking with Brian Lohan as one of the great full-backs of the last fifty years. His main memories of the game are surprising even to himself.

'Strangely, it's the little things I remember about the game. Firstly, I remember the enthusiasm and spirit of Limerick people going on the train and the little games we were playing and the jokes we were making. This was only a front for what was facing us the next day. I remember the effect on people we knew, notably a taxi-driver, John Lane, a saint in his own right, who had a tremendous sense of the importance of the occasion for a county that had been away from hurling's top table for so long.

THE GAA

'The evening before the match, the elder statesman and father figure of the team, Eamon "Ned" Rea, tried to break the ice by talking about "glamour boys" and the way rooms were being allocated in the team hotel. I suppose we were unusual in that way; we had two brothers in the squad who were both priests – Father Paudie and Willie Fitzmaurice.

'Ned, Jim O'Donnell, Seán Foley and myself headed into O'Connell Street at about 7.30 p.m. It was a sight to behold. Seeing all the Limerick people there gave us a real lift and made us even more determined to win the title, especially the way they were hooting horns at us. Some of them had been there in 1940 and were looking to see us repeat history, and others were going to attend Croke Park for the first time.

'I recall vividly the pep talk before the final. It was given to us by Jackie Power, Ger's father, who had been part of the Limerick All-Ireland victory in 1940. His voice faltered and he started to cry. Team captain Eamon Grimes like a flash stood up and took over.

'I can't remember leaving the dressing-room and I have no memory of going out of the tunnel. The next thing I remember, I was outside on Croke Park and in one din of noise.

'The weather was very bad on the day, and we got a little bonus because the wind changed in our favour at half-time. I always feel that the turning point in the game came in the second half. A high ball broke in behind our half-back line and Mick Crotty looked goalbound. Our goalie Seamus Horgan made a brilliant save, deflecting the ball so it went over the bar. A goal for Kilkenny at this point would have finished us, but the save spurred us on to victory.

'The real highlight of the All-Ireland for me came after the match with seeing a hundred people crying. It meant so much to them. That was a source of immense satisfaction.

'The post-match celebrations were not all we would have wished for. Such was the throng of people who came to the Crofton Airport hotel that we were locked in in the interests of safety. I was doing an RTÉ interview and was forced to leave by a back window. There was no dance. The tables were cleared, and guards were manning the doors so that people couldn't get in. The result was that there was no team celebration as such. There were pockets of us in different rooms. However, we made up for it the following day when we got back to Limerick to the reception in the Shannon Arms hotel. Estimates vary at the attendance between 50,000 and 65,000. I will never forget the squad car trying to avoid people as it steered us to our destination and the joy on the crowd's faces. Let's just say it was very late before we got home!'

THE PURPLE AND GOLD

In 1970, Martin Quigley made his senior debut for Wexford, and he played his last game for the county in 1989. In the course of his career, he won four consecutive All-Stars from 1973 to '76 and was chosen at centre half-forward on the Centenary Team of the greatest players never to have won an All-Ireland. In 1970, he was part of a unique piece of family history in the first 80-minute All-Ireland final when with his brothers Pat and John he was part of an all-Quigley half-forward line as Wexford lost to Cork. To add to the family connection, another brother, 'Big Dan', was selected at centre-back. An injury-stricken Wexford amassed a highly creditable 5–10, but Cork ran up a massive 6–21.

Wexford had an assembly line of new talent coming in the '50s and '60s, but the production line slowed down considerably in the '70s. This is a problem that afflicts the most successful counties. Martin Quigley was to be one of the victims of the change in Wexford's fortunes.

Asked about the greatest moment of his career, the answer comes with lightning speed.

'Our Leinster final win of 1976. Kilkenny had beaten us in the previous five finals, but we beat them by seventeen points that year. I remember looking at the clock with about ten minutes to go, and we were leading by 15 or 16 points. I thought to myself, "There's nothing they can do to us now," though with Kilkenny you can never know. It was such an unusual feeling for me to be so confident against them; that's why I remember the incident so well. The game went reasonably well for me, but nothing exceptional. It was one day, though, when it was all about the team.'

That year also saw his greatest disappointment.

'We really should have won the All-Ireland that year, having been eight points up against Cork after ten minutes. We had really good teams in Wexford those years, and we were very unfortunate not to have won at least one All-Ireland in the '70s.'

On a personal level, one of his best displays for Wexford was in a league fixture against Clare at Tulla, 'a graveyard for visiting teams', which earned him the Sportstar of the Week accolade. Apart from his pride in wearing the purple and gold, Quigley also drew great enjoyment from wearing the black and amber of Rathnure.

'I was part of a very strong Rathnure team and I have ten senior championship medals. For the bulk of my club career, I played as I did for Wexford, in the forwards. In the later stages, though, I switched to full-back and many a mighty tussle with the legendary Tony Doran. No matter what, the approach to the game in Rathnure was purist: it was about playing the game with skill and in the proper spirit. The support for the club within the parish was fantastic. The club is at the heart of the GAA – but not everyone seems to appreciate this.'

In 1972 and 1974, the Quigley family were the backbone of the Rathnure side that reached the All-Ireland club final, only to lose on both occasions to Blackrock.

In the annals of Wexford hurling, Quigley ranks as one of the comeback kids.

'I'm not sure: did I retire or was I retired in 1986? There are some who would say I had a more spectacular comeback than Lazarus! In 1988, I was a spectator at the first-round championship against Laois. Three weeks later, I scored 2–2 against Kilkenny.'

THE OLD AND THE NEW

The mid-1970s saw two interesting developments in Munster, with the emergence of Clare as a serious force in hurling and Cork winning a three-in-a-row of All-Irelands (1976–8). Ger Loughnane was up close and personal to both developments. It was a different era for player welfare.

'When we were in Dublin, Johnny Callinan and myself would have to pay our train fare home and then try to get it back from the Clare County Board. That was a really tough battle. We learned to wait till the treasurer had five or six pints in him to ask him for the money! It was absolutely terrible. They wanted you down to play, but they didn't want to pay for it!

'We started winning league games and got to the league final in '76 and drew with Kilkenny, but were hammered in the replay. We were hammered in the championship as well, but people felt a start had been made.

'In '77, we made real progress and beat Kilkenny in the league final. It was a massive breakthrough. The celebrations were not quite as good as when we won the All-Ireland in '95, but they were really great. By this time, highlights of league matches were shown on television, so we developed a great profile across the country. That year, we beat Tipperary in the Munster Championship after a replay and got to play Cork in the Munster final. The hype was unreal. Everyone thought this was going to be the big breakthrough. The game started off at a great pace with great scores. Then a row developed, and Jim Power was sent off after hitting Ray Cummins with his head. The whole scene came crumbling down for us. Everybody blamed the referee, but he had no option. There was a massive outcry, and all the sympathy was with Clare. I think Clare made a huge mistake after the game, and Waterford made the exact same mistake in '98. We failed to appreciate that the pace of our game was short, but nobody wanted to admit that. Everybody wanted a scapegoat. It would've been better to have faced up to it and said, "Right, the pace of our game is too slow. We'll correct that and take them on next year."

'In '77 to '78, we went through every match in the league unbeaten, including the final against Kilkenny. Then we qualified to play Cork again in the Munster final. The build-up to the game was something you rarely experience. The level of tension was unbearable and the air of expectancy within the county was unreal. What happened the previous year was going to backfire – blaming what happened on the referee. Now we had to deliver. There was such tension that one of our players hadn't slept for three nights before the game. In the dressing-room before the game, you could see some players almost visibly shrivel. When we went out on the pitch, the tension was everywhere. It was a terribly flat game. Most players seemed to be paralysed by the occasion. If you saw it now on video, you'd ask "Was hurling that bad back then?" When the real challenge came, the confidence wasn't there and the occasion got to us. We shrivelled up completely. I'd say only one or two of us played up to scratch. Nevertheless, at half-time it looked as if we were going to win, and as we came off the pitch, the Clare supporters stood up and cheered us. They were certain we were going to win. We had been playing against the wind, but were only four points down. We held their forwards in the second half, but we couldn't score.

'That was the end. Nobody said it was the end, but we all knew. The day had come for us to make the breakthrough, but we hadn't. From then on, we were going backwards. The door was open, but we didn't go through. After that, the door was closed again.

'We had some magical times in those three years. We'd go so far, but when the real test came, we would fail. We could beat Kilkenny on the wet days in spring, but we were caught out by Cork on the fast days in Thurles. We were as strong and tough and willing and dedicated as the rest of them. But Cork and Kilkenny always believed they would win. We never fully did. I was never as good a player again. I was only 25.'

In his playing days, Loughnane had witnessed a scene where a fire-and-brimstone speech had produced a more robust response than had been envisaged.

'I went on an All-Star trip to America in 1978. We were hammered by about 14 points by Cork in the opening match in Boston. The Cork half-back line was absolutely outstanding. After the match, we were told by the management that we were a "disgrace" and unless we upped our performance in the next match in San Francisco, there would be "severe repercussions".

'Pat Hartigan was team captain, and he gave a speech in the dressing-room before the second game. He threw his jersey on the floor in the middle of the dressing-room and said, "Anyone not prepared to die for the jersey, throw it in there and get out of here now." Our wing-forward was Pat Delaney from Offaly. He went on to become an outstanding player, but at that stage he was, shall we say, a little "impetuous". He was marking Denis Coughlan. Pat let fly the first ball that came into him, which struck Coughlan on the side of the head and split it open. Pat then moved into the centre, and the next ball that came his way he let fly, aiming for Johnny Crowley. He missed Crowley and struck his own man, Tony Doran. The game was only five minutes old, and he had sent two men to hospital! There was an immediate cry, "Get that mad man off." Pat was substituted immediately. He was very disappointed afterwards, but not in the way you might expect. He said, 'What harm, but if they had just left me on another minute or two, it would have been great. I was just going to move on Dermot McCurtin." He had taken it on himself to take out the entire Cork half-back line!

'I think, though, that little episode is a backhanded compliment to the respect that not just Pat Delaney but the entire hurling world, too, had for that Cork team. There are those who will say they were in the right place at the right time because other teams like Kilkenny were not as strong as they usually were, but look at the players they had at the time: Jimmy Barry-Murphy, Martin O'Doherty, John Horgan, Gerald McCarthy, Charlie McCarthy, Ray Cummins and, of course, the great Seánie O'Leary. You would have to take your hat off to them.'

INTO THE WEST

Galway made a breakthrough in 1980 when they beat Limerick to win the All-Ireland. Earlier, Babs Keating had been invited to coach the team:

'I was invited to coach Galway by Father Jack Solon in the late '70s. He was a great golfer. I was welcomed by the players and to this day retain great friendships with them. But I was basically a coach and had no role as a selector.

'In training, I preached the five S's – Speed and Stamina, Style and Skill, and from these four, there should emerge Scores. We got to the All-Ireland final in '79, where we lost to Kilkenny. I remember waking up that morning feeling very depressed because it was raining heavily. We had a flashy team with the Connollys, Noel Lane, P.J. Molloy and Bernie Forde – who were dry-ball players. I believe that bad, wet conditions suit an experienced team more than an inexperienced team. Kilkenny were very experienced. We weren't. I believe the wet day cost us two of Kilkenny's goals.'

Noel Lane received a call-up to the county panel for the 1977–78 league campaign, making his debut against Clare in Tulla. His build-up to the game was unusual.

'I was overawed going into the dressing-room with all my heroes from the National League win in 1975. There were some great characters, like John Connolly and Joe McDonagh, who went out of their way to give me confidence. P.J. Molloy was preparing for the game by rubbing poitín on to his legs. Poitín was hard enough to get at the time so it didn't seem a good use of it to me. I asked him for the bottle and said, "Better value to slug it than to rub it." So I had a sup. It didn't do me any harm. I was marking Johnny McMahon, who was an All-Star, and I was thrilled with my performance. I held my place after that.'

After suffering a heavy defeat to Tipperary in the 1979 National League final, a shake-up of the team was necessary. Lane was one of the casualties and was dropped from the panel. Breaking the news sensitively to him was not a priority for the Galway management.

'I got a letter in an envelope that was handed to me in the dressing-room in a club game. I smelled a rat. No reason was given for my omission. It was just: "We regret to inform you . . ." I felt it was severe to drop me like that.'

The opportunity for redemption came quickly. Galway were unimpressive in the All-Ireland final against Laois that year. Niall McInerney had been experimented with at full-forward on the day, but it had not worked well. Lane would find himself called upon to step into the breach.

'Babs Keating was training Galway at the time. He spearheaded a delegation that came down to see me to ask me back. I replied, "Not a chance." I was just playing hard to get. I was the first one in Athenry for training that evening.

'Babs was an excellent manager. As I was moved into full-forward, he gave me a lot of his time and attention coaching me on how to approach forward play and working on my solo and my passing. He gave me a lot of confidence in my own game. I really admired him as a player for Tipp. We had thought of ourselves as inferior to the big powers like Cork and Tipperary, but he was one of them and I suppose to our surprise he was a normal guy. He gave us a lot of confidence. Babs was "let go" after we lost the 1979 All-Ireland, but I believe the self-belief he gave us was a significant factor in our breakthrough the following year.'

Lane's first All-Ireland came in 1980.

'We won that day because our leaders, especially Joe Connolly, stood up and were counted. We were a powerful team, and that side should have won more than one All-Ireland. It suited us that day that we were playing Limerick rather than Cork or Kilkenny, and that gave us confidence. It felt like it was for us that day, though Limerick could have considered themselves unlucky.'

PEOPLE OF GALWAY, WE LOVE YOU

Joe McDonagh was part of the beginning of a new era in Galway hurling when he played on the county's first All-Ireland under-21 title against Dublin in 1972. And in 1979, he was the captain when Galway played Kilkenny again in the final, only to make a present of two soft goals to the men in amber and black.

'We wasted a lot in the first half. I don't think the rain suited us. Kilkenny were spurred on by the defeat at the hands of Cork the previous year and didn't want a second successive defeat. Of course, I shouldn't have been playing at all. I was ill, but didn't realise it. Afterwards, doctors were mystified that I had been able to play for 70 minutes.'

Unfortunately, illness prevented McDonagh from lining out in Galway's historic All-Ireland triumph over Limerick in 1980. However, he made a unique contribution by following Joe Connolly's tour de force of an acceptance speech with an emotional rendition of 'The West's Awake'.

THE GAA

After Clare won the All-Ireland in 1995, after eighty-one years, it created such joy that two old farmers who had been mortal enemies for more than forty years over a row about fences on their adjoining farms had a genuine and lasting reconciliation in the local pub that night. For Galway people, 1980 was such a moment, and for its hurler of the year, John Connolly, in particular. Connolly was introduced to the game by his father.

'I remember clearly being carried on the crossbar of his bike as he cycled to the official opening of Pearse Stadium in 1957. To this day, I can still see the delight and awe in his eyes as he pointed out Joe Salmon, Jim Fives and Jimmy Duggan. I really desired to emulate them that day.'

Connolly, though, was a Renaissance man. He attended school with Christy O'Connor Jnr and played for Galway minor footballers and also at under-21 level for the county.

'When I was 17, a local boxing club was started by that great boxing man "Chick" Gillen. I joined with a few of the lads and went on to win the Connacht junior light welterweight championship that year. However, I soon came down to earth when a fella called Mike Berry beat the hell out of me in a local tournamnent.'

Despite winning All-Stars in 1971 and '79, Connolly knew more bad days than good days in the Galway jersey.

'We had many frustrations, none more so than the defeat by Kilkenny in the 1979 All-Ireland final. In my opinion, it was one of the weakest Kilkenny teams ever to win an All-Ireland. Galway failed to convert opportunities, conceded unnecessary scores, and failed to capitalise on our strengths and take a grip on the game. On the way home, my wife, Nuala, turned to me and said, "Ye'll never win an All-Ireland now." Many people thought that a curse hung over the Galway hurlers like the famous Biddy Early curse in Clare. On the way home, after what Nuala said, I began to think there maybe was some substance to it. Then the Pope came to Ireland and said Mass across the road from where I grew up on Ballybrit racecourse.

'We beat Limerick in the All-Ireland final in 1980 and had whatever luck was going that day – the county's first-ever win since 1923, when

Limerick were also beaten. We won the Railway Cup. Maybe Pope had lifted the curse.'

However, the papal influence quickly waned as Johnny Flaherty's famous late goal gave Offaly a celebrated win.

'I retired in 1980, but was persuaded to return after Galway drew with Limerick in the All-Ireland semi-final. I will never understand how Galway lost to Offaly in the 1981 final. I still think of the goal I scored in the first half when the umpire waved the green flag but the referee disallowed it. The sound of the final whistle was probably the lowest moment in my hurling life. Back then, I got very upset after losing a match. I would go back over every missed stroke and all the opportunities and analyse the might-have-beens. If I could start all over again, I would promise myself to make my top priority to enjoy every match. The game has helped me to be a better person in many ways: it helped me to accept disappointment on and off the field and bounce back. Looking back on the game, though, while we didn't underestimate Offaly, we should have realised they would come at us hard in the end. At half-time, the belief was that it was our game, and we were probably a bit too confident that day. I always say that if it takes ten things to get a ball, the tenth is the most important. The problem was we weren't willing to do the tenth thing that day.'

Galway was not the only passion in John's life. The other was his club, Castlegar, which was known by everybody as Cashel. One moment with them is carved on his heart for ever.

'We won the All-Ireland club final in 1980, with five of us Connolly brothers playing and two substitutes. The team had Padraic, Michael, Joe, Gerry and myself playing, and the two *gasúrs*, Tom and Murt, were subs. It was a tradition of ours; even after us getting married with our own homes, we would all meet in our old home place the morning of a match, known to everyone in Galway as "Mamo's", which was an old name for "Grandmother's". We would chat about the game, and without realising it, we built up a kind of spirit that stood for us on the field. Then as we left Mamo's, she would always shake the bottle of holy water on us, saying, "Mind yourselves and don't be fighting, and don't come back here if ye lose!" In fairness, we were always welcomed even when we lost.

THE GAA

'Another famous victory came in the All-Ireland club semi-final that year against the Cork champions Blackrock. The Athenry ground was thronged. Parish rivalry was cast aside and every Galway man became a Castlegar man that day. I usually never remember scores, but I'll never forget that score, 2–9 to 0–9, and we beat a Blackrock team that had nine county players, including the great Frank Cummins of Kilkenny.

'No matter how high you go, there is something special about playing for your own parish or village, the people you grew up with, the ordinary five-eighths whose life is hurling, and the kick you get out of achieving something with your parish – that's the GAA for me.'

John is also retrospectively proud of his brother Joe's famous speech after Galway won the All-Ireland in 1980.

'Joe's speech probably didn't have the same impact on us as it did on everyone else at the time because we were used to hearing him talking in Irish. It was natural for him. For neutrals listening, though, it was very different from the normal speech and that is why so many were taken by it.'

His career has left Connolly with many happy memories.

'Once we were playing Gort in a tough county senior hurling championship match; Joe was playing on Sylvie Linnane at centre half-back and I was at full-forward. I had this habit of saying "*tarraing*" when dropping a ball between Joe and Sylvie. This "*tarraing, tarraing*" really fooled Sylvie. He had this idea that it was a secret code between us, and he probably conjured up this image of me telling Joe to pull on him. *Tarraing* was the Irish for "pull", and being native speakers we often spoke in Irish.

'In the 1971 All-Ireland semi-final in Birr against Tipperary, Mick Roche, who was centre half-back, came out on me in the second half. In the heat of battle, we got involved with one another, but like everything else it stopped and finished, and I remember chasing the ball into the full forward line and running down the field. I heard Mick coming after me, and I knew by his run that it was after me not towards the ball he was coming, and he bent down and caught my hurl. "God," I thought to myself, "this fella is really looking for trouble," and he took my hurl and picked this thing off the bas, which turned out to be a hairnet. He had this fine big head of black curly hair and to keep it out of his eyes he wore a hairnet. That was before the helmets. In the battle with all the hurleys, his hairnet got caught in the tin of my hurley!'

THE FAST LANE

After the disappointment of losing the All-Ireland 1981 final to Offaly, Galway had some lean years. Things took a turn for the better in 1985, as Noel Lane recalls.

'We had really a new side that year with just a few survivors of the 1980 team. We got great new players in, notably a wonderful half-back line. We beat the All-Ireland champions Cork in the semi-final. It was a wet day and there was surface water on the pitch, but we caught fire. We were always capable of doing that in a semi-final. Our problem was maintaining that right through to a final, and we lost to Offaly that year. In '86, we beat Kilkenny in the semi-final. Joe Cooney really came of age that day. Cyril Farrell used a two-man full-forward line for that game and it worked a treat. We were good enough to win in '86, but tactically we got it wrong. We repeated the two-man full-forward line in the final, but it shattered our confidence when it didn't work, and Cork grew in confidence and won.'

Lane felt the pain of that defeat in a very personal way.

'I was captain that year. We won the Railway Cup that year, but lost the finals of the Oireachtas tournament, the National League and the All-Ireland. Personally, I didn't have a good game in the All-Ireland and found the whole experience very disappointing.

'The night before the All-Ireland, I couldn't sleep, which didn't help me in Croke Park. I felt the pressure as captain and was really keen to do well. When you are young, you don't suffer from nerves as much. Back in 1979, I had got a full eight hours sleep the night before the final, but on the morning of the match I met Frank Burke and John Connolly, and they had slept so badly that they had decided to go for a walk down the streets of Dublin at three or four in the morning. I thought they were crazy then, but I understood in '86. The one thing I sometimes worry about is when I see panellists on TV almost character-assassinating players. It's not fair because I don't think they appreciate the number of reasons why a player may underperform on the big stage.'

The disappointment of '86 took its toll on Lane.

'My form suffered after that, and I was lucky to be on the panel in '87. I came on as a sub in the All-Ireland semi-final in '87. I felt very nervous coming onto the pitch and I was wondering to myself, "What am I doing here?" Then I got a goal, and it lifted the weight of the previous year off my shoulders. I came on as a sub in the final against Kilkenny and scored another goal. It might have been the worst goal ever scored in Croke Park, but it still counted!

'In '88, I was back starting on the team, but after scoring 1–5 in the All-Ireland semi-final, to my amazement and disgust, I was dropped for the final on the Tuesday night before the game. I hadn't seen it coming. I let Cyril know my feelings on the subject in no uncertain terms and in choice language. I left Ballinasloe in a hurry and went home feeling sorry for myself, believing an injustice had been done to me. I proceeded to Loughrea and drank 12 pints of beer. On the Thursday night, realising that I was lucky to be there at all, I went up to Cyril and said, "You heard what I did on Loughrea and you heard what I said to you on Tuesday night, but if you want me Sunday, I'll be there."

'I came on after half-time. It was one of the great All-Irelands. There was great rivalry and great duels. One of the decisive factors was that our full-back Conor Hayes had Nicky English in his grip. If they had moved English, we would have been in trouble. I think the captaincy played on Nicky. I got in around the square and scored a goal that was instrumental in us getting the result.'

MR PRESIDENT

One of the stars on the Kilkenny team that beat Galway in the '79 All-Ireland final was Nickey Brennan, later to become president of the GAA.

'I come from a small country parish (Conahy) with a junior hurling club (Shamrocks), but I got the big break when I went to school in St Kieran's, which was a big hurling nursery. To be frank, to survive you had to play hurling morning, noon and night between doing a bit of study. If you get on the teams there it brings you to the notice of the county's underage selectors. I played with Kilkenny from 1973 to 1985, apart from missing out on '76 and '77 because of the small matter of getting married and building a house. I was far from being the greatest hurler ever to play from Kilkenny, but I was a reliable and consistent hurler: that was probably my greatest strength.

'That Galway team had wonderful players. John Connolly was a hurler I greatly admired because he was such a stylist and had all the skills of the game. He was a complete gentleman, as were all the Connollys. I played through the era of great hurlers of whom one (Ger Loughnane) became even more famous as a manager! I felt very sorry for those great Clare players who never made it to an All-Ireland title. Certainly their emergence in the '90s was a major fillip to the game. Tony Doran was an inspiration for Wexford. Offaly's Pat Carroll was a great hurler and a very decent guy, though sadly he is no longer with us.'

OFFALY UNLUCKY

In sport, the dividing line between winning and losing is often very thin. Hard-luck stories abound. One of the cruellest pieces of luck ever experienced by any Irish sportsman was that suffered by Offaly goalkeeper Damian Martin (the first-ever All-Star hurling goalkeeper) in the 1982 Leinster hurling final against Kilkenny. He had been a hero the previous year when Offaly came out of the shadows to win the All-Ireland title in a dramatic finale against the reigning champions Galway, which saw Johnny Flaherty score the decisive goal late in the game.

In 1982, the pendulum was to swing violently in the opposite direction and Martin was to become embroiled in arguably the most controversial umpiring decision in the history of the GAA.

In a closely contested final, there is nothing to choose between the sides. A long ball is sent from the Kilkenny defence. Martin advances to the danger to shield the sliotar as it goes harmlessly wide. He is absolutely convinced the sliotar is out over the line. Kilkenny's ace forward Liam Fennelly is advancing rapidly and swings his hurley, making a sweet contact and sending the sliotar across the goal, where the ever vigilant Matt Ruth has an empty net to aim at. He does not miss.

Martin cannot believe his eyes when he sees the umpire raising the green flag. His incredulity is genuine. It is in no sense an attempt to put the blame on somebody else for an error of judgement, but the indignation of a man who feels he has been the victim of a travesty of justice. He will go to his grave with 100 per cent certainty that the umpire made a terrible blunder.

It is the turning point of the game. Kilkenny win the match and go on to win the first of two back-to-back All-Ireland titles. But was their '82 Leinster title based on an error of judgement by an umpire? Inevitably, this was the main area of discussion when I spoke to Matt Ruth about the incident. As we talked during Wimbledon fortnight, it was understandable that he should use a tennis analogy to explain the circumstances of the umpire's difficult decision.

'If you watch Wimbledon and see the speed at which the ball travels, you will notice that both the umpire and the line judge have all these fancy electronic gadgets to help them make the right decision, but still there are many times when the players think they have bad decisions made against them. The ball is hitting the line at such speed that it can be virtually impossible at times to say with absolute certainty whether a ball is in or out. The same thing can happen in hurling.

'I know Damian Martin is totally sincere when he says the ball was out. I can't say for sure myself; it all happened so fast. All I can say is that Liam Fennelly doesn't think it was out. Nobody else but Liam could have pulled it off. He is left-handed and he hit the ball at an angle that virtually no other hurler could have done to get the ball across to me. I know that it is very difficult to explain to someone who doesn't know Liam's style of hurling and his wrist action in particular. It probably sounds very technical, but I think that is most likely the reason why he was able to get the ball across without it having crossed the line, even though it seemed he had no chance of saving it.'

Nicky English was responsible for one of the most iconic scores in hurling when he kicked the ball past Ger Cunningham into the net in the '87 Munster final at Semple Stadium with a bend on the sliotar that George Best would have killed for.

'I was lucky to have scored goals in big games. I was giving out to myself that day because the one good ball I got in the whole game, I had no hurl. I was tackled by Cork's full-back Richard Browne and lost my hurley. As a youngster, I played a lot of tennis and often afterwards we played soccer with a tennis ball. I had no option that day but to kick the ball, and many times after that I tried to bend the sliotar the way I did that day, but never could. So I was really lucky it came off for me that day.

'The 1987 Munster final replay was the day of days as an event and from an emotional point of view. The thing is, though, when I look back at the game I am embarrassed. The standard is very poor and I would not want my young son Alex to see it. That's why I despair when I hear people saying hurling used to be much better in "the old days". Hurling is way better now and will be even better in a few years' time.'

Babs Keating looks back wistfully at the aftermath of that match.

'The one regret I have is that we didn't have the courage to take the team away the next weekend for a break. We had drawn the Munster semi-final and had needed extra time in the replay to win the Munster final. The team were dead, and the three of us couldn't lift the team for the semi-final. That's not to take away from the fact that Galway were a great side and deserved their two All-Irelands.'

Nicky English echoes those sentiments.

'Galway had learned a lot from losing in '85 and '86, and were ahead of us in their development. They deserved to win in '87 and '88. The rivalry between us was very strong because I think we were so far ahead of all the other counties in those years. Things came to a head in the '89 semi-final. Galway were really hyped up by "the Keady Affair" [when Galway's Tony Keady was suspended for playing illegally in New York]. They felt that a major injustice had been done to them. They were going for a three-in-a-row, and until 2008 with

Kilkenny, we saw how hard it was to do this. We knew we would be seen as failures if we returned home defeated three years in a row. Given the tradition in Tipperary, that was not acceptable. People often say you have to lose one before you win one, but losing can make it more difficult to come back, too. Jimmy Barry-Murphy said it's as easy to win your first All-Ireland as the last. By losing in '87 and '88, we maybe made it harder for ourselves in '89, but it was going to be a defining game for us.

'Both semi-finals were played on the same day. Before the match, we got the news that Antrim defeated Offaly in the semi-final. Both teams knew that our match was really the All-Ireland final and that upped the ante. It was a thundery day and there was a black cloud over Croke Park, so there was kind of an eerie atmosphere in the crowd. It was an ill-tempered game, and although we won, the fact that Galway had Sylvie Linnane and Hopper McGrath sent off took a bit of the gloss off it.'

From his Dublin home, Nicky English, with the Dow Jones index giving the most recent stock exchange figures on the television in the background, talks easily and eloquently about the complexities of the financial markets and all matters hurling. There is only one subject he is not forthcoming on. When asked directly for his opinion on Sylvie Linnane, his reply is: 'I have no comment on that topic.'

Babs Keating also regrets the atmosphere on that day.

'In many ways, 1989 was unusual. We beat Waterford in a horrible Munster final. The build-up to the semi-final against Galway was dominated by the Keady Affair. What really hurt me about that was that Galway people blamed Tipperary for setting Keady up. Tommy Barrett, the county secretary, was the Tipperary delegate and he spoke in favour of Tony Keady being allowed to play. He never remembers anyone thanking him for it. I thought it was a very noble thing, and I don't think we could have done any more. We never got involved in the politics of it. At the end of the day, Galway had delegates from their own province who didn't support them.

'Everybody knew the rules. Tony Keady knew the rules. The Galway people in New York knew the rules. Tony Keady was such a fine player that he let Galway down by playing in New York. The Galway people who played him in New York let Galway hurling down by playing him.

'The atmosphere was very bad before the game. There was a lot of aggression. From such a gentleman, Hopper McGrath did the worst thing of all when he really lashed out at Conor O'Donovan. It was a pity. Galway had beat us in the league final that year and it was a superb game.'

With typical reserve, Nicky English makes no mention of an incident in the 1991 All-Ireland semi-final against Galway when he was struck a blow above the left eye, which caused a flow of blood like a volcano erupting, required nine stitches and might have caused him permanent eye injury. Despite repeated nudges, no comment on the incident are supplied.

'We won the All-Ireland again in '91, and it was important to us that we beat Kilkenny in the final because there were those who devalued our win in '89 because it was Antrim we beat and not one of the powers of the hurling. Of course, that's very unfair on Antrim, but we had to show to the hurling world that we were worthy of a place at hurling's top table. My hamstring went in that year, and I came back too soon for the semi-final against Galway and it went again. It went a third time during the final, so I didn't make it all the way through. I think although we won the All-Ireland, the injuries were starting to catch up, and although we won the Munster title in '93 and a league in '94, we never could scale those heights again.

'I was also glad we won for Babs's sake. He knew how to get the best out of us. There was the odd blip, though. He once faced the problem of rallying us even though we were trailing Cork in a league match at half-time by eight points. After a number of inspirational words in an effort to instil confidence, Babs went around the team individually and asked each of them: "Can we do it?"

'To a man, we replied: "We can. We can."

'He could feel the surge of belief invading the dressing-room. Everything was going swimmingly until he turned to Joe Hayes and asked: "Joe, can we do it?"

'Joe took the wind out of his sails when he replied: "It's not looking good!"'

Nicky is keen to defend Babs from one long-running criticism. Keating's comment that 'you can't win derbies with donkeys' before Tipperary played Cork in the 1990 Munster final was seen as a spectacular own goal when the Cork donkeys won.

'We did make mistakes in terms of selection for that match. I think after we won the All-Ireland in '89, our first in 18 years, we coasted a bit and never had the same application as the previous year. We went to Toronto for a week in March to play the All-Stars and that was another distraction. When Cork beat us, Babs was blamed for his remarks. People said that because it suited them. It might have been used as a motivational tool in Cork, but it was not the reason we lost. Cork were hungrier than us and that was the crucial difference.'

Babs addresses his controversial comments head on.

'It was a stupid remark and no more than that. It was used against us that year. We were decimated with injuries. It was a bluff game with us. We had no sub for the backline with injuries. We took a chance with Declan Ryan at full-forward, even though he was lifting bales with his father the day before and he just wasn't fit to hurl. Mark Foley got three goals that day, and he never played like that before or since.

'The next year, both Mark Foley and the Cork full-back Richard Browne didn't perform well. Both of them are dentists. The boys in one of the pubs in Clonmel put up a sign: "Wanted for Cork: a centre-forward and full-back. Dentists need not apply."

'I knew we needed to win a second All-Ireland to be seen as a great team. We had one thing against us: lack of new players. I brought 11 subs with us on our trip to Florida and the Bahamas, but none of them really contributed to the team afterwards. We needed to find one or two new players to cover for injuries, and we didn't. The underage teams weren't going as well as I would have liked. Nicky basically didn't play in '91 because of injuries.'

Those injuries would indirectly catapult English into controversy. He found himself in the firing line when he was accused of being disrespectful to Clare while celebrating a score in Tipperary's trouncing of their near neighbours in the Munster final.

'In 1993, I was crocked with injuries. The players on my own team were having a laugh at me. When they eventually passed the ball to me, I wasn't thinking about Clare in the slightest; I was just thinking to myself that I would show my own lads that I could still do it, and when I scored, I was caught smiling. Ger Loughnane used that very successfully the next year to hype up the Clare lads, saying I had been disrespectful to them by laughing at them. All is fair in love and war, and fair play to him for taking an advantage of it, but it was misrepresented completely. It had nothing to do with Clare. It was just about proving to my own teammates that despite the injuries I hadn't lost it.'

THE CATS

Kilkenny's Nickey Brennan recalls the '91 All-Ireland from a different perspective.

'In 1991, Kilkenny lost the All-Ireland to Tipperary through a flukey goal. In fairness to Tipp, they won and good luck to them, but it could have gone either way. There were a lot of players in our side that came from the under-21 team I had managed in the previous year. Ollie Walsh was the manager and I was a selector, and I remember Ollie saying to the young players that there was a danger that the game might pass them by. His warning was prophetic because in a sense, that is what happened. The era of squads going off on sun holidays wasn't as well developed back then, but after losing that final, we went away as a squad for a weekend in Clare with wives and girlfriends – more or less as a thank you for what had been achieved. I have no doubt in my mind that the reason why we won the next two All-Irelands can be traced back to that weekend in Clare because we drowned our sorrows and built up a spirit and respect for each other.'

CHANGING TIMES

Mícheál Ó Muircheartaigh is the ideal candidate to offer a balanced perspective on the developments in hurling in this era.

'I think that hurling has changed a lot for the better, and many of the players that hurled maybe 30 years ago – and this has amazed me because generally a lot of players hang on to the theory that their own generation was the best – are admitting that the modern generation of hurlers is better than they were. I think that video evidence would swing you around to that view. There is a greater emphasis on skill now. In the past, the man was played more in hurling; now it was never as bad as football, but there was a lot of holding in the old days: for example, full-backs penned into the forwards, they held onto their man when the ball came in and kept their man away from the goalie. That would all be deemed a foul nowadays. The emphasis now is on speed and skill, and I think hurling is better for that.

'When you talk about the great teams it's not nearly as clear-cut in hurling as it is in football. If I were pushed to it, I would say that the best hurling team, with the emphasis on *team*, that I ever saw was the Kilkenny side of the early '70s – though Brian Cody's team perhaps matches them and some would say surpasses them. They won the All-Ireland in '72, '74 and '75, and played the final in 1973 against Limerick.

'Limerick had a great side in 1973, with the likes of Pat Hartigan and Eamon Grimes. They had to be to beat that wonderful Kilkenny team. Of course, they pulled off a masterstroke deciding out of the blue to play Eamonn Cregan, possibly the greatest forward Limerick ever had, at centre half-back to counter Pat Delaney.

'When I think of Kilkenny's wonderful games of the time, I especially remember those against Wexford, particularly in Leinster finals. Wexford had a great team at the time, but could not get the better of Kilkenny. I think that Kilkenny team were good in all sectors: take Eddie Keher in the full-forward line, Pat Delaney at centre-forward, Frank Cummins in midfield, Pat Henderson at centre half-back. They had super men in all parts of the field and played like a team.

'I suppose, though, I'd have to single out Eddie Keher from that team as one of the all-time greats. I always say to score, we'll say, a point in an All-Ireland final is something special for a player. I could be wrong now, but I think it's seven goals and seventy-seven points that he scored in All-Ireland finals alone. What memories must that man have? That tally is a measure of the man's greatness.

'D.J. Carey was a star. There was no doubt about it. The crowd got very excited when the ball came towards him. He had speed and tremendous skill. On his day, he was unbeatable. You'll often be asked on the day of a match when a guy shines if he is the greatest player you ever saw. I always say that you have to wait a few years after a guy retires to judge him properly. Eddie Keher played senior for Kilkenny for the first time in 1959, having starred in the minor All-Ireland final that year. The senior final ended in a draw and he was drafted on as a sub for the replay. He was still playing for the seniors in 1977, so, apart from his superb skill, that he remained at the top for so long is also a factor in considering his greatness.'

John Connolly, too, was a big fan of that Kilkenny team.

'I wonder if we will ever again see a forward line unit like the one Kilkenny had in the mid-'70s: Crotty, Delaney, Fitzpatrick, Brennan, Purcell and Keher. Could you ever trump that again for class?'

9

A NEW ERA

EUGENE MCGEE TELLS THE STORY OF A NEW MANAGER WHO IS dismayed with the drink culture in the squad he has just inherited. He comes up with a brainwave to illustrate the error of their ways. He summons the team into the dressing-room and places two glasses on the bench. One he has filled with water, the other he has filled with vodka. He then drops a worm into each glass. In the glass of water the worm lives, but in the glass of vodka the worm dies. Afterwards, the manager asks: 'Now lads, what can we learn from this?'

One player snaps up his hand immediately and says: 'Drink plenty. It will kill all your worms.'

HEFFO'S HEROES

As manager of the Dublin team that changed the face of Gaelic football in 1974, Kevin Heffernan never had any problems with being clearly understood. Yet when Dublin played their first game in the Leinster Championship that year as a curtain-raiser for the National League football final replay between Kerry and Roscommon, nobody realised they were looking at the All-Ireland champions. Surprisingly,

THE GAA

Joe Brolly has the inside track on the turning point of their season.

'I didn't go through the St Pat's Maghera, Jordanstown or Queen's production lines. I went to Trinity. One of my teammates there was Tadhg Jennings. He has a unique claim to fame. He is Kevin Heffernan's godson, and in 1974, Dublin were struggling to find a free-taker. Tadhg was only eight at the time and he said to Kevin, "I've seen a man up in Marino and he never misses a free." Heffo was intrigued and went to see for himself. The rest is history. So many a time during my Trinity career, I would hear Tadhg saying, whenever he had a pint or two, "I'm the man who discovered Jimmy Keaveney."'

Keaveney's prolific skills were the missing link in the team that Heffernan assembled that brushed aside Galway to win the Sam Maguire Cup. Surprisingly, that is not the game that year that their star corner-back Gay O'Driscoll remembers most fondly.

'I think the most significant game for that great Dublin team was the Leinster quarter-final of 1974 in which we beat Offaly by a point. Offaly had a really great team at that point – having won the three previous Leinster titles and two All-Ireland finals. When the final whistle blew, and I can still remember it as clear as anything, I was about halfway up the field on the Cusack Stand side. That was when our great run really began. I will never, ever forget that tingling sensation that went down my back. It was like a premonition that great things were in store for us. Nothing in sport, not even the All-Ireland finals, compared with that moment.

'At the time, Dublin football was in the doldrums. I remember in the early '70s, we lost to Kildare in the first round of the championship. I was sitting with Jimmy Keaveney on the bus back and he said to me that he would get an awful slagging from one of his mates at work the following day. I thought to myself at least nobody knew that I was playing for Dublin because I never told anyone about it, nor would I ever admit I played for Dublin.'

Asked the reason for Dublin's startling transformation into a team of thoroughbreds from a bunch of no-hopers, O'Driscoll pauses for deliberation.

'It's very hard to put your finger on it. There were several reasons, and the transformation was like a snowball. Although eight or ten of the players who played in '74 were there in '70 and '71, we got a few new players in '74 – notably Brian Mullins, who had a big impact. Of course, Kevin Heffernan's role is well documented at this stage – though it should be remembered he had great players to work with.

'One thing I observed that I'm convinced did make a big difference was that there were no cliques in the team any more. I had played for Dublin since 1965, and up to '74 there were always cliques in the team; for example, players from the one club sticking together and togging out together. That changed for some reason in '74, and Heffo capitalised on that by making us the fittest team in Ireland. The final wasn't one of our greatest games. I suppose the highlight was Paddy Cullen's penalty save, particularly as Liam Sammon had never missed a penalty for Galway.

'Tactics didn't come into it in '74. The only instruction the backs were given was to win the ball and get it quickly to the forwards. Their instruction was to win the ball. I would kick the ball straight down to Anton O'Toole. After losing to Kerry in '75, tactics and a more professional approach came in the following year, like watching videos of our opponents. I remember we watched a video of Kerry beating Cork in the Munster final and picked up one of Kerry's key tactics. They tried to pull out the opposing full-back line and pump the ball over their heads and get their forwards to turn around and run in. We countered that by keeping either Robbie Kelleher or myself back to act as a kind of sweeper.

'In hindsight, the '77 semi-final was a classic football match. We were trailing all the way until the last few minutes. Never did I think it was gone; nor did I ever think we would win. In that cauldron, you never thought about victory or defeat. Such was the intensity of the games against Kerry that you knew you had to give 110 per cent for every ball, and your concentration was total on what was happening in the here and now.'

Dublin trailed by two points with only six minutes remaining, but goals from David Hickey and Bernard Brogan gave the Dubs a 3–12 to 1–13 victory.

'There was a mutual respect between the teams. Many people remember that there was a clash between Brian Mullins and Ger

Power, and Brian had already been booked. He put his hands up over his face fearing he would be sent off. He said to the ref, "If I do it again, I will walk off myself." There never was any rancour between the teams, and Brian's clash was the result of fierce competitiveness rather than malice.

'I couldn't afford any lapse of concentration because I was marking John Egan, who was probably the most underrated Kerry forward of them all. The only way you could stop him was to prevent him getting possession because he never, ever wasted possession – once he got the ball, you were finished. The one thing John didn't do was to forage hard for balls. By sticking tight to him, you cut off his supply of ball.'

MIKEY CHEEKY

The high of '77 gave away to the crushing defeat the following year at the hands of Kerry in the All-Ireland final. A pivotal point in the game was one of the most famous goals of all time when Mikey Sheehy famously chipped Paddy Cullen.

'After 20 minutes, I was willing our forwards to make a mistake so that we could get some of the ball, we were so dominant up front. Myself and John Egan could have gone for a pint in the first 25 minutes and nobody would have noticed. There were great rumours afterwards that Jimmy Keaveney hit Paddy Cullen in the dressing-room. That was total rubbish. We weren't shattered at all, and there was no panic.

'It was not what the goal did to us but what the goal did for them. The goal lifted Kerry out of their boots. They came like a storm in the second half. The Bomber [Eoin Liston] started to perform and caught some terrific balls. The Kerry forwards fed off him very well.

'Kerry were a team with all the roles. The teams that are most successful are the ones that gel as a team. If a team has one or two great players, you can always blot them out and you can take them, but you can't blot out six class forwards. You couldn't single out any one player on that Kerry side. They were a team of stars.

'I marked Mikey Sheehy in his first match for Kerry in Killarney when he was picked at top of the left. He never played on me again.

Before we played Kerry in a league final, Kevin Heffernan came to me and reminded me about that and encouraged me to renew my acquaintance with Mike. I went in on him early in the game with a hard shoulder and knocked him over, and a free was given against me. As he pulled himself up, he said, "Ah sh*t, Gay, that's not your game." It completely took the wind out of my sails and was a brilliant piece of psychology on his part.

'People think that final must have been the biggest disappointment of my career, but in fact that came 11 years earlier when we lost the 1967 All-Ireland under-21 hurling final to Tipperary. We were only beaten by a point in the last minute by John Flanagan. He did nothing all day in the match, but popped up to score the winner. Hurling was my first love. At the club, it is said I was a natural hurler and a manufactured footballer.

'We had great players on that team and great characters, too, like the late Mick Holden, who was one of the great characters of Gaelic football. Coming up to an All-Ireland final, Kevin Heffernan spoke to the Dublin team about diet and proper preparation. He told them if they had any problems sleeping before the final, they should get tablets from Pat O'Neill. The first person in the queue was Mick Holden. Heffo said to Mick, "I never thought you'd have any problems sleeping." Holden answered, "Oh, these are not for me. I sleep like a baby. These are for my mother. She can never sleep the night before a big match!"'

ME AND EUGENE MCGEE

Dublin's status as kingpins of Leinster was abruptly ended by Offaly in the 1980 Leinster final. Offaly's manager Eugene McGee was to mastermind one of the biggest upsets in football history when his Offaly team beat a Kerry team seeking five-in-a-row in the 1982 All-Ireland final. The undisputed star of that team was Matt Connor.

'The build-up suited us very well because all the pressure was on Kerry. They were probably the best football team ever. They had a lethal forward line, an extremely good back line and a great midfield. They really had no weakness. We had to work hard on the day and never give up. One very important thing was that Eugene McGee put my brother Richie in at centre-forward. That was a key decision on that day because the year before, Tim Kennelly had absolutely cleaned up. He was going to make sure that the main reason we were beaten in 1981 wasn't going to happen again. McGee put him as a kind of stopper and a playmaker at centre-forward, and that worked a treat. Another thing was that Eoin Liston was the key man in the Kerry forward line and we had to stop him and stop the supply of ball to him. Liam O'Connor did quite a good job in that sense on the day, and the players out the field did a lot of hard work and hard grafting to stop the ball going into the Kerry full-forward line.

'The first half was open and it was a very good game of football. The second half it started raining fairly heavily and the game deteriorated a good bit. Kerry dominated for a long time and we were lucky enough to stay with them. Martin Furlong's penalty save was very important. If they had scored that, I don't think we would have come back. The rest is history. We were four points down and we got two frees to put us two points behind. Then a long ball came to Seamus Darby and he banged it into the net. It was a super shot. All Croke Park went wild, but there was still a minute and a half left in the game and we had to hold on with all our might.'

A sadness so deep that no tears would come fell over football fans everywhere two years later with the news that at the age of 25, Matt Connor's career had come to a premature end.

'I was going home from Tullamore on Christmas Day to my Christmas dinner. My car went out of control and I was thrown out of the car and landed on my back. I damaged my spine and I suffered paraplegia from the accident. That finished my football career. When I had the accident, I suppose football wasn't the main priority at that stage. It was just a complete change of life that I was not able to walk again.'

MIGHTY MEATH

One test of fame is a person's ability to define an era. The Beatles did in the 1960s; Princess Diana did in the 1980s; and for Meath football fans, Seán Boylan did in the '80s and '90s. Boylan became team manager in 1982 at a time when no one else wanted the job. Meath football was in the doldrums, and the great powers in Leinster were Offaly and Dublin. During his 23 years as Meath manager, Boylan drank from a glass that continously refilled itself, the last long, cool swallow as necessary as the first, his thirst unquenchable.

Nonetheless, it was the same old story in 1983 as the Royal County lost to the Dubs in the early rounds of the Leinster Championship. He laughs at the memory of one comic incident from that match.

'It was shortly after I became manager, and Dublin were playing Meath in Croke Park. I wanted to make a positional change during the match, so I walked down along the sideline behind the goal in front of the Hill, and all the Dublin fans were jeering me and slagging me. It was all in a good-natured way and there was no malice in it whatsoever. Because I was so new in the job and Meath weren't having huge success at the time, this Garda came racing up to me and thought I was just a fan! I had a fierce problem convincing him that I was actually the Meath manager. After a lot of cajoling, I eventually persuaded him of my identity and I said to him, "You do your job and look after the spectators, and let me do my job and look after these lads on the pitch." After we had finished our "chat", I walked back in front of the Hill again. This time the Dublin fans gave me a great ovation. They thought I was a hero because I had stood up to and had a big row with a guard!'

Meath seemed to have turned a corner when they won the Centenary Cup in 1984, to mark the GAA's 100th anniversary, by beating a strong Monaghan side in the final. Later that year, they reached the Leinster final and ran Dublin to four points. It was back to the bad old days in 1985, when they suffered a humiliating defeat at the hands of Laois in the Leinster Championship by 2–11 to 0–7 in Tullamore. Questions were asked about Boylan's stewardship, and he had to survive a vote at a county board meeting to remain in office.

Although it was without doubt a low point for the Meath team, it proved to be a blessing in disguise. Boylan found six new players who would play key roles in the coming years: Terry Ferguson, Kevin Foley, Liam Harnan, David Beggy, P.J. Gillic and Brian Stafford.

THE GAA

The tide finally turned when Meath beat Dublin in the 1986 Leinster final. Meath went on to win back-to-back All-Irelands in 1987 and '88, and to win five out of six Leinster titles from 1986 to 1991 in the greatest run in the county's history, losing All-Ireland finals in 1990 and '91 to Cork and Down respectively.

Dublin reigned supreme in Leinster from 1992 to '95. Boylan faced another apparent crisis in '95 when Meath lost the Leinster final to their great Dublin rivals by ten points. Boylan had to face another election. Again, Seán reacted to major defeat by rebuilding the Meath team and was rewarded with another All-Ireland title in 1996. Not for the first time, Boylan's career served as a parable of the power of persistence. Three years later, he took Meath to another All-Ireland title. It was a series of four games that most carved the Boylan era into the public consciousness. If the *Titanic* had been made of the same stuff as that Meath team, it would never have gone down.

EPIC

'How can you win four battles and lose the war?' This was the question posed by one Dublin player after a four-game saga that enthralled the nation in the first round of the Leinster Championship in 1991. At a time when Ireland was going through soccer mania after Italia '90, and when the nation was under the spell of Jack Charlton, that series of games showed that reports of the GAA's demise were premature. Territorially, Dublin were dominant in all matches, but still ended up as the losing side, which continues to puzzle Tom Carr.

'There were stages in each of the four games when I thought we had won. The memory of the games is all blurred into one, apart from the last fifteen minutes of the final match, which is frozen on my mind for ever. I was watching the game from the sideline having gone off injured at the stage, and it was literally sickening to see the way we snatched defeat from the jaws of victory.'

Colm O'Rourke was at the heart of Meath's triumph.

'What I remember most is the intensity of the games. Kevin Foley's goal would have been the most dramatic in anybody's sporting life. There were stages in all the games, particularly in the last one, when I thought it was gone, but we were mentally strong, having been together so long. We didn't play well in some of the games, but did just enough to hang on. Morale was very good in the camp. We did very little training between the matches. It was mainly rest and recuperation. There was a very simple explanation why we emerged victorious in 1991 – we were the best team.'

Armagh star Enda McNulty is awestruck by one aspect of that classic confrontation.

'I was talking to Mick Galvin and Keith Barr about those games. I assumed that the boys were straight into the pool after such tough games. They told me that was not the case. What they did after each of the games was to go out drinking. Not only that, but they went out drinking the night after the games, and the night after that again! I was shocked.'

The 1991 victory did not mean as much to Colm O'Rourke as the victories over Dublin in the mid-'80s.

'For a long time in the '70s and '80s, Dublin had a hold over us. There was a feeling of the inevitable in our camp about Dublin's victory. All that changed in 1986 when we reversed that pattern and paved the way for our All-Ireland titles in '87 and '88. We had a settled team at the time and they hadn't, which gave us a significant advantage.

'Winning the first All-Ireland was obviously a very sweet one for me, but '88 was even better, when we won both the league and the championship. I felt that I had made my greatest triumphs all the sweeter because they came towards the end of my career, particularly as I had so many disappointments and injuries early in my career.'

The importance of O'Rourke to the Meath side was never more clearly demonstrated than when he came on as a sub in the second half of the 1991 All-Ireland final, having gone down with viral pneumonia in the week leading up to the final.

'The year ended on a real downer (no pun intended!) for me when we lost the final to Down, particularly because I missed most of the match.'

Paradoxically, O'Rourke feels Meath's place in the affections of the Irish people was greatly heightened by the defeat. The ill-tempered clashes with Cork in the '87 and '88 finals had left Meath with a reputation, at least in certain quarters, of being a dirty side.

'After the game, it would be fair to say I noticed a big change in the attitude to Meath of people outside the county. I think we won a lot of friends because we didn't crow about it or rub it in when we beat the Dubs, and accepted our victory graciously and our defeat to Down equally graciously.'

Leitrim legend Packy McGarty was not a fan of aspects of Meath's style.

'I remember Colm O'Rourke writing an article explaining how Meath beat Cork in the All-Ireland replay in 1988 when Gerry McEntee was sent off early in the game. Their tactic was to foul an opponent out the field and then they were no longer a man down because a Cork player had to take the free. It was very effective, but it was no way to win because it's much too negative and ruins the game as a spectacle.'

Former Mayo star Martin Carney provides a wonderfully economical view of that Meath team.

'I loved playing Meath. They were a fierce, manly and honest team, though if it was needed, they would rearrange your features!'

Meath's ace midfielder Gerry McEntee told a story to Enda McNulty that confirms the toughness of the team. Enda recounted the tale to me.

'In the pre-Seán Boylan era, Meath were playing Kildare and Gerry was being pulled and dragged on all through the match by his opponent. It got to the stage where Gerry said to himself, "If he pulls out of me one more time, I am going to have to give him a box." Gerry admits he's not very proud of this, but he struck out and visibly broke his opponent's nose. Gerry didn't wait for the referee to send him off; he just turned around and pointed to his jersey and said to the ref: "Number 9, McEntee." Then he walked into the changing-rooms. He was taking a cold shower to cool off and was contemplating his football future when somebody came in for him and asked him to go outside. Gerry asked, "What's going on?"

'He was told, "Your father is in a bit of trouble out here."

'Gerry walked out underneath the tunnel in Navan and the referee was lying on his back on the ground, and he said, "What's after happening here?"

'He was told, "Your father is after striking the referee, Gerry."

'Gerry turned to his dad and asked, "Dad, what did you do that for?"

'Gerry's dad replied, "Didn't he send you off? Didn't he f***ing send you off?"'

I'M FOREVER BLOWING KISSES

Joe Brolly had some memorable encounters with Meath in his playing days. His distinctive style was diametrically opposed to the Meath way – notably his penchant for blowing kisses during games.

'That whole thing started by accident. Eamonn Coleman was away and Down were the All-Ireland champions, so when they came up to Celtic Park for the first game of the league, they gave us a guard of honour. Eamonn would have been horrified if he'd heard about that. Eamonn's deputy Harry Cribbin was in charge and he didn't select me to start. He thought I was too big for my boots. I would have been as cocky as anything. There was a massive crowd because it was such a big deal for an Ulster team back then to have won an All-Ireland. With 15 minutes to go, Derry were struggling and I was brought on. The first ball I got I put it over the bar. The second ball I put over the bar. The score was tied and I can still see a beautiful ball 60 metres over the top. The Down defender thought he could get it and was back-pedalling and he missed it. I caught it and the Down goalie came out to me and I lobbed the ball in the far corner. It has been shown a number of times on TV, and the crowd were really animated. Of course, I ran down the length of the field blowing kisses as a way of saying, "Harry, you dirty bastard for not picking me." One of the boys told me that Harry Gribbin said, "Oh, that wee bastard's trying to sicken me." It was the talk of the place and everyone really enjoyed it. So that was the start of it.

'Down's heads went down after the celebration, and I could see after that it became a sort of psychological weapon. It became a thing that if I scored a goal in the Ulster Championship, it had a demoralising effect on the opposition. I remember Fergal Lohan telling me that he had said to the Tyrone team when he was captain, "The key thing is to stop that f***er from scoring a goal." Ten minutes into the second half, I scored a goal. It just deflated them. It always had a very heavy effect on the opposition. In Celtic Park especially, the fans came to expect it. I remember watching the TV one night when we had played a championship match against Monaghan. I got a goal after 15 minutes and ran the length of the pitch blowing kisses, and the cameras swept up along so I could see the whole Derry crowd laughing, so it was fun. I must say I enjoyed it, but I wouldn't do it now.

'My flamboyant celebrations were not universally popular among opposing players, though. I had my nose broken twice after scoring goals. The physical exchanges used to be a lot heavier then.

'I remember lobbying the Meath keeper in Celtic Park. He was a big, tall fella and I just popped it over his head. Colm Coyle came charging over to me as I began my celebrations and drove his boot into me. I needed about 13 stitches. Brian Mullins was managing us at the time and said, "You deserve that, you wee bollix!"

'One of my favourite memories is of marking Kevin Foley in particular. A high ball came in-between us; I fielded it and danced around Foley and blasted the ball over the bar. A second high ball came in-between us with the exact same result. I, though, was aware that the Meath crowd had gone very quiet and noticed Foley and Liam Harnan exchanging signals. The next ball that came in, I noticed both Foley and Harnan coming at me at top speed, so I ducked, causing Harnan to catch Foley with his elbow. Foley was stretchered off unconscious. Last summer I met a man who was at that match and he was saying how serious it looked for Foley. I became a hero in Derry not because of any score I ever got but because I was the man who "floored" Kevin Foley! I am often asked since how hard I hit him. I just say, "Auch, I didn't go too hard on him."

'I think the excessively physical reputation of that Meath team was exaggerated. They don't deserve the bad press they sometimes get.'

Sharing the sofa with him on the *Sunday Game*, it often appears that Brolly is no great fan of Colm O'Rourke. Who said the camera never lies?

'He's a top guy. As an analyst, there's nobody better, and look at all the titles he has won coaching his school and see how well he did managing the International Rules Series. He's quality through and through.'

Brolly's generous assessment of Meath is not shared as enthusiastically by former Mayo great T.J. Kilgallon.

'Meath were always too prone to play mind games for my liking. Gerry McEntee would always stand nearer the opposing free-taker than he was supposed to, and would try and put the kicker off by saying something like, "You're going to miss." He would tell you that you would put it to the right or the left, but never over the bar. Colm O'Rourke was not shy on the field. He would always be passing a smart comment to you. Some of the lads thought he was trying to get you irked enough to punch him so that you would be sent off. He was certainly trying to distract you and put you off your game. I think Ryan McMenamin is probably the main exponent of that "art" today.'

MAGIC MOMENTS

In the 1990s, Kildare fans had the pleasure of seeing their county at last come in from the footballing wilderness. Pat Mangan's analysis of the reasons for the team's breakthrough is very concise.

'I think it's all down to one man. Mick O'Dwyer brought the organisation and the skill to the football that was lacking over the years. He's a very, very strong personality and the most positive guy that you could ever talk to. A negative would never get into his head. If you were talking to him, he'd have you convinced in ten minutes that you were going to win. He came to Kildare when they were at their lowest. Kildare people love their football and are great supporters, but because of that they expect a lot from their team. There's a tremendous tradition of football in the county so that created a lot of pressure, and his arrival was headline news so there was a lot of media scrutiny.

'I watched a lot of the trial matches he held at the start, and in my opinion, Kildare had a very, very ordinary bunch of players. He moulded them together, gave them confidence and got them exceptionally fit. I would honestly say that in the beginning he got them winning matches against better teams because they were so fit, and got them to a league final. Kildare were so fired up by O'Dwyer that they felt they could walk on water. After that, he got them to two Leinster finals, but when they lost both, the hatchet was out again. They literally ran him out of the county in 1994.

'Unfortunately, Kildare had two bad years after that. In fairness, his successor, Dermot Earley, was on a hiding to nothing. Kildare, having built up all their expectations, found themselves without O'Dwyer. Morale among the players was low and I think Dermot was expected to perform a miracle. They got knocked out in the first round of the championship in consecutive years and the hatchet fell on Dermot. Attendances at club matches were down, and Seamus Aldridge and all his henchmen realised the mistake they had made and brought O'Dwyer back. It was a difficult situation for him. He did an incredible job to lift that team. He had a few good young players coming through and our "imports" were a big help. It's an amazing achievement, and I think he was unfortunate not to win an All-Ireland final in 1998 because of all the injuries they had in the run-up, though Galway gave a tremendous display on the day.'

SINGING THE BLUES

A recurring feature of the championship in recent years has been the hype that attends Dublin's early games. However, the footballing realities generally puncture all the propaganda by the time the Sam Maguire Cup is presented in September. Tom Carr knows this anguish at first hand.

'Although I was very, very down after the Meath saga in 1991, to miss out on captaining Dublin to an All-Ireland the following year was devastating.'

Why did Dublin not live up to expectations in the decider?

'You always think you are preparing properly for a game; you always like to think that, anyway, and that you will be right for the game, but subconsciously things are playing on your mind telling you things are not as they should be. We didn't play well on the day; everybody knows that. I can't explain what went wrong. Psychologists have tried for years to figure out why does an individual or team not give their normal performance on a particular day, but have never come up with a proper answer. It's not a physical thing – it must be mental.

'I personally feel it had to a lot to do with what the Americans call "focusing". We weren't properly focused. There were just too many distractions and external activities – guys modelling clothes and going on radio shows and so on. In isolation, there was nothing wrong with any of them, but when you added them all up, the focus was badly distracted. They all mounted up. The test of players' focus is the way they perform on the pitch. You judge a player by the way he plays, and clearly we weren't up to it on the day. Donegal won and deserved to. They were up to it and we weren't. It was that simple.'

One of the first casualties of Dublin's defeat was their manager Paddy Cullen. Was the Dublin camp really driven apart by strife as some media reports suggested?

'You'd have to be a blind man not to know there were major differences in the Dublin camp in 1992, but if we had won, all that would have been glossed over. Defeat brought the cracks and divisions more closely to the surface. Without saying too much, Pat O'Neill would have taken a very different approach to Paddy.

'The bad reaction to the defeat would not have happened in the '70s because everybody realised that Kerry were an exceptional team and that there was normally only a bounce of ball between the two teams. In 1992, it was different because 99 per cent of the population thought that Dublin would win. I thought we were the form team that year and we should have won. That was an All-Ireland we should have won. That is not to take away in any degree from Donegal's achievements. They performed out of their skins on the day. We did the opposite.'

There were particular criticisms levelled at the Dublin forwards after the game – was that criticism justified?

'I don't want to be unfair to anybody, but I'd say it's correct to say that whereas Donegal had exceptional forwards, we didn't. I was on the panel when we beat Galway in the All-Ireland in '83. I don't want to hurt anybody's feelings or be disrespectful, but in '83 we had exceptional players like Barney Rock, who was at his peak, having scored a great goal in the semi-final that paved the way for us to win the All-Ireland that year. Again, his quick thinking in the final when he lobbed the goalie gave us the decisive goal. We had nobody of that ilk in '92, and that was the crucial difference.'

Was Charlie Redmond's failure to score a goal from the penalty a major factor in Dublin's defeat?

'It didn't bother me too much at the time because it was early in the game and we were winning at that stage. If it had been late in the game, I would have been gutted. It shouldn't have affected us, but looking back on it afterwards, I think it must have. It certainly gave a great boost to Donegal.'

While Dublin did win an All-Ireland in '95, Carr would again experience frustration when he managed the Dubs. One of the Dublin players of that time was Declan Darcy, who had previously led Leitrim to a historic Connacht title in 1994.

'The easy thing for me to have done would have been to stay in Leitrim, where I would always be a hero because of '94. But I wanted to win an All-Ireland, not a popularity contest. Part of me had always been curious about whether I would have been good enough to win my place on the Dublin side, particularly when they won the All-Ireland in 1995. I remember meeting Paul Bealin, and he said to me, "I'll give you balls for doing it alone." I wanted to test myself, and if I failed, at least I had given it a go.

'I had a good first year or two with Dublin, but I made a big mistake when I came into the dressing-room first and didn't say to players like Keith Barr, "Get the finger out of your arse and start playing." They were all experienced and gifted players and part of me thought, who was I to be telling them what to do? I should have let loose, but Dublin is a closed shop and I wanted to make friends. Mickey Whelan was the trainer in my first year and I felt his training was very advanced, but it needed the players to take some of the responsibility themselves, and they were letting him down. I felt I was a newcomer and held my tongue. Towards the end, I did say what I felt ought to be done, but I should have done that so much earlier.

'We came very close in 2002 when Ray Cosgrave almost equalised against Armagh, but to be honest, I believe Tommy Carr had a better team. John Bailey, then the county chairman, told us after the drawn game against Kerry in the All-Ireland quarter-final in 2001 that no matter what happened, Tommy Carr would be staying for the next year. He actually cried with emotion as he said that, but less than a month later, he put the knife into Tommy. Players would have done anything for Tommy, but we didn't do enough for him. I felt sorry for him because he was very unlucky, none more so than with the Maurice Fitzgerald sideline that drew the match for Kerry the first day. Tommy was as honest as the day was long and was fiercely driven. There was nothing he wouldn't have done for Dublin. He was probably a better manager at the end, but had more to learn, and I think it's a shame he didn't get the chance.'

Darcy continues to be involved in the game through coaching St Brigid's, a side managed by Gerry McEntee. 'Gerry manages the way he played!'

With Jim Gavin, Darcy coached the Dublin under-21 side to an All-Ireland in 2003, though the team was officially managed by Tommy Lyons. What was their relationship with Lyons at the time?

'It was frosty enough. If Tommy walked into this room now, I would have great craic with him, but I don't agree with his approach to management. To me, management is all about the team. It's not about courting popularity with the media or putting yourself or your profile ahead of the team. He had a very different agenda to Tommy Carr.'

Many of that under-21 team have graduated into the senior ranks. Who were the players Darcy knew would make it?

'Alan Brogan was always going to be a great player. Bryan Cullen stood out as a player and a leader. He had that serious drive and determination that you need to be a winner. We had a celebration after we won the Leinster title, and after it, all the boys went to pubs or nightclubs, except Bryan. When I asked him why, he said, "I've won nothing yet. I want to win an All-Ireland."'

More recently, Alan Brogan has experienced the bitter taste of defeat in big games with Dublin with depressing regularity.

10

GLORY DAYS

NO PLAYER ON THE GREAT KERRY TEAM BOUGHT MORE INTO THE
ethos that 'pain is temporary, glory is eternal' than Pat Spillane. What
can't be cured must be endured. A ruptured anterior cruciate ligament
in his left knee threatened his career.

'I was told by quite eminent orthopaedic surgeons in the country
that I would never play football again, but I was determined to prove
them wrong and I did.'

Spillane had exploded into the national consciousness in 1975
when, as a raw 19 year old, he collected the Sam Maguire Cup when
Kerry beat Dublin and team captain Mickey O'Sullivan was en route
to hospital.

'It was a dream, only that it was actually reality. I was very immature
and it was something I took for granted. After that, for all of us, there
was only one way to go and that was down, which we did. We were
a bunch of youngsters, mainly bachelors, fun-loving lads. We had a
great time. We cruised through '75 and thought we were great guys
altogether. Success went to our heads and Dublin cut us down to size
in '76 when they beat us easily in the All-Ireland final. We got exactly
what we deserved – a kick in the pants.'

THE GAA

KERRY'S DUB-LE TROUBLE

Kerry and Dublin renewed their rivalry in 1977 in a classic All-Ireland football semi-final. Kerry's corner-back Jimmy Deenihan was more concerned about the result than its entertainment value.

'It was a very fast game, played at a very high tempo with quick movement of the ball. The physical competition was intense, and there was a great atmosphere because we were craving revenge after losing to Dublin the previous year. We had a large following from the north of Ireland at that stage. But from our point of view, it's no good going down in history for having played in the greatest match of all time when we didn't win it.

'Our preparations for that match were hampered by injuries. I had a bad shoulder injury; it was dislocated. Seán Walsh had a serious ligament injury. He played well and got a goal. We were out on a mission to prove that the '76 result was not real. We trained very hard in '77 and went in with reasonable confidence. We felt we had the edge after beating them in the league final earlier that year.

'We had the initiative from the start and were playing comfortably. The only fly in the ointment was that Anton O'Toole had the edge on Ger Power that day and scored a couple of points before half-time. Early in the second half, a high ball came in from Tommy Drumm and landed between John McCarthy and myself, but there was hesitancy on everybody's part, including our goalie, Paud O'Mahony, and the ball ended up in the Kerry net. Late in the game, a soft ball came in towards the Kerry goal. John O'Keeffe had been going well on the day and tried to deflect the ball away from Jimmy Keaveney, but he made a boob and knocked it straight to Tony Hanahoe, who passed it to David Hickey, who scored a goal. Then Seán Doherty made the catch of his life to thwart us as we attacked.'

Does he agree that selection blunders cost Kerry the match, particularly a failure to redress obvious midfield problems?

'The selectors were caught with an embarrassment of riches in terms of players. Páidí Ó Sé was chosen at midfield. He was a great footballer, but he was never a midfielder. We had three natural midfielders in the squad at the time: Pat McCarthy, John Long and Mikey Connor, who were all playing well at the time. Selecting Páidí at midfield caused an

172

imbalance in the team. Pat was brought on when the game was lost. As I said, Ger Power was getting a roasting from Anton O'Toole. Both problems were obvious from an early stage, but no corrective action was taken. Losing that game, though, was the inspiration for our win the following year. It was a terrible blow for us, worse almost than losing the five-in-a-row in '82. We got a worse reception than we got in '82 when we came home. There was sympathy for us that year, but there was none in '77. For the league games, I was rested, as well as Pat Spillane, Ger Power and Paud O'Mahony: I had gone through a run of injuries and I think that they may have felt I was imagining some of them; I think they felt Spillane was too individualistic and not enough of a team player at the time; Ger had not been playing well for a while; and I think the selectors blamed Paud for Dublin's first goal. Kerry had a very poor league campaign, and only the width of the post prevented them from being relegated in the final match.

'There had been a lot of criticism of management. A challenge had been made openly on Ger MacKenna's position as county chairman. Some of the selectors were replaced. Mick O'Dwyer was booed at a league match in Killarney, I think it was against Galway. That hurt him a lot. We were all irked at the media adulation of the Dubs and the way Kerry were presented as not being in the same league.

'I played rugby all winter for Tralee and was coached by former Irish international Barry McGann, which kept me fit, and I made my comeback to help Munster win the Railway Cup in '78. A big plus for Kerry came in May of that year when we beat Dublin in a game at Gaelic Park, New York. It was a very red-blooded match in every sense! I got my nose broken. Tommy Doyle, Eoin Liston and Pat O'Neill were sent off. We took it very seriously, but they took it less so. It was a milestone for us: psychologically, we proved to ourselves that we could beat them.

'There was a lot of pressure on us to beat Cork in the Munster final, particularly as Cork had a strong side at the time, but we did and cruised past Roscommon in the semi-final. The final was a big confrontation for us. We were superbly fit for the game. Most of us lived like hermits. None of the lads went near Tralee races or to the craic in Ballybunion. There were no late nights or alcohol. People who

173

later became heavy drinkers were not drinking at that stage.

"We were very careful with the media that year. O'Dwyer pleaded with us to be very cagey with journalists. We had a press night when all the journalists came down, but O'Dwyer changed the training routine just for that night! In both '76 and '77, Kerry were affected by the media. There was a lot of hype and we believed it. We were a mature outfit, hungry for victory in '78. There were a lot of damaged egos in the side among both the players and the management. O'Dwyer acknowledged that he had been badly hurt by the booing incident in Killarney.

'We went into the final with a very changed-about team from the previous year, with a lot of positional switches and a much better balance. Eoin Liston, Mick Spillane and Charlie Nelligan came into the side, adding youth and freshness. We were really stretched in the first 15 minutes. I thought it was going to be an avalanche. We were just about hanging on. I remember Robbie Kelleher (the Dublin corner-back) had a shot for a point at one stage, which summed up how bad things were for us. I think they were deluded by the media attention and adulation so much that they left John Egan unmarked. John was not the type of player to be bothered what his marker was doing up the field. He stayed in his position and his goal turned the tide. Then came Mike Sheehy's goal, and we were on our way.'

For Deenihan, there was a personal disappointment about the final.

'We went in at half-time having absorbed total pressure in front. We just destroyed them in the second half. Everything went our way and we finally produced the type of football we thought we had been capable of for the previous three years. We exploited gaps in the Dublin defence. Their backs were not great second-phase markers.

'A scuffle broke out in front of the goal, and John McCarthy and Charlie Nelligan were sent off. I was the loose man and went in goal briefly, but the selectors sent on Paud O'Mahony and I was the one taken off. It would have been nice to have finished out the game.

'After that game, I remember going back to Killarney, where we got a tumultous reception having defeated "the unbeatable Heffo machine". I remember saying, "We're now a mature team. We're savouring the victory, but aren't going to get carried away like we did in 1975." I knew then we could win more All-Irelands.'

Two years later would prove to be an eventful time for Deenihan.

'In 1980, my club, Feale Rangers, won the Kerry County Championship. To celebrate, we decided we would go on an American tour to Pittsburgh and New York. I was organising the trip and didn't want to bring the Sam Maguire Cup, but I was persuaded to do so. Pittsburgh Steelers had won the Super Bowl the previous year and another Pittsburgh side, the Pirates, won the World Series. Two of the most prestigious trophies in the world would be in the one city. Tom O'Donoghue felt it would be a good idea to have those two trophies photographed with the Sam Maguire Cup.

'We were staying in the Abbey Victoria Hotel next to Rosie O'Grady's pub in Manhattan, initially. We had a function on the Saturday night before playing a game the next day in Gaelic Park. Everybody wanted to see the Sam so I reluctantly brought it along. We left the cup in the safe in Gaelic Park. It was a big strong one.

'The following morning, I got a phone call informing me that one of our travelling party had been involved in a serious accident. I went to see him in the hospital. I only got back to the ground in time for our match against the famous Ardboe club from Tyrone. I had to go back to the hospital after the match. I returned for the cup that night. The watchman told me that someone had come for the cup already, but no one knew who he was.

'We had to go to Pittsburgh for our match at the Pittsburgh Steelers' ground. There were a lot of dignitaries there, all the leading politicians and so on, and former Steelers' stars like Rocky Blair. Everybody was full of expectation. It was a total anticlimax when we arrived without the cup.

'I went back to New York on the Thursday to take up the matter with the local police. Initially, they didn't take much notice, but when they saw newspaper reports from Ireland, they realised its importance and carried out investigations. I was due home to play a National League semi-final against Galway. I stayed on to get the matter sorted out because obviously it would be terribly embarrassing for me to have returned without the cup. It would have been a national scandal. Eventually I was told if I turned up in Gaelic Park on Monday, I would find it waiting for me. I did, but never bothered to find out who had taken it. The cup was scratched and the words "Up the IRA. Up Roscommon" were inscribed on it, though I suspect that the person involved was a sympathiser of neither. The irony was that six months later I received Sam when I captained Kerry to win the All-Ireland.'

THE MEN BEHIND O'DWYER

Jimmy Deenihan offered an anatomy of the most successful trainer in history, Mick O'Dwyer.

'He was very discerning. He could look at a player and know if he was drinking. He was a great judge of a player's condition. He could smell the drink on an individual. If he thought people weren't serious, he would crucify them in training and give extra to anyone not toeing the line. He had a good understanding of people. Some would call it cunning. He was quick to make his mind up about someone, and if you entered into O'Dwyer's confidence, you had a supporter for life. He could read your mind and he could detect when someone was not sincere. He punished mediocrity.'

The heart becomes a different place when a few All-Ireland medals are stored on the mantelpiece. It would take exceptional powers to keep that Kerry team motivated. In conversation with this scribe, the late Tim Kennelly credited Mick O'Dwyer as the main catalyst for Kerry's success.

'O'Dwyer was a bit of a rogue, and a really cute rogue at that, but he knew how to get the best out of us. We took everybody by surprise in '75. Going into the '76 All-Ireland, we thought we were world-beaters. All the back-slapping got to us. We were as good as Dublin, but we just weren't mentally ready for that final. The semi-final in '77 against the Dubs was one of the great games. The match was there for the taking. Most of the Kerry players were in tears after the game in the sanctuary of the dressing-room. We had put in a huge amount of training that year, but still we had lost to the Dubs again. That certainly dented our confidence. Some of us were thinking, "Will we ever beat the Dubs again?" The next year, we got the Bomber on board, and I think he was the final piece of the jigsaw.

'It was a massive disappointment to lose in '82, and it's a memory that has never left me because we were minutes away from immortality. We had plenty of chances to win the game, but we became too defensive when we went four points up, and this allowed Offaly back into the game. People say if Jimmy Deenihan had been in there, the famous Seamus Darby goal would have got in, and they were right. Jimmy knew how to "put manners" on anyone. I think it was a bigger deal for our supporters than for us. I think we were the better team, but the result said otherwise.'

The decision to become a county selector hastened Kennelly's retirement.

'There was talk in north Kerry that I was selecting myself on the team, and I didn't want to be in controversy so I stepped down in 1984. I have no bitterness. I had three great years as a selector and we won three All-Irelands. We had great times – maybe, if I'm honest, too great, as some of us got too caught up with the drinking culture. There is a price for fame – let no one ever tell you different.'

PAT ON THE BACK

Pat Spillane has invested considerable reflection into his time with that Kerry team.

'Nostalgia can be a dangerous pastime when it clouds the memory and impedes our ability to recall accurately the strands of the past. I am sometimes criticised when offering opinions about Gaelic football today that I am forever harking back to the past and to the great Kerry team that I played on. Maybe I do. I suppose we are all guilty of eulogising about our own era at the expense of the present day.

'When it comes to comparing standards from one generation to another, the pundit who is an ex-player is always on difficult ground. It is easy to lose track of the boundary between proud self-belief and triumphalism. Training methods, tactics, diet and general preparation for the game have altered dramatically from when Mick

O'Connell stopped playing in 1974. It makes it almost impossible to make judgements on how players from the distant past would have performed had they played in a different time. There are players, though, who would have survived in any era. They had that X-factor that set them apart in their own dreams. They had the vision, determination, imagination and, above all, the sheer skill to rise above the players around them, and Jack O'Shea and the rest would do just the same if they were playing today.

'What also would have made those Kerry players stand out in any era is that they were an exceptionally intelligent bunch. Their speed of thought was most evident in the way Mike Sheehy cleverly chipped Paddy Cullen with a quick free, which turned the 1978 All-Ireland final in our favour. After Seamus Darby's sensational last-minute winner for Offaly against Kerry in 1982, that Mike Sheehy goal is the most famous ever scored in an All-Ireland final. Paddy Cullen's frantic effort to keep the ball out was memorably described afterwards by the legendary Con Houlihan, who wrote it was like "a woman who smells a cake burning".

'I was just watching the tape of the goal recently, and I heard Michael O'Hehir describe it as "the greatest freak of all time". You would have to take him to task for that comment. It was a moment of pure genius in the speed of thought and the execution of a very difficult skill. Absolutely magnificent. Of course, it wasn't a free. But that's beside the point.

'I can honestly say there is no group of people I admire more than the members of the Kerry team. I have to be honest, though, and say the love affair is not entirely reciprocated. When I wrote my autobiography a number of years ago, I wasn't prepared for the kind of reaction it provoked, especially from what I thought was the most innocuous chapter in the book, on my teammates on the Kerry side. I had gone through it carefully and did not think that anybody would take offence. I had a little section of comments about each of them and talked about their playing abilities and so on. I really didn't think I could have upset many people, but I did. There are several who continue to talk to me since the book came out, but there's certainly a detectable coolness to me there.

'Ogie Moran was a great player. He had to be to win eight All-Ireland medals, all of them in the centre half-forward position. He had great skill, outstanding speed and total unselfishness. As a pundit, I was a strong critic of Ogie's management of Kerry – though never of Ogie as a person. Ogie has never forgiven me for that, and it saddens me.'

THE GENTLE GIANT

Mick Galwey could have been one of the Kerry greats, but in his native county he chose 'the road less travelled' and opted for rugby as his main game. His decision was vindicated with forty-one caps for Ireland, captaining his country in four of those games; over one hundred and thirty appearances for Munster; a place on the Lions tour in 1993; and the award of an honorary doctorate in law from Trinity College in 2002 for his services to rugby. It is only when you meet someone like Mick Galwey, or 'Gaillimh', that you really understand the phrase 'larger than life'. Although he was the epitome of lionheartedness when under the fiercest pressure during a match, he is modest and unassuming off the field. Time passes quickly in his company. As a boy, his childhood hero was Mick O'Connell.

'I came from a football area, Currow, near Castleisland – the same area as Moss Keane came from. I played for them every year from when I was nine until I was thirty-two, when contractual obligations prohibited me. Football was my first love until rugby came along. After school, my interest increased when I started working as a baker with Charlie Nelligan, who was a star with the great Kerry team. I got minor trials with the Kerry team and played at midfield for them in the Munster minor final in Centenary year, when we lost to a very strong Tipperary team. Three years later, we beat them at under-21 level only to lose the All-Ireland final to a very strong Donegal side.'

Galwey reaped the benefit of the internal discord that prevailed in Kerry at that time in the wake of the controversy about their infamous 'Only Bendix Could Whitewash This Lot' advertisement. On the morning of the All-Ireland final in 1985, two Sunday newspapers carried full-page ads that showed several Kerry players in a state of undress as they posed around a washing machine. The controversy blew up again the following spring over the team holiday that was to compensate the Kerry players for their venture into modelling.

'The Kerry team were on strike and they were looking for 15 lads to go to Tourmakeady in Mayo, so I was brought in because I had played under-21 the previous year. It was a weekend away and I'll never forget it, especially because we all got Aran jumpers after the match, which was great. Then I was called into the Kerry panel for training.

'I was 19 at the time, and it was a great experience for me to be rubbing shoulders with all these great players and Mick O'Dwyer, who were not just very talented but also totally committed. I was very impressed by their professional approach, and what I learned from them probably stood me in my rugby career and gave me a competitive edge. Every game with them was very competitive, which is not a bad thing.

'It was very intimidating going in to train with such great players. Mick O'Dwyer was a great man to push the young fellas, especially. The training back then was like the way we train in rugby now – short and sharp. Sometimes lads would get sick in training, but he never managed to make me sick! Afterwards, it was a case of us going down to the Imperial Hotel in Tralee, and we used to have steaks and chips and onions and a pint of milk. Now it's different and you're not advised to eat like that, but it didn't do that Kerry team any harm.

'Mick O'Dwyer had a great way of making things very competitive and of getting the very best out of his players. He would get old lads sprinting against young lads on a one-to-one basis. Wire to wire, it was called. Then it was backs against forwards, which was awesome. Some of the tackling was ferocious and you'd never see anything like that in a proper match. It was kind of like the law of the jungle, but it really prepared fellas for championship football.

'In fairness to O'Dwyer, he really knew when to push and when to rest players. I remember in 1986, up to the Munster final he hadn't really pushed the players too hard, and after the match he announced that the team were to have a few days off, but that six people would have to return early for extra training. Everyone's ears cocked straight away. Páidí Ó Sé, the Bomber and Seánie Walsh were three of the names. They were all exceptional players, but for different reasons probably needed a bit of extra training. I was brought in with them because I wasn't sharp enough then and I needed extra training. The six of us were given extra laps and push-ups and sit-ups. It was hard work, but it had to be done.

'O'Dwyer would pull you aside from time to time and say you were going well or whatever. At the time, Jack O'Shea and Ambrose O'Donovan held the midfield places, and Dermot Hannafin and I were challenging for them. We were never going to get ahead of them, but we kept them honest. I can remember Seánie Walsh saying one time that the contests between the four of us in the midfield were very good.'

Galwey could hardly have chosen a more auspicious occasion for his championship debut in 1986.

'That summer, I came on as a sub for the Bomber in the final ten minutes of the All-Ireland semi-final against Tyrone when he went off with a hamstring injury. It was very thrilling to come on in Croke Park against Meath, who were a "coming" side while Kerry were on the way down. It was a baptism of fire because I went in on Mick Lyons! Mick obviously was a great footballer, but I wasn't two minutes on the pitch when he gave me a dig in the ribs. I was still very nervous so I swung back at him, but I didn't connect. I have to tell you, he didn't waste time in letting me know he was still the main man! Some young fella wasn't going to steal his glory. I played a few times on him after that and he turned out to be a grand fella, but my first introduction to Mick Lyons wasn't the nicest!'

The Meath match was the summit of Galwey's Gaelic career.

'I touched the ball once in that semi-final. I caught it, and I'll always remember passing it on to Ger Power, who in turn gave it on to Mike Sheehy, but the goalie made one of the saves of the year. I really felt that I was part of the set-up because I had actually played a game.

'Coming up to the All-Ireland against Tyrone, I injured my ankle, but in fairness to Mick O'Dwyer, he kept it quiet and carried me along for the final. Having got the taste of Croke Park in the semi-final, it was a step up again to be there for the final. It looked bad for us when

Kevin McCabe stepped up to take the penalty, but after he drove the ball over the bar, we got into our flow. I remember Timmy O'Dowd coming on as a sub and playing a stormer, as did Pat Spillane. That was the great thing about that Kerry team: there was always someone who could turn the game for you.

'Earlier that year, I had won a Munster Senior Cup medal with Shannon. Shortly after, we played the league champions Laois in a GOAL challenge. After the match, we were going into O'Donoghue's pub, which is a real Kerry haunt, and Ogie Moran turned around to me and said, "Jesus, Mick, you could be the only man to win a Senior Cup medal in rugby and an All-Ireland medal in the one year." I remember thinking that would be a wonderful achievement if it came to pass.

'The following year, Larry Thompkins and Shay Fahy put an end to our dreams. A lot of players retired after that so it was the end of an era. I played for Kerry for a few years after that mostly as a sub. My main commitment was to rugby, which probably didn't go down too well in Kerry at the time. I do regret not being able to play more for Kerry, but overall I have no regrets about my career.'

Galwey had the good fortune to play in a team full of characters.

'They were all great characters. Páidí Ó Sé was a great personality. He stood out because he was so committed and enthusiastic. Even back then, you knew he'd be the one to make his mark in management. Football was his life then. Tommy Doyle was actually very funny. Publicly he kept to himself, but with the lads he was great fun. Charlie Nelligan was also a great character. The young fellas had to show a bit of respect to them.

'Dermot Hannafin was a gas man and was always in great form. Dermot and I had the distinction of playing together at midfield for Kerry in an under-21 match when we lost to Clare. No disrespect to them, but at the time it was the worst thing in the world that could happen to lose to Clare. Dermot brought a breath of fresh air to everything. He was a great mimic and was always going into Mícheál Ó Muircheartaigh mode, but he was also great taking off O'Dwyer. Micko would be wondering why the lads would be collapsing with laughter, not realising he was being "done". O'Dwyer was always very keen to keep an eye on all the balls at training so that he had the same number at the finish as he did at the start, but there were always fellas trying to steal them on him, which did nothing for his blood pressure!

'The best fun, though, came after training as soon as O'Dwyer left the dressing-room! If somebody got a bit of a bollocking from O'Dwyer, the whole squad would take the mickey out of him.'

How does Galwey react to the criticism that Mick O'Dwyer held on to his team too long and didn't sufficiently introduce new players?

'There's probably something in that, but to be fair to O'Dwyer, it was hard to change such a successful side. I don't think that he ever left better players on the sideline. Anyway, O'Dwyer's record speaks for itself.'

WHERE WE SPORTED AND PLAYED

Kerry's difficulty would be Cork's opportunity, and Billy Morgan led the county to four consecutive All-Ireland finals – initially losing to Meath in '87 and '88 before beating Mayo in '89 and old rivals Meath in 1990. Morgan had captained Cork to an All-Ireland in 1973.

'It was hugely important for Cork to win that year. It was 28 years since we had last won a senior football All-Ireland, and the longer it was going on, the harder it was becoming. We beat Galway easy enough in the end, but what I most recall was the homecoming. When we got into Cork, there were crowds in the station and all the way up MacCurtain Street. The biggest thing is when we turned Barry's Corner; looking down on Patrick Street, it was just a sea of people. I'd never seen anything like it before. You couldn't see the streets; it was just people all the way down to the Savoy.

'In 1988, I had thought we might be getting such a homecoming when we played Meath. They had deservedly beaten us the year before, but we had a year's experience behind us in '88. We drew the game even though we should have won it. In the drawn game, Dinny Allen had caught Mick Lyons with his elbow, and Barry Coffey had tackled Colm O'Rourke and caught him with his shoulder behind the ear. People said Niall Cahalane had "caught" Brian Stafford. All the talk between the drawn game and the replay was that Meath were going to sort us out. My own instructions were that if that was the case, if there was any trouble, stand together and be united.

'It didn't come as a huge surprise when Gerry McEntee hit Niall Cahalane. All our lads got involved in the flare-up. When it was over and McEntee was sent off, I said to our fellas: "OK now, that's it, we'll play football from hereon in, no retaliation." I repeated the same message at half-time. It was the biggest mistake I ever made as a manager. What I should have said was: "Meet fire with fire, and if necessary, we'll finish this game ten-a-side." Fair play to Meath: they beat us with 14 men.

'I suppose it was sweet then to beat them in the final in 1990. It was a great feeling to manage my county to an All-Ireland in 1989.'

After the acrimony of the previous year, the '89 final was a game for the purists. That was of little consolation to the defeated Mayo team, which included Kevin McStay.

'We were millimetres from winning the All-Ireland in '89. We hit the post twice and the ball bounced back into play. They hit the post twice, but each time the ball went over the bar. One of their players double-hopped the ball and scored a point, but the ref, Paddy Collins, who was normally an excellent referee, missed it. After scoring the goal, Anthony Finnerty got another chance, but the late John Kerins got a touch to it. The umpire backed away because he was afraid the ball was going to hit him. He missed John's touch, and instead of giving us a 45, he flagged it wide. Our free-taker Michael Fitzmaurice was on fire that day and hadn't missed a placed ball, including a 45. If we had got a point at that stage, it would have been a big help to us. Cork were a more experienced team than us, having contested the All-Ireland final the previous two years, but they were very brittle at that stage of the game. As a forward, I could see their nerves in the way the backs were shouting at each other, but we allowed them to settle rather than keep them on the ropes.'

ON A CLARE DAY

Munster football is dominated by the old rivalry between Kerry and Cork, but John Maughan would briefly change that. In 1990, to his great surprise, he found himself at the age of 28 being offered the opportunity to manage the Clare senior football team. He famously coached them to a historic Munster final over mighty Kerry in 1992.

'It was a magical experience, but I didn't fully appreciate it at the time. Clare hadn't won a Munster title since 1917, and for many people, the "Milltown Massacre", when Kerry clocked up a score of 9–21, was fresh in people's minds. When I first took the job, no one suggested anything about winning a Munster Championship to me. I was brought up with a very positive outlook and my main priority was to set about giving an improved performance. The Meath game in the quarter-final of the league in '92, when we nearly beat them even though we had two men sent off, gave me an inkling as to how good we were. The one thing I emphasised very strongly afterwards was that I did not want to see any celebrations for running Meath so close. Our time with being satisfied with moral victories was over. After that game, we thought we were ready to take a Munster title. We got 26 players together and we got a great spirit going. I wasn't worried when we missed a penalty in the Munster final – a penalty miss so early in the game has little significance. It was almost a unique performance in the sense that all our 15 players played to the maximum of their potential. I felt for the Kerry trainer, Mickey Ned O'Sullivan. I was afraid he would be made a scapegoat for Kerry's performance – which he was.

'The next morning, I got a phone call at seven o'clock. I spent the next four hours sitting at the bottom of the stairs answering one call after another. Then it started to sink in how big a deal it was. I got a call from the county board and was summoned down to Clare for a tour of the county with the team and the cup.'

THE GAA

The appointment of Páidí Ó Sé as Kerry manager ushered in a colourful era for Gaelic football. His reign brought mixed reviews, but his former teammate Pat Spillane sees his term in a positive light.

'When people talk about the great managers of today, they speak about John O'Mahony and Mickey Harte, but Páidí's record compares favourably with anybody's. He did bring a National League and under-21 All-Ireland to Kerry, and two All-Irelands in 1997 and 2000. I think people who doubted Páidí's credentials when he was appointed Kerry manager have been proved wrong. Not alone, I believe Páidí as a manager has been completely underestimated. Everyone knows his passion, but what many people miss out on was his cunning, astute footballing brain. We saw it in 2004 in the switches he made for Westmeath against Dublin. He brought an All-Ireland to Kerry in '97 with what I have publicly stated was the poorest team to ever win an All-Ireland.

'The wheels came off the wagon in the 2001 All-Ireland semi-final when Meath beat Kerry by no less than 15 points. Kerry went through a 29-minute spell in the first half without scoring, and then could only muster a single point from substitute Declan Quill in the second half. After the match, Marty Morrissey asked a Kerry fan, "Where did it all go wrong in Croke Park today?"

'The fan replied: "The green bit in the middle."

'Inevitably, when a Kerry team lost by 15 points in Croke Park, serious questions were asked, particularly when Páidí refused to start Maurice Fitzgerald. You can train for all conscious eventualities, but your greatest moments are when your instinct takes over, and afterwards you cannot remotely explain why you did what you did. Maurice's career is peppered with moments of genius like that. His finest hour was the 1997 All-Ireland, when he regularly broke through with Mayo defenders falling around him like dying wasps and kicked incredible points from all angles. There was a time I would have joked that if my mother had been marking Pat Holmes that day, she would have been man of the match. Not any more! Let us instead simply observe that Pat made Maurice's job a lot easier that day. Along with

Mike Sheehy, Maurice was the most skilful player I ever played with in the Kerry jersey.

'Maurice is very quiet. However, some of the people surrounding him liked publicity. The people advising him had Maurice's best interests in mind, but not necessarily the best interests of Kerry football, although they purported to have the good of Kerry football at heart. He had two very high-profile people backing him in the media: *Goal*'s John O'Shea and the editor of the *Sunday Independent*, Aengus Fanning.

'You can argue that Páidí was right or wrong. At the end of the day, Páidí was proved right. There is a very thin line between success and failure, and on the basis of your decisions, you have to be judged on whether you were right or wrong. Páidí was proved right in 2000. Maurice was most effective as an impact sub. It was a big gamble, but it delivered an All-Ireland.

'I was looking forward to reading Páidí's autobiography because I thought it would be the perfect opportunity for him to finally tell us what his problem with Maurice was, but on the single issue that most exercised Kerry people he said absolutely nothing. Ronan Keating was wrong. You do not say it best when you say nothing at all.'

One of Fitzgerald's biggest admirers is RTÉ radio's Gaelic correspondent Brian Carthy.

'I was at a social function when a man berated me for praising Maurice on the basis that he claimed Mikey Sheehy had been a better player. I replied, "Maurice is a rare and wonderful talent, as was Mikey Sheehy. To praise one is not to diminish the other."'

Pat Spillane sees the Maurice Fitzgerald controversy in a wider context.

'No football manager is an island. He needs a good team behind him on and off the field. It would also have been nice to near the real story of Páidí's relationship with John O'Keeffe. Johnno is a lovely guy and a real gentleman. Páidí initially wouldn't have been given the Kerry job because people thought he was a loose cannon. These people underestimated Páidí. At first, he was given Seamus McGearailt to "mind" him. There is no doubt that Seamus kept Páidí under control and made a massive contribution to Kerry's success in

1997. What people don't realise, though, is that if Páidí was unsure about something, he was always willing to get advice, but he would do so indirectly and not get it from anyone close to the Kerry camp. Then, when Seamus moved on, Johnno was parachuted in on him because certain people would have thought Páidí was incapable of training the team on his own. The nature of the imposition put a strain on the relationship straight away. A comparable relationship would have been that of Eddie O'Sullivan and Declan Kidney. At the best of times, Johnno and Páidí would not have been bosom pals.'

The two big controversies of Páidí's reign, the Maurice and the 'animals' disputes, were played out in the full glare of the media. In January 2003, he gave an interview to the *Sunday Independent* and famously said: 'Being the Kerry manager is probably the hardest job in the world because Kerry people, I'd say, are the roughest type of f***ing animals you could deal with. And you can print that.'

A short time later, he was forced to meekly apologise: 'I regret very much if I have offended all or some of my Kerry supporters who have been very loyal to me.'

'He was unlucky insofar as the "animals" controversy blew up at a very quiet time of the year when there was nothing else for GAA journalists to write about, and as we all know, paper never refuses ink.

'A lot of Páidí's most vocal critics were people with agendas. His interview in South Africa was ill-advised. It was not good for Kerry football to have its dirty linen washed in public or to have colleagues and former colleagues on opposite sides. There were no winners in that situation, and it left a bitter legacy and a sour taste.

'In Kerry, we like to think Páidí is the greatest magician of all time. He made Kerry disappear for the entire second half of the 2002 All-Ireland final against Armagh. An old joke was revisited: "Why aren't the Kerry team allowed to own a dog?"

'"Because they can't hold on to a lead."

'This is a match, a classic case of nouveau riche versus old money, that I will never be allowed to forget. Don't think I haven't tried. At half-time in the 2002 All-Ireland final, I was "sceptical" about Armagh's chances of beating Kerry. I caused consternation among Armagh fans when I said, "My mother has arthritis but even she has more pace than the Armagh full-back line." In the second half, I was left looking a right idiot and, understandably, one banner featured prominently in the subsequent media coverage. Against a backdrop of the Armagh colours, it said simply: "Are you watching, Pat Spillane?"

'Most people thought that Kerry had underachieved in the previous two years, but that 2003 was going to be the year that Kerry made up for lost time and reclaimed the Sam Maguire trophy. Fate was destined to booby-trap Kerry once again that summer. It also landed me in hot water when I described the manner of Tyrone's victory over Kerry that day as "puke football".

'Where did it all go wrong for Kerry in Páidí's last three years? There are a number of different theories on success. I believe, though, there are two things you need to succeed as a football manager and in life. First, you need common sense. A few years ago, the Americans experienced a setback to their space programme. They discovered that on moon landings they did not have a biro that worked. Over the next few years, they made correcting this problem a priority. They spent $12 billion to invent a pen that would work in any environment on earth, underwater and in space. What did the Russians do? They used a pencil.

'In a lot of counties, common sense went out the window in Gaelic football with managers having their teams doing adventure courses and doing weight training like Olympic weightlifters. There was no common sense because there were too many training sessions without the ball. Football is a game with a ball, and to become good at it, players must use the ball.

'The second thing you need to do is to be able to read and adapt to a situation. The successful sportsperson and businessperson can size up a situation and react as the circumstances demand. When the going got tough for Kerry in Croke Park in successive years against Meath, Armagh and Tyrone respectively, Páidí was unable to come up with a Plan B to reverse the situation.

'The players, though, must take their share of the blame. The hallmark of a great player is one who knows that his usual ploy isn't working and can adjust his game according to the circumstances. The players on the great Kerry team could do that because they were very intelligent and could read games well and adapt and change tactics when needed. The great captain is one who can motivate his troops and can sort things out with a calm head when they are not going according to plan on the pitch. In recent years, there has been a clamour for "runners" on the field in Croke Park who can give the manager's instructions because they find it impossible to communicate with their players from the sideline because of the noise. That is why they need a captain who can read a situation on the pitch. The classic example of this was Tony Hanahoe. Tony was the thinking man's footballer. Páidí had nobody like him.

'The wounds from those three losses cut deeply not because we lost but because we lost so tamely on each occasion. That is not the Kerry way. To lose abysmally once was bad; for it to happen twice was shocking; but for it to happen to Kerry three years in a row in Croke Park, the ground we think of as our second home, was the end of the world. In some counties, success is accidental. In Kerry, it is compulsory. After failing so spectacularly three years in a row, Páidí's days were numbered. The only problem was that Páidí himself didn't see it that way.

'Apparently, shortly before he died, someone suggested to John B. Keane that he should write a play on Páidí Ó Sé's reign as Kerry manager. He replied, "I don't write tragedies."

'Páidí's year of the U-turn was 2003. After his reluctant resignation as Kerry manager in October, he said: "I wouldn't rule anything in or out, but I couldn't see myself at the present time having the bottle to go in and train another team against the green and gold jersey."

'A week later, after taking over as Westmeath manager, he said: "I now want to transfer all my professional allegiance to Westmeath and will endeavour to coach and improve the team and achieve success in the future."

'My view is that whatever Páidí was getting, he was worth every penny because he raised the profile of the game within the county, really put Westmeath on the football map by taking them to a Leinster title in his first season and created a buzz within the county and a feeling of togetherness and identity that led more and more youngsters to wear the Westmeath jersey.

'The other story is that Páidí was supposed to be getting a helicopter to fly him from Kerry to Westmeath for training sessions. During our days on the Kerry team, Páidí had an amazing fear of flying. Paudie Lynch shared that fear, and when we were travelling on trips abroad, the way the two of them coped was to get totally inebriated before the trip. I remember one day when we got to Dublin airport, I said, "Look here, Páidí: if it's your day to go, it's your day to go."

'Páidí turned around to me and said, "But if it's the f***ing pilot's day to go, he's going to bring me down with him!"

JACK'S BACK

Páidí's successor as Kerry manager was the more low-key and low-profile Jack O'Connor. He led Kerry to what were seen as two soft All-Irelands over Mayo in '04 and '06, and Pat O'Shea led them to another All-Ireland in '07 – but against a Cork side that never got out of the starting blocks. The Kingdom, though, were plundered by Tyrone in '03, '05 and '08. After the defeat in '08, O'Shea stepped down and O'Connor came back as Kerry manager. There was the odd controversy on the way. Joe Brolly found himself embroiled in one of them.

'On television, you make a casual remark and people become suffused with rage. The odd time people will berate you for that. I recall travelling on a train to Dublin when a fella in a Meath jersey got up and said to me: "You f***ing bollix." During an ad break in the Wexford–Armagh quarter-final in 2008, a man in his 70s burst into the studios and said to me: 'You're a f***ing joke, yourself and O'Rourke. You're Dumb and Dumber." They almost had to push him out because the ad break was nearly over. I'm not sure if punditry has any point at all, but if it has, you've got say what you believe.

'I'm not like Pat Spillane, who has to do hours of work presenting the *Sunday Game* because his job is very technical. I just walk in a bit before the game and talk about football because I enjoy it. The odd time people will cross the road when they see me coming because they've been told: "Don't talk to that f***er."

THE GAA

'I can say something relatively trivial and RTÉ gets a thousand emails. I once compared Ciarán MaDonald's braids to those of a "Swedish maid". The phones were hopping. A furious priest wrote a long complaint to the local newspaper.

'I said something about Paul Galvin after an "incident" against Armagh in '06. I said, "That's unbelievable, and he's a teacher. That's real corner-boy stuff." Jesus Christ. All hell broke loose.'

Brolly was unfazed by the controversy.

'The Kerry manager Jack O'Connor was supposed to be furious. I am told that in his book he has a go at me for "crossing the line", but I never read it. I reviewed it, but I never read it! I'm like Alan Partridge. He's interviewing a woman and asks her: "Is it true that you . . . ?"

'She answers: "Of course I did. Did you not read my book?"

'Alan replies: "No, I never read the books."

'In my review, I said O'Connor's book was unlikely to trouble the Pulitzer Committee!'

11

THE WEST'S AWAKE

JOHN O'MAHONY HAS A WEAKNESS. HE CANNOT WATCH A FILM OR programme on television unless he knows it is going to have a happy ending. After 32 years of misery, he wrote a happy ending for those of us from the west.

A litany of woes. Defeats snatched from the jaws of victory. Close calls. Demoralising trouncings. For 32 years, that was the story of Connacht football. A procession of what-might-have-beens. The gods tend to write depressing scenarios for fans west of the Shannon. A history of disillusion shared by a whole generation. Each defeat remembered, like beads on a rosary. A legion of Connacht fans had learned the hard way that to falter is to be swept aside. It was written into the nation's consciousness that Connacht football did not merit serious consideration. To television pundits, Connacht football was little more than a joke.

Gaelic games, more than any other sports, are about place. In the west of Ireland, tribal loyalties run particularly deep and serious slights are not easily forgiven or forgotten. You attack our football teams and you attack us all. To us, Croke Park induced the bitter bile of regret as crushing disappointments there went through Connacht teams like a recessive gene.

193

THE GAA

The appointment of John O'Mahony as Galway manager in October 1997 would change all that. He had qualities that were hard to define, but easy to recognise. A man of self-reliance, of candour, he was not a prisoner of the uncertainties or the enforced servility of the previous decades. Yet nobody predicted the benign revolution that was at hand.

Love hurts, as John Wayne Bobbitt painfully discovered when his wife cut off his most private part after she found out that he was cheating. So do heavy losses at Croke Park. Few fans have learned this lesson more harshly down the years than teams from Connacht.

THE ROSSIES

In 1972, Roscommon seemed set for a breakthrough, as the county's greatest-ever full-back, Pat Lindsay, recalls.

'We beat Mayo in the Connacht final with a very young side. Our oldest player was Jimmy Finnegan, who was 26. We were badly beaten by Kerry in the All-Ireland semi-final. The big disappointment was not that we lost, but that we didn't play as well as we could. The same thing happened against Kerry in the semi-final in 1978. Losing but playing well may not be much of a consolation, but it is a consolation. When you get to Croke Park and play one of the top teams, you want to play to your best, and it hurts when you fail to do so. I should say I always looked forward to playing Kerry. They are the aristocrats of football. They are the yardstick to measure how good you are, personally and as a team.'

Two years later, Kerry were to ruin Roscommon's hopes again.

'We completely outplayed them in every sector of the field in the National League final, but John Egan got a last-minute goal to equalise the game. They beat us easily in the replay. To beat Kerry in a national final in Croke Park would have been a huge boost to that team and would have set us up for greater things. Instead, we were again badly beaten in the Connacht final by a very strong Galway side who were unlucky not to have won an All-Ireland final in the early 1970s.'

Although on a personal level 1977 saw Lindsay rewarded with an

All-Star award, it was to be another year of might-have-beens for Roscommon.

'We were seven points up with ten minutes to go in the All-Ireland semi-final against Armagh, but we lost concentration and let them back to draw the game. You could feel the giddiness running through the team. We thought we had one foot in the All-Ireland final. We were shell-shocked in the dressing-room afterwards. We had been much better than them, but in the replay, they beat us by a point.

'It was pretty much the same story two years later, when we somehow contrived to lose against Dublin in the semi-final. If we had won either of those two semi-finals, the experience of having played an All-Ireland final would have been invaluable when we took on Kerry in the 1980 final.'

Again, there were some crumbs of comfort for Lindsay in 1979 when he captained Roscommon to its first and only National League title, with a crushing defeat of a star-laden Cork team. His Roscommon colleagues would not allow him to get too big for his boots, though.

'Eamon McManus said to me, "If you ever get up the midfield area that's for skilful players, pass the ball to someone with a bit of skill!"'

Roscommon had won the All-Ireland under-21 final in 1978 and had picked up some really class players from that side: Tony McManus, Seamus Hayden, Mick Finneran and Gerry Connellan.

'The spine of the team were very experienced, but the new lads brought another dimension. Tom Heneghan had come in as our manager. He was ahead of his time as a coach. With Tony, Mick and John O'Connor in our forward line, we had three guys who could get you scores. Their worth was really shown in the All-Ireland semi-final in 1980 against Armagh, when, after failing in four previous semi-finals, we finally qualified for the All-Ireland. Tony McManus's goal that day typified what our forward line was capable of. Tom once said to us, "Our tactics are very simple: get the ball fast into the forwards." There was none of the passing to the side, or even backwards, that you see today.

'It was just incredible to reach the All-Ireland final in 1980. Tom had us really well prepared. He arranged for us to get two weeks off work, and for those two weeks, we trained twice a day, at noon and in the early evening. By night-time you couldn't wait to get to bed. We had Kerry reeling early on, but I feel we lost because we weren't attacking enough. We had great attacking half-backs and on the day they did a good defensive job, but we didn't use them to attack Kerry. Offaly beat Kerry in 1982 by attacking them. We had the class to do the same, but we didn't.

'We were gutted afterwards, especially for the supporters. They gave us a massive reception when we got home. Every year Roscommon plays in the Connacht Championship there's an expectation that we can do something significant. The Roscommon supporters really rally behind the team, as was shown in Ennis in 2006 when Roscommon beat Kerry in the replay of the All-Ireland minor final. The atmosphere was incredible, and judging by the massive traffic jam on the way home from the game, every man, woman and child in the county was at the game. That Roscommon team played football the way I think it should be played: with great support play, no fouling and enormous commitment.'

Sligo shocked Roscommon in the first round of the Connacht Championship in 1981, as Pat recalls: 'We were complacent and I think by that stage some of the hunger had gone out of the team.'

The disappointment of losing the 1980 All-Ireland to Kerry has never faded for Tony McManus.

'I still feel aggrieved by the refereeing that day. It was outrageous. The ref was from Monaghan, and I still have Monaghan people apologising to me for it. It seemed to us as if he had a preconceived idea that Kerry were destined to win, and when it wasn't going according to the script that they had to get every decision their way.

'I am not one to hold a grudge, but I still am annoyed by Mick O'Dwyer's reaction to it. He said nothing at the reception the next day, but down in Kerry he said that dirty tactics would never beat Kerry. That still sticks in my throat. There was reference made to the treatment of John Egan. The implication was that Harry Keegan, who marked him in the final, was a dirty player. John would be the first to admit that Harry was not that sort of player. I think the only time that I ever saw Dermot Earley angry was at those comments. I felt that O'Dwyer conveniently overlooked a few tackles that our forwards had to take. Every time I went for the ball that day, I had my jersey pulled. I accept that as part and parcel of the game, but then to hear his comments after the match, you would think that all the sinning was on one side and that Kerry were above reproach.

'I never had a problem with any of the Kerry lads. Myself and John O'Gara were very friendly with Ogie Moran, Bomber Liston and Mikey Sheehy. All of the Roscommon players got on very well with the Kerry lads, apart from Pat Spillane.

'We were sick after losing, but I thought I would be back again the next year and many times more afterwards. How wrong I was. Looking back, the real one that got away was when we lost to Dublin in the semi-final the previous year, a game we should have won. We wouldn't have won that year, but the experience of having been in a final would have helped us to win in 1980.'

Five years later, a Roscommon footballer found himself the unwitting centre of controversy. The late Mick Dunne had the inside track on that story.

'The famous John Kerry O'Donnell of New York was a wonderful character. Back in the 1960s, I was involved in selecting the team that would travel to New York to play in the Cardinal Cushing Games to raise money for the cardinal's mission in Peru. It was almost the precursor of the All-Stars. We tried especially to pick some good players from the weaker counties. In fact, the former GAA president John Dowling always maintained that one of the reasons why Offaly eventually made the breakthrough in hurling was because of the boost it got when players like Paddy Molloy got one of these trips.

'John Kerry dined out for years in America on the story of what happened when this gang of Irish journalists got together. The importance of picking players from the weaker counties led us to speak about the terms of reference in selection decisions. One of our number blurted out immediately, "Let's pick the team first and we'll sort out the terms of reference later!"'

For many years, Dunne was secretary to the journalists who selected the All-Stars. The fruits of their deliberations often generated controversy – for their perceived sins of omission as much as their actual selections. Selecting the best 15 often provoked passionate disagreements among the journalists in question.

'When he was president of the GAA, Pat Fanning said after seeing us picking the teams, "The amazing thing is that they are such good friends after a night fighting like this!"

'The president and director general of the GAA sat in as observers. The only time they ever intervened was if there was a tie over a particular position when somebody abstained. They then, having listened to all the arguments, went out of the room and decided who got the nod.

'The only time I ever got "approached" was when I got a phone call from a manager of a team the day before the team was picked. After a bit of casual conversation, he blatantly started talking up some of his players with a view to influencing my selection. I simply said, "It would be much better for their chances if you didn't interfere in this way."'

Controversy erupted in 1985 when Roscommon's Paul Earley was chosen at full-forward on the All-Star football team ahead of Monaghan's Eamonn Murphy. An article was written by a prominent GAA personality in Monaghan that claimed that Earley was awarded the honour because he was an employee of the sponsoring bank. Was there an 'informal canvassing will disqualify' policy in operation?

'The accusation that the bank interfered in Paul's selection was totally wrong and very unfair to his abilities as a player. If they had tried to persuade us to pick Paul, it would have ensured that he wouldn't get the All-Star!'

YEATS COUNTY

In 1974, Roscommon needed a replay to beat Sligo in a National League semi-final. Sligo's centre half-back Barnes Murphy was rewarded for a string of fine performances through the year with an All-Star award. The trip was to have an unintended side effect.

'Getting an All-Star really meant a lot to me, and it was great to get to meet Kevin Heffernan and his team on that tour. I feel that the GAA owes them a lot. Gaelic football was not fashionable before them, but they did a massive PR job for the game, as was seen in the number of Dublin jerseys being worn at the time, which later spread to Mayo jerseys, Sligo jerseys and so on. That helped us in Sligo enormously in 1975. We need Dublin to win an All-Ireland every decade because of the hype they generate.'

On that tour, Murphy befriended a man who in west of Ireland parlance was 'a horse of a footballer'.

'I remember Galway's Billy Joyce was a replacement on that team. I thought he was an awful so and so, and he thought the exact same about me! As a result, we didn't even talk to each other at Shannon before flying out. On the trip, though, I got to know him very well, and I found out he's the soundest guy ever and great fun. Billy and the Galway lads on the trip, like Johnny Hughes and Tom Naughton, said to me that Sligo always put it up to Galway for fifty minutes, but Galway knew they would always take us in the last ten minutes. I was coaching the Sligo team at the time, and after hearing these comments a number of times, I was really fired up that was going to stop. When I got home, I passed that fierce drive on to the rest of the team.

'When we played Galway in the Connacht Championship in 1975, every time Billy Joyce went for the ball I shouted "Judy", because that was the name of Billy's love interest at the time. He got more and more annoyed, and once he shouted back to me, "If you don't shut up, I'll go back and hit you in the lug." I was delighted because it showed he was distracted from the game. In the end, we won easy enough and then went on to win a Connacht final at last.'

As coach and captain, Murphy saw the euphoria generated by the victory as a mixed blessing.

'We had three weeks to get ready then for Kerry in the semi-final. I am a non-drinker, but for the first week, I couldn't get some of the fellas to keep their heads out of drinking from the Nestor Cup. I was marking Mike Sheehy, and he wasn't getting a kick of the ball so he had to be replaced. I gave out to our corner-backs, who gave Mike a belt because he wasn't doing us any damage. Instead his replacement came on and scored a goal. We were in the match until the second half of the second half. Kerry got three goals and two points in the last ten minutes. It ended up as a bad defeat, and for over 20 years, that would be the story of Connacht football.'

MAYO'S MISERY

Over the last 50 years, no team has learned more about bad defeats in Croke Park than Mayo, as Dermot Flanagan is all too keenly aware. His early years were spent on the Mayo side of Ballaghaderreen.

'So split is the town between Roscommon and Mayo that I joke that even the marital bed could come under pressure when the two counties meet in the Connacht Championship.'

The family came to live in Dublin when he was still in primary school. With the encouragement of his father, Flanagan played a lot of soccer in his new home of Clontarf, once playing against Ronnie Whelan.

'I think I brought some of my soccer training into my Gaelic football. I was the first to pass the ball back to the goalkeeper, which was considered very avant-garde at the time.'

In 1982, having just established himself on the Mayo team, Flanagan found himself training with Dublin's Kerry-based players. In the best GAA tradition, this was an accidental by-product of a controversy. Mícheál Ó Muircheartaigh was training players like Mick Spillane and Jack O'Shea in University College Dublin (UCD), but a newspaper made a big issue of the fact that none of the players involved were attending UCD. A Gaelic football solution to a Gaelic football problem had to be found. As secretary of the UCD club, Flanagan wrote and invited the Dublin-based Kerry players to join the UCD players involved in summer training.

'Mícheál was very welcoming. The first night, he pointed to me and said to the Kerry lads, "You'll see that man winning an All-Ireland." I deeply appreciated his comments. His training methods were very modern and sophisticated. When I went back to train with Mayo, I was noticeably sharper because the training was so crisp. The big thing for me was that in March they were training for September, whereas counties like Mayo were only training in four-week bursts until the next match. Psychologically, I found that the Kerry way made you believe you were an All-Ireland contender rather than hoping you might possibly be one.'

Flanagan holds a unique, albeit poignant, distinction.

'I was the last person to mark Offaly's Matt Connor before his horrific accident. He would've been one of my heroes.'

In 1985, Mayo reached the All-Ireland semi-final against Dublin. Flanagan's background was to prove a mixed blessing in the run-up to the match.

'There was a lot of media attention on me before the game because I was the only link to the '50 and '51 teams, and that drained me. In the first half of the first game, I was feeling the effects.'

Nonetheless, his performance on Barney Rock in the replay, keeping him scoreless from play, helped Flanagan to win the first of his two All-Stars that year. His next semi-final, against Meath in 1988, was at once memorable and unremembered.

'It was a very physical game and I was knocked unconscious. I swallowed my tongue and was a little perturbed to find out afterwards that I could have died.'

The promise of reaching the All-Ireland final in 1989 was not built on, and Flanagan looks back on the experience as a lost opportunity.

'The winter of '89 saw a form of euphoria because we had reached a final after such a long time and had played well, which really took away from our focus. What should have happened was that we should have cleared off for a week and realised we had lost. People thought we were on the crest of winning an All-Ireland, which created a lot of distractions and left us vulnerable in '90.'

To this day, Flanagan finds it difficult to assess the way events unfolded after Mayo's defeat in the Connacht final replay to Roscommon in 1991.

'John O'Mahony departed in controversial circumstances. John has never spoken in public about all the details, and I suppose we should let him have his say on that. It is probably fair to say that part of the reason was that he was not allowed to choose his own selectors. Looking back, the circumstances of Mayo football were not right then.

'Brian McDonald came in as his replacement, and a year later would find himself in a huge controversy. Were there any winners?

THE GAA

Everybody was a loser to a greater or lesser extent. Brian had been a selector with Liam O'Neill in 1985. To be fair to Brian, he had a lot of good ideas about the game, but whether he was the man to get the best out of players was another question. The first thing he asked me when he took over as manager was if I was committed to Mayo football. I was totally committed. I was the first guy to do stretching before training and after training. Long before it was fashionable, I was doing acupuncture, watching my diet, reading sports-injury books and doing power weightlifting – anything that would give me an edge or improve me as a player, so it came as a shock to be asked that.

'The issue that got into the media was about the players pushing cars as part of a training session. That was not the underlying problem. You needed to have a very strong skin to be able to handle Brian's comments in a training session. That was OK for the senior players, but repeated exposure to this for the younger players could have undermined their confidence. We had a lot of younger players in the squad at the time.

'Again, in fairness to Brian, we did win a Connacht final in 1992 and could have beaten Donegal in the All-Ireland semi-final. We were not in the right frame of mind for an All-Ireland semi-final. There were a lot of problems with organisation. I was a man marker and I was on Tony Boyle for a short time in the game and did well on him, but I wasn't left on him and he played havoc with us.

'Afterwards, the controversy broke in the media. The team was going nowhere. There were no winners in that situation. The tumultuous saga reflected very badly on the whole scene in Mayo. The county board had been deaf to any complaints. John O'Mahony had left under a cloud. These situations don't come from nowhere. A lot of mistakes were made.'

The sins of the father were revisited on Flanagan.

'My Dad wouldn't have been hugely popular with the county board in his playing days. One day, he turned around and asked the county chairman if he wouldn't mind leaving the dressing-room. For that reason, some people believed that I was the most likely instigator of the "revolt" against Brian, but I had nothing to do with it. I never had to push cars because I was training in Dublin and was too busy in my legal career to be "masterminding a coup".'

Although he won an All-Star that year, T.J. Kilgallon's memories of the All-Ireland semi-final in 1992 are not very happy.

'There was kind of a bad vibe all year, and even though we won the Connacht final, there was a sense in the camp that things were not going well. Probably the most memorable incident that happened in that game was that Enon Gavin broke the crossbar in Castelbar and the match had to be delayed. The management had brought back Padraig Brogan earlier that year – I'm not saying it was a popular move with the players. When we played Donegal in the All-Ireland semi-final, it was probably the worst game ever seen in Croke Park. Padraig had played for Donegal the previous year, and when the Donegal lads saw him warming up, you could see that it gave them new energy.

'Things got ugly after that. It was more personal than it should have been. It was probably an early example of player power. We said that if there wasn't a change of management, a lot of us would walk away. I was asked recently if we really did spend a training session pushing cars. We did! It was the Dunnes Stores car park in Castlebar, and the cars were really big. There was not a great humour in the camp and the manager had to walk the plank. John O'Mahony had stepped down in 1991 because he was not allowed to choose his own selectors, and maybe that's when we should have acted.'

It was hoped that Jack O'Shea's appointment as manager would revive Mayo's fortunes, but it was not to be, as Dermot Flanagan found out at first hand.

'We were very lucky to beat Roscommon in the Connacht final in 1993. I picked up a cruciate ligament injury, and had to decide whether to retire or have surgery knowing that it might not be a success.'

John Maughan's appointment as Mayo manager would usher in a new era for Mayo football. Having recovered from his operation, Flanagan was happy to know he had not been forgotten.

'I really wanted to get involved again, not just because of John but also because of his backroom team of Peter Ford and Tommy O'Malley. Peter rang to invite me back. I told him I was going on holiday for two weeks in Portugal. I told my wife I was going back to play for Mayo so I spent the two weeks running up and down sand dunes. It was a huge psychological challenge for me. I was 34 and in the winter of my career. I knew the media scrutiny of me would be much greater, to see if I had become a has-been. I played in a challenge game against Donegal, and Peter told me I had done fine. I was then selected to play against Galway in the league, and that night Peter rang me to say that people had come to bury me, but I had proved them wrong. I knew, though, that there would be ongoing questioning of whether I was the weak link on the Mayo team.'

It is clear from the tone of his voice that Flanagan still nurses a sense of frustration on one aspect of the events of 1996.

'We played some super football that year and were tremendous when we beat Kerry in the semi-final. Not winning the All-Ireland that year remains the big disappointment of my career.'

Flanagan has a more personal regret about the loss to Kerry in the All-Ireland final in 1997.

'I had got a nick in my hamstring ten days before the final, as had Maurice Sheridan. Both of us thought we were good enough to do the job, but neither of us lasted the match. The ironic thing was that psychologically I never felt better in my head for the game. I had taken a month off work and was really psyched. There was no point in me going in for just five minutes if that's all I thought I could last – which is all I did. It is a huge regret of mine that I never got to contribute more to the team that day.'

Asked about his dream team, Flanagan says the team he would most have liked to see playing was his father's Mayo All-Ireland-winning team. Since his retirement, Flanagan has had ample time to appraise his career.

'Eugene McGee once asked me, "Why don't you play gobshite football?" I didn't understand what he meant then, but I do now. Maybe if we had been less keen on sportsmanship in Mayo down the years and had been a bit more cynical, we would have won more silverware.'

Mícheál Ó Muircheartaigh points to the importance of Mayo's relative success for Connacht football.

'Sport tends to go in cycles. If you look at Gaelic football, for example, all has changed in the west. If you look back to the '60s, after the demise of the Down team in 1968, people felt that if you were drawn against an Ulster team in the '70s and much of the '80s, the belief in Leinster and Munster was that you were already in the All-Ireland final. That belief was dead and buried once the Ulster counties took over in the early 1990s. Then it seemed that Connacht was the soft draw. Mayo changed that. They had it for the taking twice in 1996. It was their own fault, though they had some ill luck. I thought they'd have done it in 1997. They started well and played excellently against Galway, but they were going downwards from then on. I think because they got over Galway so early, unknown to themselves, they had it in their minds that all they had to do was take it up there from September. It doesn't work like that.'

LAST NIGHT I HAD A PLEASANT DREAM

The fact that both Declan Darcy's parents were from Leitrim was the catalyst for his immersion into club football in the county, though initially the move was shrouded in controversy because he was born and living in Dublin.

'I was playing illegally with Aughawillan. I was not living or working there, but I put my father's home down as my address. Some people in other clubs didn't want me because I was giving Aughawillan an advantage, but the club arranged for me to play with Leitrim, and that certainly made things easier. The great thing about playing with Aughawillan was that I found myself playing in big club tournaments at the age of 16 or 17, like playing in a final in Cavan against Navan O'Mahony's, up against Joe Cassells, Finian Murtagh and David Beggy, which was surreal for me.'

A senior intercounty debut soon followed.

'I made my debut against Fermanagh wearing some ridiculous thing on my nose, having broken it just beforehand in a hockey match. I then played against Offaly. I started at wing-forward and was doing OK, but then moved to centre half-back. Every ball seemed to come to me then and I was the hero of the day, and that was where I lined out from then on.'

Darcy soon learned an important footballing lesson.

'I was marking Greg Blaney in a Railway Cup. I was just a nipper, and because I respected him so much, I was marking him very tightly and hanging on to him for dear life. Eventually, he lifted me with an elbow and it was lights out. I couldn't see a thing. Greg is a dentist, but he knocked out two or three of my back teeth! He remembers the incident well, and we've often laughed about it since. It taught me an invaluable lesson: that when you are marking a top player, you can't be hanging out of him. Finbarr Cullen famously found out the same thing marking Paul Curran. I learned that day that you don't cross the line, and the next time I played on Greg, I marked him very differently.'

Darcy's early years with Leitrim coincided with a significant upturn in the county's fortunes.

'Things started to roll when we beat red-hot favourites Mayo, managed by John O'Mahony, in a Connacht under-21 semi-final, and then Galway in the Connacht final. Aughawillan were doing well and should have beaten Clan na Gael to win a Connacht title in the famous "battle of the fog".

'Jerome Quinn played for Aughawillan against Clan na Gael that day, and really dished it out to some of the Clan lads and developed a reputation as a hard nut. That was one of the reasons why Aughawillan versus Clan was renamed "the Provos versus the Guards". We were playing Roscommon in the Connacht Championship in 1990 and before the match, our manager, P.J. Carroll, had an unusual mind game planned. He said: "Jerome Quinn, they all think you're f***ing mad in Roscommon; what you need to do is pick up a clump of grass, stick it in your mouth and eat it in front of your marker's face. He'll sh*t himself." Jerome was wing half-back and was marking a lovely, skilful player. Sure enough, Jerome did as he was told, and you could see the Roscommon player's legs turn to jelly!

'At one stage, we were playing a league match in Antrim. A special train from Dublin was run for Leitrim fans, and ten or twelve coaches from the county came to the game. That level of support gave you energy when you went back to training the next Tuesday and created a great buzz. Looking back now, though we didn't realise it at the time, we were giving the county a great lift in the dark days of the early '90s. It was heartwarming stuff.'

Things moved up another gear when John O'Mahony became county manager.

'The first thing was that he came. Before he did so, he had seen us play when he was Mayo boss and we beat them out the gate in Carrick-on-Shannon, so he knew what we could do. When he agreed to manage us, we knew that he was coming because he believed something was going to happen.'

O'Mahony's Midas touch worked its unique magic in 1994. One of the iconic images of the year was Darcy, as captain of the Connacht champions, holding the Nestor Cup with Tom Gannon, who had captained Leitrim to their only previous Connacht title in 1927. That was the start of an unforgettable adventure.

'I stayed in the Bush Hotel in Carrick the night after the game. The next morning, the receptionist apologetically rang me and said she was being hounded by somebody who wanted to speak with me on the phone. I asked, "Who is it?"

'"Pat Kenny."

'I thought somebody was winding me up, but sure enough it was Pat, who came on the line and asked, "Where are you?"

'"I'm in bed."

'"With who?"

'"With the Nestor Cup."

'After the interview, I went out on the main street and was surprised at how quiet it was. I had expected a bit of a buzz. I went across the road to the pub, and when I opened the door, it was like a nightclub. The place was jammed and hyper, and it was only 10.30 in the morning and Shannonside radio were broadcasting live in the corner.

'My abiding memory of the whole thing came that day in Ballinamore. When my father was asked where he was from, he had always said "West of the Shannon" rather than Leitrim. We did a tour of the county and it was very special. All the players went to their own clubs. The emotion was unbelievable, but as someone who grew up in Dublin 4, I didn't have that local base. I found myself on the stage in Ballinamore not sure what to do when my father ran on, grabbed the cup and threw it in the air like a mad lunatic! It was raw and real. It was about passion and pride. It meant so much to him. It is an unbelievable memory that will stay with me for ever.'

Although Leitrim were to lose the All-Ireland semi-final, Darcy was literally to leave his mark.

'As captain, when I shook hands with John O'Leary, as the photo shows, I was so fired up I nearly squashed John's hand. He told me afterwards that I nearly broke two or three of his fingers and that he thought I had done it deliberately, but it was just because I was pumped up.

'It was a fantastic achievement for the team, and when I led them out onto Croke Park, although it meant a lot to the county, I was really thinking about all those training sessions we had suffered in Strandhill. This was the reward for the sacrifices, the endless travel to training sessions, and the blood, sweat and tears.

'For Leitrim people, just to be in Croke Park one day in their lives was such a proud moment for them. That's the magic of the GAA. It is so much more than football.

'We didn't do ourselves justice in the semi-final, and the next year we left the game against Galway behind us in the Connacht Championship. If we had won, I believe we would have retained the Connacht final and given a much better showing in the All-Ireland semi-final. I know Armagh's Enda McNulty, and he often says that they should have won more than one All-Ireland. I tell him that they were lucky to win one because it is so hard to make a breakthrough when you have no tradition of winning.'

When John O'Mahony stepped down as Leitrim manager in 1996, it was obvious that things were on a downward spiral. What was it about O'Mahony that made him achieve success with Leitrim?

'One thing is his man management and the belief that he gives you. I remember a very tight game against Galway in Carrick-on-Shannon, and we got a potentially decisive free about forty yards out. Two or three of our lads ran over to take it, but John came running to the sideline and roared at the top of his voice, "Dec, I want you to take it." He believed in me to score this vital kick, and because he believed in me, I had confidence that I would. To an outsider it

Star Trek: The Next Generation: Victorious Roscommon minor manager Fergal O'Donnell signs an autograph for a young fan after the 2006 All-Ireland final replay. (Photo courtesy of John Boyle)

Raising the banner: Roscommon and Kerry parade before the replayed All-Ireland minor final in 2006. (Photo courtesy of John Boyle)

Earley to rise: Paul Earley greets two of his young fans.

The Harte of the matter: Micky Harte with Máirín McAleenan
and former Down forward Paddy Doherty.

Keep your eye on him:
Kerry's Tomás Ó Sé keeps
close to his opponent.

The man in black: Kerry's Mike Frank
Russell gets an earful from the referee.

Meet and greet: The Mayo team meet the
president before the 2006 All-Ireland final.

Courting success: Kevin Walsh and family take to the basketball courts.

One man and his horse: Eddie Macken was one of the many Irish sports stars lost to Gaelic games after showing promise as a footballer in Longford.

One of a kind: The late, very great Lulu Carroll.
(Photo courtesy of Ozzie Dunne)

The clash of the ash: The joys, thrills and
spills of wheelchair hurling.

Ladies of the ash: The 2004 All-Star camogie team.

Driving home:
Babs Keating declines the
public transport option.

A grave matter: The tombstone of James
Burke in St Nahi's graveyard, Dundrum.
He was killed aged 45 by the Black and
Tans on Bloody Sunday in Croke Park.
(Photo courtesy of Niall Sloane)

She was lovely and fair: Ladies' Gaelic footballer
Aoife Kelly becomes the Rose of Tralee in 2008.

Hurling out of Africa: Galway's Alan Kerins, one of the last of the
great dual stars, spreads the hurling gospel in Zambia.
(Photo courtesy of Damien Eagers)

looked a pressure kick, but I felt totally calm because of what Johnno had said.

'John was brilliant at getting into the heads of individual players. Colm McGlynn was a great full-forward for us, but he always liked to think he was a bit special. He once told John that he could not train one evening.

"Why?"

"I have exams in college. I can't train Thursday, either."

"Why?"

"I have exams in college."

"Well, when are you free?"

"Ten o'clock on Wednesday night."

"OK, I will meet you in Ringsend at ten o'clock."

'John travelled all the way to Dublin and ran the sh*t out of him. Colm never asked for special treatment again! That's the way John was. What he did for Leitrim was priceless. It was very emotional when John left – both for us and for Johnno.'

Although Leitrim were not to reach those dizzy heights again, they did find themselves in the headlines once more.

'We were playing Mayo on a live game for RTÉ, and a melee broke out and the Mayo manager John Maughan came running onto the pitch in his shorts. He passed a comment to Gerry Flanagan and Gerry floored him. In our view, Maughan definitely deserved it, but it's probably not the thing to do on live TV! Pat Spillane and the pundits were outraged, but it did Flanagan's reputation no harm in Leitrim!'

Some of the same fans who were throwing bouquets at Darcy in 1994 were swinging cleavers when he decided to transfer to Dublin, though many of his friends and Leitrim fans wished him well.

'Once the offer was made, I had to give it serious thought. At the time, the '94 Leitrim side were disintegrating. The changes weren't to my liking. One little incident encapsulated it for me. The day before we played a Connacht Championship match, we were having lunch and were given steaks. In pretty much his last championship game, Mickey Quinn said he wouldn't eat steak; he would only eat chicken because it was the best meal for the match the next day. Here was this Leitrim legend on his last legs worrying about his diet, but when I went out of the hotel, I saw two of the new players, very talented guys, smoking. That was their way of preparing for the biggest game of their lives. To be honest, if Mickey was going to continue playing, I wouldn't have been able to walk away from Leitrim because I looked up to him so much and so admired his great commitment to the county.'

MAROON AND WHITE FOR EVER

Having taken Mayo to an All-Ireland final appearance in 1989 and Leitrim to a historic Connacht triumph in 1994, John O'Mahony became Galway manager in 1997. He had been great at making teams good, but would he be good enough to make that Galway team great?

For years, defeat had jostled the Galway team's elbow and dogged its steps, imposing unbearable strain on the players' fragile spirits. Once O'Mahony was at the helm, the injection of his unique spirit and his talent for inspiring people brought meteoric progress. It does not require special perception to detect the solidity of the confidence behind his quiet persona. Who dares wins. He dared and he won.

Every team, to a greater or lesser extent, reflects the personality of its manager. It is no coincidence that O'Mahony's Galway represented a fascinating combination of wit and grit, of steel and style. Within 12 months, he had taken his side to an All-Ireland final.

On 27 September 1998, it was not just a victory for John O'Mahony and Galway. It was for all of us born and reared in Connacht. Turning points are generally the creations of novelists and dramatists, necessary plot mechanisms to distil morals from sequences of actions and to give the audience something unforgettable to mark a character's growth. This was different, like a gift wrapped up in deliciously pretty paper to be given, with discretion, to the right people. Galway's victory transcended football. It was about identity and how we felt about ourselves, individually and collectively. This was a defining moment, an experience that redirected the revealed truth by whose light all previous conclusions must be rethought.

210

It was a story whose historical accuracy was of less significance than the function it served, a drama that seemed to be enacted just for us.

The win restored the hope that sport can still be the simple, challenging life enhancement it was first meant to be. The Galway team gave all of us from the west of Ireland back our dream. John O'Mahony is acutely aware of the importance of that All-Ireland win to all Connacht people.

'For much of the '80s and '90s, Connacht football was in the doldrums. The nadir was probably the trouncing Cork gave Mayo in the 1993 All-Ireland semi-final. So to take back the Sam Maguire trophy west to the Shannon for the first time in 32 years meant so much to so many, and we were very aware of that. The memory of the celebrations will live with me for ever. However, what I really appreciate now is going around the west of Ireland and seeing young children wearing their county jerseys or displaying the flag of their county team with pride. You really can't put a price on that.'

Asked about his recipe for success with a team, O'Mahony's answer seems very simple.

'Being together as a team is ultimately more important than winning. If a side is not together as a team, success will be transitory, but if a side achieves togetherness and unity of purpose, success will follow.'

THE BYRNE-ING ISSUE

In the glory days of Jack Charlton's reign as Irish soccer manager, one of the best-known faces on Irish television was the team's physio, Mick Byrne. Mick is the archetypal Dub. Yet he also played a role in Galway's historic All-Ireland in 1998.

'Gaelic football and hurling have always been my sports. John O'Mahony was managing Leitrim, and they were training in Navan and he needed someone to give the players a rub-down and look after them, so John invited me into the set-up.

'Players are the same no matter what sport they play. John would collect me on the way to training and bring me back afterwards.

Leitrim won the Connacht final in '94 after such a long time, and it was wonderful to be part of that adventure.

'When John got the Galway job, he rang me straight away to invite me to join the set-up there, but it would involve me making a big commitment because of the amount of travel involved. The hospitality there from John's wife, Ger, and his four daughters was fantastic. One of the girls, Cliona, was always dumped out of her room to make way for me. It was like staying at home for me.

'I remember we played Offaly in the league quarter-final in '98 in Hyde Park, in Roscommon. Strangely enough, I had been part of the Dublin set-up with Kevin Heffernan that opened Hyde Park. After losing to Offaly, I said to John, "We're going to win the All-Ireland this year. I have a gut feeling." We had played really well that day, but had 19 wides.

'I'll never forget beating Mayo in Castlebar that year. That was fantastic. I was really hoarse afterwards. Then we went on to win the All-Ireland. It was incredible to be in the dressing-room afterwards and have all the greats like Frank Stockwell and Seán Purcell congratulate you. I had watched them play and it was such a privilege to greet them at that special moment, especially as Galway had waited so long to win the Sam Maguire again.

'We should have won the All-Ireland in 2000, the first day. I was away in Portugal with the Irish side on World Cup duty in Portugal for the replay. I was sick for John when Galway lost. He's such a professional man in everything he does. He would have made a brilliant soccer manager because of the professionalism he brings to everything. He does everything right: the hotels, the accommodation, the food. It's no fluke that Galway were so successful once he took charge.'

Yet Byrne witnessed one or two moments when O'Mahony's high standards were not matched by his players.

'After we won the All-Ireland in '98, we played in the GOAL challenge a couple of days later. Some of our players hadn't slept for three days. After the match started, I was going to give a rub to some of the subs. When I got to the subs' bench, a few of them were asleep and one of them was snoring loudly! I had to shout to wake him up. He didn't know where he was!'

Mick has a treasure-trove of stories about his association with the Irish soccer team, particularly of the glory days with Jack Charlton. He struck up an immediate and enduring friendship with Jack. His face lights up when he talks about soccer. Yet it is perhaps a very revealing insight into his character that the most emotion comes when he recalls the most difficult moment for him in the Charlton era.

'It was John Giles who first brought me on board with the Irish side. I was very close with John and then with Eoin Hand. When Jack Charlton was appointed, first he asked to meet me. He asked if I would be willing to act as physio for the Welsh game because he had to find out if he could work with me. I replied, "I will certainly, 'cos I've got to find if I can work with you!" He was a bit taken aback by that. We lost the Welsh game 1–0. He blamed the defeat on me, 'cos he said I picked the team! If we had won, he'd have picked the team! That night, though, he came to me and said, "Thanks very much. I'm very happy with you. The job is yours if you want it."

'When Jack came on the scene, I never dreamed we would qualify for the major championships. We were always a "nearly" team, content with moral victories. Yet Jack changed that. He was a great manager, and I saw a number of qualities in Jack that I later saw in John O'Mahony.

'First, they both have self-belief. Jack brought Ireland to a soccer tournament in Iceland shortly after we took over. I don't think there were any press people there from Ireland because there were few expectations at the time, but we won the tournament. In the dressing-room afterwards, and I'll never forget this, Jack said to the lads, "Do as I ask you to do. Play as I ask you to do, and you'll be successful." I thought of that moment after we famously beat England in the European Championship in 1988. There was a great photo taken of me immediately afterwards kneeling on the ground in a prayer of thanks for our victory. John believed that when he took the job in Leitrim and Galway, he would bring success to both counties.

'Second, they both can take hard decisions. The saddest thing in my sporting life came during our World Cup adventure in 1990. The incident involved Gary Waddock.'

Waddock was the man at the centre of one of the most controversial episodes in Irish soccer. In 1990, at the last moment in the training camp in Malta, Jack Charlton created a sensation by calling up Alan McLoughlin and dropping 'Waddo' from the World Cup squad for Italy.

'Gary is such a lovely lad, but Jack had to make a decision. I remember going at four in the morning with Gary to the airport and it was a gut-wrenching experience. John has also had to make tough decisions about which big-name players to leave out.

'Third, they kept people around them who weren't simply yes-men. I could talk to Jack like no one else could. I would go to him and look him eye to eye and talk to him about particular players. There were times he resented this. Once I went to him and took the side of one of the lads who he was unhappy with. He said, "Remember whose side you are on."

'I replied, "Yeah. You remember who plays for you." With that I walked out and slammed the door. Ten minutes later, I was in my treatment room. Jack walked in and put his arm around me. He didn't say anything and just walked back out. That was the type of relationship I had with Jack and I loved him for it. I have a similar relationship with John, and he had strong people around him like Pete Warren and Stephen Joyce. They have to have people around them who will say no to them. Any manager who surrounds himself with yes-men will achieve nothing.

'Fourth, they both believe in keeping their squads happy. When we went to Italy in 1990, we went first to acclimatise to the heat in Malta. The only problem was that it was raining there all the time and the weather was actually much better at home in Ireland! The second problem was that our hotel was worse than any German prison. Even though we had great characters in the side like Andy Townsend, Tony Cascarino, Aldo and Ray Houghton, the lads would get a bit down at times. So it was important to provide light relief. I remember one time we were playing Scrabble. At the time we had a Monsignor with the squad to say Mass for us. Jack was losing so he got a bit miffed and told the Monsignor he was sacked. The lads were falling around the floor laughing at him losing his cool like that.

'When we moved to Sicily a little later, we were staying in a shocking hotel. It was like Fawlty Towers. The waiter was a ringer for Manuel! So we knocked great fun out of that. The hotel owner's pride and joy was a model boat he had on display in the foyer. He told us it was a priceless antique. One evening, I could see the lads were a bit low so I decided to organise a sing-song. My enthusiasm got the better of me at one stage, and I swung back my elbow and knocked the boat on the ground, smashing it to smithereens. I nearly died. To this day, the players still speak to me about the expression on my face when I broke the boat. The whole squad got a great delight out of my embarrassment and it gave everyone a lift.

'Another thing we did to boost morale was to dress up our kit man Charlie O'Leary in various costumes. When we sent him to the players' rooms dressed like that, it always gave everyone a laugh. Jack really encouraged that.

'John, too, wanted to create a good spirit in his sides. I remember Galway going to play a tournament game in Wicklow and John brought us to Druids Glen on the way. All these little things make a big difference.'

FAST EDDIE

O'Mahony brought another man destined to become one of the biggest names in Irish sport into his backroom team: Eddie O'Sullivan.

'Back in 1997, I was working in America. It was seasonal work because I was in Ireland for the winter and in America for the summer. I got a phone call from the Galway manager, John O'Mahony, and he asked me if I'd be interested in running the fitness programmes and being the physical trainer of the Galway football team. At the time, I said I'd like to help but I couldn't be there on the ground, so I would write the training programmes and he could run them himself. So we said we'd try that for a while, and we did. In '98, Galway won the All-Ireland and that sealed it. I kept in touch with John. I devised the plans and he implemented them.

'I only met the players three or four times a year, but they knew I was always there in the background. I'd usually take them in winter for a weights session and in early spring for a running session, and perhaps do some flexibility work at another stage. My on-the-ground input with the Galway team was minimal, really, but I was in constant contact with John O'Mahony over the phone.

'It was like being the fitness advisor at long range. It worked very well for the team, and John is a pretty special guy himself and was able to utilise the plans on his own. It was an unusual relationship, but it seemed to work well.'

Why does O'Sullivan believe O'Mahony is a 'special guy'?

'I think he's got a lot of good management skills. He's a very knowledgeable football coach. However, I think the most important thing of all is that he elicits huge respect from his players. They see him as a very good manager, very knowledgeable and a guy who manages his players very well. Ultimately, that's the key to your success as a manager, how well you manage your players, because if you manage them well you maximise their potential, and if you maximise their potential then you've achieved your goal as a coach.'

FROM THE HEART

A good team can win an All-Ireland, but it takes a great one to win a second All-Ireland. O'Mahony's Galway team achieved that against the raging-hot favourites, Meath, in 2001, as the victorious manager recounts.

'Meath had demolished Kerry in the All-Ireland semi-final, and we had been beaten by Roscommon in the Connacht Championship. At that stage, people thought we were dead and buried, but we had a great team and we came back. I would like to think there is a lesson there for everyone. It is not about the setbacks you confront in life that matters, but the key question is how you cope with these setbacks.'

A major setback seemed to the sensational decision of Michael and John Donnellan to withdraw from the county panel in the middle of the championship campaign. Youth, impetuosity and the intense will to win go together in a highly combustible concoction. The news of the Donnellans controversy burst so dramatically, when so much of what seemed so stable was shifting unnervingly around them, that some of the Galway camp gave convincing impersonations of skiers in an avalanche, struggling to keep their feet as the old world crumbled beneath them. For O'Mahony, caught in the full glare of media attention, and with the fate of his team seemingly on the edge of the abyss, the possibility of anonymity, of assuming another identity entirely, was momentarily delicious. Despite the media frenzy, O'Mahony worked quietly behind the scenes and the brothers were soon back in the fold with the minimum of fanfare.

After Meath sensationally trounced reigning All-Ireland champions Kerry in the 2001 All-Ireland semi-final, Kerry manager Páidí Ó Sé said, 'Meath football is honest-to-goodness football; it's from the heart, it's passionate. To succeed, you need the two ingredients, and you have both in abundance.' Ó Sé could just as easily have been talking about the Meath manager, Seán Boylan, a man who always wears his heart on his sleeve.

That year, his Meath side were hotly fancied to add another Sam Maguire victory to their collection, but in an amazing match, Galway ran out as easy winners. The football world was shocked and frantically searched for an explanation for this tale of the unexpected, but not the then Meath manager.

'It was very simple: Galway were a better team on the day. It was very tight for a lot of the game. Then a few things happened very quickly that changed the game. Firstly, Ollie Murphy broke his arm. Secondly, Nigel Nestor was sent off. People talk about Trevor Giles missing the penalty, but that wasn't the reason why we lost the match. Galway won because they produced outstanding football. Nobody wants to lose an All-Ireland, but if I had to choose to lose to another manager, it would be to John O'Mahony. A lot of the credit for that All-Ireland has to go to John.

'John is a wonderful manager. All you have to do is to look at his record, not just with Galway but with Mayo and Leitrim, too. What he has done for football in the west is remarkable and he's brought it on to a whole new level. He's very professional in his approach and he has the most basic quality a great coach needs: the ability to get the very best out of his team and to get them to believe that they can and will succeed.

217

THE GAA

'It wasn't easy for him in 2001. He had to face a lot of problems early on in the season, but he dealt with the problems in the dressing-room in his own way. He worked at it behind the scenes. What is said in the dressing-room is like what is said in the confessional: it's not for outside consumption.

'John also played the media very well in the build-up to the game. He fed in the notion that Meath were red-hot favourites and Galway were really only there to make up the numbers. I never believed that for a second, but a lot of people did because of the way we had beaten Kerry in the semi-final. That was just a freak day. Everything went wrong for Kerry and right for us. It would have been much better for us if we had only won by a point, but in a match like that you can't tell your players to take their foot off the pedal. What John wasn't saying in public, though, was that Galway had a great hunger to win, having lost the All-Ireland in a replay to Kerry the previous year. John was able to channel that hunger positively and get his team to produce wonderful football on the day. The best team won. We've no complaints.'

12

THE 'LOVE ULSTER' CAMPAIGN

AFTER THE 2004 ALL-IRELAND FINAL, WHEN KERRY BEAT MAYO, Tommy Lyons sent a text to Pat Spillane saying: 'Football is coming home.' Spillane had been the most high-profile critic of the blanket defence tactics employed by both Armagh and Tyrone in their marches to their respective first All-Irelands in 2002 and 2003. Spillane had provoked consternation the previous year when he described Tyrone's performance against Kerry as 'puke football'. It had all been so different a decade earlier, when everybody loved Ulster.

UP DOWN

Former Irish schoolboy basketball international Joe Brolly believes that Down's All-Ireland victory in 1991 and the three consecutive All-Irelands for Ulster teams that followed it were fuelled by one man.

'Looking back at the 1970s and the '80s, the reason why the teams from Leinster and Munster always wanted to play an Ulster team in the All-Ireland semi-final was because Ulster teams were defeated before the match even started due to psychological reasons. Deep down, they didn't believe they could win.

'I'm as sure as I can be about anything else that the man who changed the face of Ulster football was James McCartan Jnr. He changed everything. In part, it was because his father had played on three All-Ireland winning teams in the 1960s and James had inherited the winning mentality from his dad. The Down team was moribund until he came along. Ross Carr, Greg Blaney, Mickey Linden were all there before. Then McCartan comes in as an 18 year old. He had scored three goals in a McCrory Cup final and taken Down to an All-Ireland minor title. He was a force of nature. I had never seen anything like him. I still haven't. Dermot McNicholl was the closest: like James, he had that exciting, swashbuckling quality, but he didn't have the fine skills that James had. McCartan changed that entire team. In a way, I think he shamed them all because of his bravery, his courage, the way he played and his electrifying confidence and self-assurance.

'I think the famous story told about him sums him up. When he was nineteen, he played for Ireland against Australia in the Compromise Rules and was rooming with Jack O'Shea, one of the most iconic names in Gaelic football. An Australian journalist asked him, "What's it like to room with a legend?"

'James shrugged his shoulders and said, "You'd have to ask Jacko."

'In 1991, James was in his second year with Down. He was irresistible. He scored five points in the All-Ireland final against Meath. He changed everything. If Down hadn't won that All-Ireland, you could have forgotten about Derry winning an All-Ireland, you could absolutely forget about Donegal winning an All-Ireland, and there wouldn't be Tyrone or Armagh All-Irelands. All of those titles were grafted on the back of Down's '91 win. Donegal realised they could win an All-Ireland, and there was a sense of the inevitable that Derry would win the All-Ireland in '93, and Down came back to win another final in '94. If you had to isolate one reason for all of that, it would be James.

'The strange thing was that he burnt out so quickly. Perhaps it was his size. He wasn't big and took a lot of hits. He was a constant target because of the way he played. He was a phenomenal athlete and is the seminal influence in the way he changed Ulster football.'

Brolly's admiration for that Down team is shared by Armagh's Enda McNulty.

'Mickey Linden was a class player. I played with him in an ex-All-Stars match in '08, and he was still in better shape than 90 per cent of players I have come across in the last five years. He was unbelievably quick and he was 42 years of age. I would be a massive fan of Greg Blaney. The number of balls he put into Mickey Linden's hands was incredible. I would be a big fan of James McCartan, who I would say was one of the greatest players of all time because of his ability to lose a player, his ability to tackle, his ability to score and his ability to catch a high ball even though he was only five foot six or seven.'

THE HOMES OF DONEGAL

Seamus Bonner first played for Donegal in 1970, when he was only 18, and had an unbroken record of service with the county until 1985. For the first eight years he was a star midfielder, but as he got a bit older he got moved closer to the goal, and the latter part of his career was as a full-forward. Football is obviously in his genes as his son Kevin has played with the Dublin senior team.

The highlight of Bonner's playing career with Donegal came in 1972, though earlier in the year, few could have predicted the end of the county's provincial subjugation.

'We played Leitrim in the League in Carrick-on-Shannon. I think the score was 4–13 to 1–3 to Leitrim. Brian McEniff was their player-manager at the time. He got us into a room in the Bush Hotel in Carrick-on-Shannon and said, "Right, boys. The only way we can go is up. Today was the lowest we could possibly go. The championship is coming up soon, and are we going to make an effort for it or are we not?" We all made a vow there and then that we would all train hard for the championship, and we did.

'We beat Down after a replay and Tyrone in the Ulster final. It was kind of a fairy tale after so bad a start to the year. As it was Donegal's first-ever Ulster title, the whole county went wild. It was like winning the All-Ireland. We had a great week afterwards! The celebrations probably affected us in the All-Ireland semi-final against Offaly, the reigning All-Ireland champions. We were playing very well up to half-time, but we gave away a very bad goal to Kevin Kilmurray. Even though we lost, we were probably happy enough with our performance because Ulster teams weren't doing well in Croke Park at the time. I'd say Offaly got a bit of a shock that day.'

Donegal were brought to earth with a bang the following year.

'In 1973, we were beaten in the first round of the championship by Tyrone. Tyrone were a coming team and went on to win the title. Ulster was always a graveyard for reigning provincial champions. I played that day, but earlier that morning I had buried my grandmother, which is not the sort of preparation you should have for a big match.'

In 1974, though, Donegal were back on the glory trail, and Bonner was at the forefront.

'In the Ulster Championship, we beat Armagh and Monaghan in the semi-final. We beat Down in the Ulster final in a replay. At one stage in the second half, we were eight points down with about twenty-two minutes to go. We were lucky enough to get two penalties, and I took both. There wasn't much pressure on me for the first one because we were eight points down, and I thought if I scored, it would make the score respectable, but if I missed, we were getting hammered anyway and it didn't matter much. There was much more pressure on me for the second one because we were three points down and it was to tie the match. My technique was to get it on target and hit it as low and hard as possible. Thankfully, both penalties went in and we got another goal in the last few minutes to win by three points.'

Coincidentally, Donegal also got two penalties the next time they won the Ulster final in 1983.

'We had nine barren years after 1974. Brian McEniff stepped down as player-manager, and there were a lot of changes on the panel and in the backroom personnel. In 1977, Derry gave us an awful hammering in the Ulster Championship and a lot of the old team retired. A few of us kept going on.

'One of the new players that came on the scene in the mid-'70s was Packie Bonner. I played with Packie at midfield against Sligo in Tubbercurry. He was about 17 at the time and he had the offer of going to Glasgow Celtic, and I remember him asking me, "Seamus, what do you think I should do?"

'I replied, "If Celtic offered me a contract, I'd be gone in the morning." Packie went, and the rest is history. Despite his success with Celtic, he stayed close to his GAA roots and trained with us many times in the summer months, and remained a huge fan of the Donegal team.

'In 1979, we qualified for the Ulster final against Monaghan, but they beat us well. The match is best remembered for an infamous incident. The referee threw in the ball. I won possession, sent in the ball to the forwards and one of our lads popped it over the bar. The only problem was that the band was still on the far side of the pitch and it was playing the national anthem! The referee had to restart the game and our point was disallowed.

'In 1982, Donegal got a massive boost when we won the All-Ireland under-21 title. We picked up a lot of new players, like Anthony Molloy, Martin McHugh and Joyce McMullan. We had a nice mixture of young blood and experience. To add to the factors in our favour, Brian McEniff was back in charge of the team.

'We were fortunate enough to get two penalties against Cavan in 1983. I scored a goal from the first one, but there was only a minute to go for the second one and we were three points up. I tapped it over the bar for an insurance point.'

Although Seamus Bonner won three Ulster championships, Donegal failed each time at the penultimate stage.

'It is always disappointing to lose when you are one step away from playing in an All-Ireland. The biggest disappointment was losing to Galway in 1974. We were very unfortunate. At one stage, Donal Maughan and Patrick Shea went up for the one ball and collided with each other. Johnny Tobin stood back, and as they were falling down, he was collecting the ball and racing through to score a goal. Johnny was on fire that day, but Gay O'Driscoll tamed him in the All-Ireland final. Galway raced into the lead, but we pulled them back. I was playing good football at the time, but after about 25 minutes, I had a collision with Gay Mitchell and had to be carried off. I was no sooner in the dressing-room than Brian McEniff came in with a split thumb. I always feel that was the semi-final that got away because Galway only beat us by a few points, and if it wasn't for those injuries, I think we would have won.

'In 1972, we didn't really expect to win. We had achieved our main goal – to win an Ulster title – and I suppose at the back of our minds, we had settled for that. Nineteen eighty-three was a big disappointment as well because I knew it was probably my swansong at that level, and my chances of playing in an All-Ireland final were gone.

'I continued on for another two years, until Monaghan beat us in the Ulster Championship. They were a very strong side then. They had some great players, especially Nudie Hughes, who was a class player and very versatile. Few people could win All-Stars as a corner-back and as a corner-forward, the way he did. At that stage, I was 35 and my mind was telling me what to do, but my body couldn't keep up with it.'

In 1989, Brian McEniff took charge of training Donegal again and he invited Bonner to be a selector. The offer was readily accepted despite the fact that it committed him to extensive travelling up and down to Donegal from his Dublin base. McEniff's Midas touch was soon in evidence again as Donegal won the Ulster title the following year. Bonner was party to McEniff's innermost team secrets.

'As a forward, he's the sort of guy I would really hate to have marking me. He was very tough and tenacious. He'd be standing on your toes almost, and wouldn't give you much time on the ball.

'His dedication is total. Although he's got his own business, if he heard a Donegal man was playing football in Cork, he'd drop everything and travel down to Cork to see him play and it wouldn't cost him a thought. He never missed a single training session in the 1992 campaign, and this encouraged the players to do the same. His willpower rubbed off on the players. He's also got incredible enthusiasm, and that's infectious.'

The Bonner–McEniff double act had their finest hour in 1992, when they masterminded Donegal's All-Ireland 0–18 to 0–14 triumph over red-hot favourites Dublin. Before they reached that stage, controversy had erupted about Padraig Brogan's appearance in the All-Ireland semi-final.

'Padraig had made his name with Mayo, but had declared for us a couple of years previously and played for us. Then he switched back to Mayo, and a year or so later, Mayo brought him on against us in an All-Ireland semi-final. Mayo would consider themselves unlucky not to have won the match, but when they brought on Padraig, instead of lifting Mayo, it lifted our lads. The feeling among our lads was that Padraig had left Donegal because he thought he had a better chance of winning an All-Ireland medal with Mayo. Although we were playing poorly, when our boys saw him coming on, it made them more determined than ever not to lose the game. The sight of Padraig coming on the pitch caused them to up a gear.'

In conversation with this writer, Padraig Brogan candidly admitted that his arrival on the pitch had the opposite effect to the one intended, in fact inspiring Donegal players and fans alike, and was a serious tactical blunder. His reason, though, for transferring back to Mayo was that 'blood is thicker than water'.

In the Bonner household before the semi-final, tension was high for a different reason as Seamus's wife Cathy is from Achill Island. Bonner's inside knowledge of the Dublin players was to prove invaluable in the final.

'Having played club football so long in Dublin, I knew the Dublin players better than McEniff did. One of the highlights of my career had been captaining Civil Service to the Dublin Championship in 1980.

'Basically, I was keen to do two things in the All-Ireland. First, that we would keep very tight on Vinnie Murphy. I knew he was their target man, and if we kept him quiet, the other Dublin forwards would struggle. It was also vital that we curbed the Dublin half-back line because we didn't want the likes of Keith Barr running at our defence with the ball. We took steps to do both, and after we got over their penalty chance, which Charlie Redmond didn't take, we were always holding our own.

'We had been so unimpressive in the All-Ireland semi-final against Mayo that nobody gave us a chance against Dublin. I think that gave the Dublin players a false sense of security. The media really built them up, and I think the Dubs started to believe their own publicity.

That's a dangerous game. I think something similar happened to Kildare in 1998. In contrast, there was no hype about us because we hadn't done anything to deserve it. None of our fellas were going on radio shows blowing their own trumpets.'

Although the excitement was unprecedented, Donegal's marvellous victory came with a price tag attached for Bonner.

'The hardest part of my time as a selector came in the run-up to the final. Tommy Ryan had played for us in the All-Ireland semi-final, but we felt that Manus Boyle could do the job for us on the day. He scored nine points in the final so our judgement was vindicated. But nobody wants to miss out on the chance to play in an All-Ireland final so it was incredibly tough to have to tell Tommy that he was going to miss out.'

McEniff and Bonner gave leadership from the sideline, but who were the Donegal leaders on the pitch?

'You can't win an All-Ireland without leaders on the pitch, and we had four of them in 1992: Anthony Molloy at midfield, Martin McHugh at centre-forward, Tony Boyle at full-forward and Martin Gavigan at centre-back were all leaders in different ways. Molloy was a superb leader. He could catch a ball in the clouds and that would lift the team. If you could get past Martin Gavigan, you were doing well. Tony and Martin could get you a score from nowhere. After his success with Cavan, Martin is seen now in Donegal as the man who can lead the team back to glory. He would be the people's favourite if he wants the pressure again of being a county manager.'

NO ORDINARY JOE

When Derry succeeded Donegal as All-Ireland champions in 1993, Joe Brolly was fast becoming a star name in Gaelic football.

'I always wanted to play for Derry because of the great team of the '70s that won back-to-back Ulster titles. It was very clear from an early stage that the team was going somewhere. We had a lot of very strong characters on the team. An important catalyst for our success was Lavey winning the All-Ireland club title in 1991. Our captain was Henry Downey from Lavey, and he was driving us on. He would tell us we were not training enough. So when Lavey won the All-Ireland club title, we all bought into the belief that the Downey way was the right way. We were training five nights a week.

'Our manager, Eamonn Coleman, was also crucial. He was jolly and a great character. He always played cards with the lads down the back of the bus. He was a teetotaller himself and didn't understand drink. Eamonn was a small man so it was a sight to see him berating a giant like Brian McGilligan about drinking. The most enthusiastic drinker in the squad was Johnny McGurk. Eamonn would say to him, "Wee man, wee men can't drink." The boys would be laughing because Johnny could drink any member of the squad under the table!

'Eamonn was a rogue, but his heart was in the right place. He wasn't a great tactician, but he was a real leader: the boys loved him very dearly because he was a man's man. He once told me I needed to do weight training, saying, "Brolly, you're like a girl." This was before advanced training methods or anything. We often started with ten four-hundred-metre runs. It was masochistic stuff.

'Then Mickey Moran came in. He is a quiet man who is a terrific coach and a football fantatic. He worked very well with Eamonn. The broad-brushstroke man who had the philosophy behind everything was Eamonn, while Mickey was the nuts-and-bolts man. I know in hindsight that Eamonn was not a good trainer, but when Mickey came in, all of a sudden everything was right.

'The other thing that was important to us was Down winning the All-Ireland in '91. We had nearly beaten them that year in a titanic game in the Athletic Grounds. We were a point up at the end when they got a free 60 yards out. I was close to the ball at the time, and I heard Ross Carr saying to Enda Gormley, "I'm going to drive this over the bar."

'Enda told him, "Wise up, you f***ing eejit." But Ross sent it over the bar and they went through instead of us, but when they won the All-Ireland it inspired us because it made us realise how close we were.

'I didn't see either the 1993 semi-final or All-Ireland final, but anyone who did told me they never had the slightest worry that we would win either, although it was very close against Dublin in the semi-final; and even though Cork got a whirlwind start scoring 1–2 in the first five minutes in the final, we beat them without any problems.

'The strange thing for me was the sense of anticlimax. I thought to myself: "Is this what it's like?" I thought it would open up some promised land. We went to the Cat and Cage, and nobody knew what to do! That was before the time sponsors looked after everything. The reward was the fulfilment of a lifetime's ambition.

'It was a massive thing for the people. Derry is a huge football county. Over the last fifteen years or so, six different Derry clubs have won the Ulster title. So when we won the All-Ireland, people were delirious. To this day, people speak about time – by talking about winning the All-Ireland to fix other things by. I especially recall people queuing for the Credit Union because nobody worked for two weeks. We had a banquet in the Guildhall. It was organised by people who wouldn't know if a football was pumped or stuffed. It was like the end of the world. The spiritual side was very important. To Kerry, winning an All-Ireland is just routine, but to Derry, it was cathartic. At last, we could take our place among the football counties with self-respect.'

It can be exclusively revealed that despite the amateur ethos, the Derry squad were the first to engage in pay-for-play when they got an unexpected reward for their achievements.

'Eamonn brought us to Ballymaguigan one night and said, "Lads, there someone who wants to speak to you." In comes Phil Coulter. He was wearing a lemon suit and a lime tie. He presented each of us with a signed photo of himself and a commemorative copy of "The Town I Loved So Well". The reason he gave us that was that when the *Sunday Game* came to film our celebration the night of the final, we sang that song for them. On the cover of the record, Phil had his arm outstretched in a Liberace pose. It was ghastly. It is gathering cobwebs somewhere in my house. There are few signs in my home that I ever was a footballer. My mother has my All-Ireland medal and three National League medals.'

THE FIRST CUT IS THE DEEPEST

Derry's first All-Ireland win in 1993 was a source of great pride to their legendary player from the 1950s, Jim McKeever.

'It was very emotional when the full-time whistle went. The magnificent players on that team personified not only their own accomplishments but also the sacrifices of generations of Derry people who had made that moment possible. I was very conscious of all the people who organised games and travelling arrangements down through the years, regardless of personal inconvenience or harsh weather. Without those people, the sequence of events that led to Derry's historic success would not have been started. The fact that all the years of disappointment have been wiped out with the 1993 side gave me a certain amount of pleasure. It was a unique occasion. The first time that something great happens is special because there can never be another first time.'

Like so many others, Joe Brolly expected more great things from that Derry team.

'I remember John O'Keeffe wrote in the *Irish Times* that: "This Derry team will dominate Gaelic football for the next ten years." We had a lot of advantages like our midfield. Brian McGilligan was astonishing. There was never a tougher or better athlete than him. He never did weights, but he was like granite.

'Brian was as tough as they come. His big break in football came from Kevin Heffernan. Hurling is big in Derry, and Brian started out as a hurler. After he was appointed manager of the Irish Compromise Rules side, Heffo saw him playing hurling one day in Dublin and was very taken by his physical presence and said: "Can you play football, son?"

'Brian replied: "I'll give it a try, sir."

'The rest is history.

'Anthony Tohill loved playing with him because Brian did all the donkey work while Anthony played all the football. Tohill was a brilliant finisher. He always wanted to be a professional athlete. He is a huge physical specimen. As a teenager, he had gone to Australia to try his luck at Aussie Rules, but came back when Derry started to motor. I think Eamonn Coleman was keen to get him back. When he was 24 or 25, he went on trial to Manchester United. At one stage, he was playing in a training match with the United squad. Although there was a hundred million pounds' worth of talent on display, Anthony was doing sliding tackles and bashing into people. Andrei Kanchelskis went to Alex Ferguson and said, "Take that f***er off before he kills someone." Fergie went over to Anthony and said, "Son, I think we've just got to you a bit late in life."

'Anthony was a very popular and respected member of the squad. At one stage, we were all in a bar when Anthony got his results from university. When we heard he got first-class honours, someone piped up: "The bastard's got no chink in his armour." We call him "Highlife" because he's always enjoying the high life, drinking the best champagne or playing golf or staying in some posh hotel in Chelsea or hanging round with Tony McCoy. He loves being on the television in his role as pundit.'

After the high of 1993, Derry made an early exit from the 1994 championship.

'Down beat us in an epic game in Celtic Park. Eamonn Coleman took them for granted because we had beaten them by 18 or 20 points the year before. Eamonn positively laughed at the notion that Down could beat Derry in Celtic Park. Mickey Linden kept them in it in the first half. Then in a classic smash-and-grab, they beat us with a late goal. After one game, we were gone.

'There had been a lot of discomfort in Derry about Eamonn. He was a players' man, not a county board man. He would have literally told them to f*** off, and there was a lot of jealousy. All of a sudden, he was sacked. In his first year, he won a National League. Derry's previous league title was in 1947. In his second year, he won an All-Ireland. He had won a minor All-Ireland himself as a player and had coached Derry to an All-Ireland minor title, with his son Gary as captain. He had coached an All-Ireland under-21 team. When he was sacked, it killed the spirit within the team. It had been a very special group, but Eamonn's sacking spread a poison through the team. It was impossible to pick up the pieces. Mickey Moran stood on and took complete charge in controversial circumstances. He never had the team with him. We won the National League the following year on autopilot. The interest was gone.'

A legend of the game would revive Derry's fortunes.

'Brian Mullins was terrific. He was just what we needed after the poison of the previous years because he was so honest. He was teaching then on the border of Derry and Donegal. We were so lucky to get him, and we had a great adventure with him. He built a new team, which, although not on a par with the '93 team, won a National League and an Ulster title. He tended to philosophise. Most of those musings went straight over the heads of many of the lads. He was very powerful and dogmatic, yet at the same time we liked him a lot. Although he wasn't the perfect tactician, he was an absolute warrior for Derry, like the way he played for Dublin. He would stand out in freezing cold nights with hailstones pelting down as he trained us. In this way, he was illustrating to us all those important virtues of loyalty and togetherness. As a trainer, he was exactly as he was when he played for Dublin. I must say we retain a great affection for him and we keep in touch with him.

'Derry still have the players to succeed. We need a manager who understands tactics and strategy.'

THE BOYS FROM THE COUNTY OF ARMAGH

The next Ulster team to make a breakthrough was Armagh. John Evans, trainer of leading Carlow club team Éire Óg, famously said some of his team he wouldn't insult by sending them to a sports psychologist and others he wouldn't insult the sporting psychologist by sending them to him! One of Ireland's leading sports psychologists, Enda McNulty, has been crucial to the 'Orange Revolution' in recent years.

'I started playing for Armagh in 1996. Myself and Aidan O'Rourke and Barry Duffy were asked onto the Armagh panel at the same time. I remember we got a phone call to the house, and the two boys were out on the drink and arrived back at three or four in the morning in very good form to say the least! So let's say I had a struggle to make them believe that we were really on the panel. There was bit too much partying done after that. There was a door broken and a window broken. The next morning, I had to break the news to the two boys that we were required to go to training that night. A phone call was made that afternoon saying we had a prior engagement because the two boys were in a very bad way, and we started off the following Thursday night.

'Brian McAlinden and Brian Canavan were coaching at the time, and they probably haven't got due credit for what they have done. They did a massive job between 1996 and 2001. They took us from being the whipping boys of Ulster football to a side that was a year away from winning an All-Ireland. Brian McAlinden in particular deserves a lot of credit: the discipline, the ethos, the work ethic he created is probably still in the squad.

'We won an Ulster title in '99, beating Down, who had defeated us so often. I wouldn't even say we were second-class citizens – we were third-class citizens when compared with Down because of all their titles. It was much more special to win the Ulster that year than it was in '08 for Armagh, because we had won it so often at that stage.'

However, 2000 would bring heartbreak for Armagh when they lost an All-Ireland semi-final replay to eventual champions Kerry.

'We knew we were good enough to beat Kerry that time, but I'd say we just weren't smart enough. I think if we'd had a bit more cuteness on the pitch, we could have won either of those games. The master Maurice Fitz created all sorts of havoc when he came on as sub in both games. Looking back, if he had been there in 2002, he could have done something special, either a score or a pass, to win the game for Kerry. Losing in extra time in a replay was shattering, but on reflection it was a positive thing. It made us stronger as individuals and as a team.

'In 2001, we were playing Galway in the All-Ireland quarter-final. We were doing a warm-up on Na Fianna's pitch and were due to get a Garda motorcycle to lead us to Croke Park. We were waiting on the coach for over half an hour, maybe 40 minutes, when the motorcycle finally came. We got to Croke Park ten minutes before the match. We had no time for a warm-up or a team talk. I remember pulling on my shorts and socks very quickly, and as I ran onto the pitch I saw Barry O'Hagan coming out and he was still in his jeans, and I remember thinking: "How are we going to win an All-Ireland? This fella isn't even togged out here." We had to sprint out into the tunnel and I remember thinking: "There's something not right here." We gave Galway a seven-point lead early on but only lost by a point and Galway went on to win an All-Ireland. If only we had had a bit more composure, we would have taken our time and realised that the match couldn't have started without us. Had we had that bit of composure and experience, we would have won that game.'

Joe Kernan would bring Armagh to football's top table when he was appointed Armagh manager, as McNulty recalls.

'The biggest thing that Joe brought to the table was belief. When Joe walked into the Canal Court Hotel in December 2001 for his first team meeting with us, he had already won All-Irelands with Crossmaglen. So when he sat down with us, you knew you were in the presence of a winner in Croke Park. Allied to that, he had already played for Armagh in an All-Ireland final. Of course, when Joe walks into the room, he brings a great presence because of his physique. All he said was: "Get me to Croke Park and I'll ensure ye'll win." You believed him. We knew we were on the edge of winning an All-Ireland and believed that Joe was the final piece of the jigsaw – and he was.

'We played Louth in the league in 2002, and Louth are always tough to play against. I think we were level at half-time. I remember vividly Joe saying to us at the break: "Do you think that just because I have won an All-Ireland with Crossmaglen, I have a magic wand? Boys, there's no magic wand. You have to make more blocks than you ever made in your life. You have to kick the ball in to the forwards better than you ever have in your life. It's not about anything that I can say or wave. It's about what ye do. It has to do with what ye do in the middle of the game." That struck a chord with me.'

McNulty feels that it was a variety of factors coming together that paved the way for the team's ultimate success.

'I read a very interesting article about Lance Armstrong a few years ago that described him as "the god of the small things". I believe sport is the kaleidoscope of a whole range of small things made perfect. I think that is the road Armagh went down.

'In 2002, Armagh started to get more of all the small things right than all the other teams. From a mental point of view, we got some unbelievable guys in to coach us. We worked on team cohesion and did some good bonding sessions. The other thing we did was to bring in Darren Campbell, whose basketball background meant his statistical analysis skills were on a different level. I remember him handing me a sheet before we played Tyrone in the 2002 Ulster Championship with a diagram showing me where exactly Peter Canavan had received every ball on the pitch in the previous five games. From a mental-preparation point of view, that was great for me. Not only that, it also pinpointed to me when Canavan liked to get the balls in those positions – so as the game went on, I could predict whether he would move out or in. That was invaluable. Then we went on a training week in the sun – which was very innovative then, though everybody does it now. Apart from the bonding, it was a very serious trip. Not only was there no alcohol or nights out, there weren't even any discussions about nights out or alcohol. It was very tough training, and the mental resolve that trip gave us was important.

'We were walking up the hill in Clones like an army before the Tyrone game. Everyone knew we had been on the trip to the sun, and one of the Tyrone fans shouted at us, "I don't see any suntan, lads." When Joe got us in the dressing-room, he used that incident and said, "We'll show them a f***ing suntan before the end of the match." That was the spark we needed.

'There were numerous small things. A nutritionist was brought in. Physical conditioning was brought to a new level, which probably reflected how driven the lads were. Joe brought a good team all around him. Every little detail was sorted out.'

Things came to a happy ending for Armagh in the All-Ireland final against Kerry in 2002.

'We knew we could win if we played to our potential and most of our team performed, but didn't know we would win. We knew our conditioning was better than Kerry's. We knew we were a tougher team than Kerry despite what anybody said. There was bit of a myth about how good that Kerry team were, and the press had built them up the way they've built up Dublin in recent years. We weren't under any illusions, though, that it was going to be easy. We knew it would probably go down to one kick of a ball, and that's what happened.

'It hadn't gone well in the first half, but what hasn't gone into folklore is that we began well. I started on Gooch Cooper and then moved on to Mike Frank Russell. Then Kerry had a period of dominance and Oisín McConville missed a penalty, and we sort of went off the rails after that, but we finished well and only went in at half-time trailing by four points. I remember having slipped on the pitch a few times in the first half because I'd used studs instead of blades on my boots. I knew I had to pick my game up, so I changed my boots at the break and that made a big difference in the second half. I remember looking around the dressing-room and thinking the mood in the team wasn't unbelievably spirited and the body language wasn't very strong. Joe came in and he started talking: "Listen, boys, we weren't playing well. I played in the 1977 All-Ireland final and I remember going home on the bus crying, and with all the boys crying. Do ye want to be like f***ing me?" It wasn't really what he said next, but the impact of him physically throwing his loser's medal from that game against the shower and it rattling down the wall and shattering into little pieces and the plastic breaking and the coin or whatever it was rolling all over the floor. I again vividly remember looking around and seeing the body language change immediately. Before that, everybody was sitting kind of slumped, and suddenly everybody was sitting up as if we were all saying: "That's not going to be us." To use a term from sports psychology, we all went up into a "peak state". It was as if we were all saying to each other: "Jesus, boys, we're going to win this." Then Kieran McGeeney brought us into a circle and you knew by looking into the boys' eyes that everybody was ready for a battle. There were other games when you'd look into the boys' eyes and you'd see a bit of uncertainty, but there was none at that stage.

'It was total euphoria when we won. The first thing that happens is hundreds of supporters jumping on top of you. I remember my little brother Patrick coming into the dressing-room afterwards, and that was very important to myself and my brother Justin. It wasn't that I had realised my lifetime ambition; it was more about seeing the impact it had on the fans. I also remember the next morning, it wasn't: "We're the men here." It was: "How can we win another one?" I remember feeling this drive to become the first Ulster team to win back-to-back All-Irelands since the great team of the 1960s. Going on a tour in south Armagh with all the bonfires lit was very powerful. The disappointing thing was that we only had one chat as a team without any hangers-on, on the Wednesday afternoon in Paddy McKeever's bar in Portadown. There had been a bottle of whiskey that had not been opened since 1953 – when Armagh had been beaten in the All-Ireland final – and we all had a drink out of it. It was very powerful because it was just us. There is a time to meet the supporters, family and friends, but we had too many of those and not enough with just ourselves. Again, there were too many hangers-on when we were presented with our All-Ireland medals. Any team I am ever involved with in the future, I will always get the boys together on their own, whether it's a win or a loss, have a few drinks, decide what happens next and have closure.'

The glory of 2002 was not to be repeated the following year.

'There's a lot of regrets about 2003. Probably, on reflection, we played better football in 2003 than we did in 2002, but we made a big mistake. Two weeks before the All-Ireland final, we changed a few crucial things. We changed the way we played the whole year, which was a critical mistake. We picked some players in different positions, which was a big error in hindsight. Not only the game plan and the positional changes, and I have spoken to Kieran about this many times; even more important was the change in our attitude. In all the games up to the final, we had a "take no sh*t" attitude. We got stuck in and used our physical capacities, not in any dirty way, just harnessing the physical strength of the team: Francie Bellew, Kieran, the McEntees, Paul McGrane. In the run-up to the final, there were a lot of articles in the press saying that not only were Armagh a dirty team; they were over-the-top dirty. One of the articles stated that somebody was going to be left in a wheelchair because of the way we played. I remember reading that article, which was written by a Fermanagh player, and thinking to myself, "Oh dear, what's going to happen if some of our players are affected by this?" We probably subconsciously decided not to be as physical as we had been in the previous games, which was an absolute disaster. Armagh's game has been built on our physical nature, and in a lot of games in 2002, we crushed teams just by our physical exertions. Because we were so well conditioned, we could easily deal with anyone else in that respect. Against Tyrone in 2003, we decided we were going to show the whole country that we could win by playing nice football. We tried to play less tough football and more champagne football. We needed to marry the skills with the physical dimension. We could also have been more intelligent on the day on the pitch – I'm not talking about management. For example, I was marking Canavan, who wasn't fit to walk, and I marked him man to man. I should have come out in front of him and covered Eoin Mulligan as well. So I am taking the blame for my own performance. The player I always knew I had to be unbelievably focused on when I was marking him was Peter Canavan. You knew you had to be incredibly switched on for every single ball because if you even blinked, he would stick the ball in the net.

'We must all shoulder the blame. I wouldn't blame the management for any of our defeats.

'We don't despise Tyrone, though we have a great rivalry with them. You have to respect any team that wins All-Irelands. They were probably smarter than us in the games in which they beat us. I think the media have not picked up on the fact that winning Ulster Championships so often has been a big disadvantage. We have won way more Ulsters, but Tyrone have won more All-Irelands. Playing in the qualifiers gives them more games and, above all, the opportunity to iron out their weaknesses when they lose. When we lost, we were knocked out and learned our weaknesses too late. It's not the only reason Tyrone have won more All-Irelands, but it has been an advantage to them. I would say the rivalry has been a positive thing for football.'

THERE'S SOMETHING ABOUT KIERAN

Like the Clare hurlers in 1995, myths abound about the obsessiveness of Kieran McGeeney, which Enda McNulty is in a privileged position to comment upon.

THE GAA

'There was a bit of a legend about Armagh that we got our motivation from Joe or Kieran. I believe that motivation is something that comes from within, and that all our boys were incredibly driven and didn't need anybody else to motivate them. They all have the Michael Jordan concept of "driven from within". That was there before Joe came. Joe nurtured that and it took a smart man to do that, but Brian McAlinden had already inculcated that discipline before Joe arrived. When Joe brought in a nutritionist, the Paul McGranes of this world were going to lap up everything that would give them an edge or anything that would make them leaner, fitter or meaner athletes.

'Kieran is a leader. When he walks into a dressing-room and talks about dedication, players know that nobody is more dedicated than him. But Kieran would be the first to admit that there were other leaders – like Paul McGrane, Diarmaid Marsden and the McEntees, as well as guys who got very little credit, like Andrew McCann, who drove to training every single night from Armagh to Dublin on his own. Andy was a leader in actions rather than words.

'Kieran is a great friend, but more than anything he has a desire for excellence and is unwilling to settle for mediocrity in anything he does, from weight training to nutrition to skills training. And you always know that even when a game looks as if it's gone, he's not going to throw in the towel.

'We were trailing by seven points to nil in that match against Galway in 2001, and they were on fire. I remember I was out of breath and Kieran was out of breath as we were both trying to fight off the waves of Galway attacks. I can still hear in my ears Kieran saying, "Weather the storm, weather the storm, weather the storm." I'm sure he said that to the other boys too, and we did very nearly haul them back.

'We fancied ourselves, not in a joking way, as a band of brothers. We knew each other better than some of our own brothers, we spent so much time together. One of the things that encapsulates Kieran is that in every one of the big games, when he talked to us in the circle beforehand he'd be nearly crying: that's how emotional he would be. He was very focused. After we won the Ulster finals, he'd say: "Boys, take a good look at the cup. That's the last time ye're going to look at it. The next cup we want to see is the All-Ireland." He was very good at bringing guys down to earth. He would be very good at calling a spade a spade. If one of the guys was not pulling his weight, he'd say: "What the f*** is going on here? You're dossing, Enda," or "Oisín, you're not up to your own high standards. I'm disappointed in you." Because he was able to walk the walk, you could never argue with that.

'Just last night, I was club training with Kieran at Na Fianna. Paul Grimley was doing a blocking session with us. Kieran, at 36 years of age, was throwing himself at every ball so that his teeth and nose were literally on top of it. There were no half measures. Every single ball with him was all or nothing. Every single ball last night was like the famous block he made against Dara Ó Cinnéide in the 2002 All-Ireland final. That's something I can learn from him. I try and lead the boys too much in a verbal sense during a match, whereas all Kieran's communication on a pitch would be through actions. Kieran would only ever say a few words on the pitch. I've learned from him to taper down my words and to try and amplify my actions. He is a master of leading by actions on the pitch and by words off the pitch.

'Myself and my brother Justin and Kieran have trained every Christmas Day since we were about 15, no matter what we've done the night before. Last Christmas Day, myself, Justin, our younger brother Patrick, Kieran, his brother Declan, and Kieran McKeever trained on the local pitch at home. We'd all had a good breakfast and some of the boys had had a few beers the night before. We played a match: three on three. At this stage, Kieran was the Kildare manager. I left the pitch that day totally physically drained and, with absolutely no exaggeration, having being hit harder than I would in a championship match. The three lads were giving everything in body and mind to be better than the three other fellas, and Kieran McGeeney was literally boxing the heads of the boys to get a ball. Even though he had retired, even though it was Christmas Day, he was unbelievably fit, unbelievably driven to win every f***ing ball. It was Kieran who set up the game, with the pitch only 20 metres long and with small goals. Just to see the fella who wanted to be that good in that game even though it had no consequences, more than anything else exemplifies his ethos, his attitude, his drive.'

McNulty is keen to pay tribute to the lesser lights of Armagh football.

'My own brother Justin never got very much credit. Yet he got his hands to three balls in the last fifteen minutes of the 2002 All-Ireland final, and had a Kerry forward got possession even one of those times, they could have scored and we would have been beaten. In the 2002 All-Ireland semi-final when Ray Cosgrave's free struck the post, four Armagh backs jumped for it, but only Dessie Farrell jumped for it in the Dublin side. It was Justin who got his hands to it and cleared it. I was training with Dessie last night. He's got injuries not only to every limb but to every part of every limb, and still he soldiers on.'

Regrets, I have had a few is as much a sentiment for Enda McNulty as it was for Frank Sinatra.

'I think Armagh are like Dublin: we need to focus less on physical conditioning and go back more to skills. Dublin have got carried away with the media hype in recent years.'

Like many Armagh players, McNulty is less than happy with the media portrayal of his team.

'In recent years, even Kerry, while they have played nice football, have pulled more men behind the ball than Armagh ever did. As I was watching Kerry play Cork in the 2008 All-Ireland semi-final, I got texts from my brother Justin and Kieran McGeeney both saying they couldn't believe how many men Kerry had behind the ball. Yet when Armagh pull men behind the ball, it's negative. It's all about perception. In the media, perception is reality.'

PETER THE GREAT

Tyrone would become the team of the decade at the start of the noughties. Joe Brolly traces their success back to the lessons learned a decade earlier.

'I think it was because of the way Down played that inspired other Ulster teams. They were electrifying. They had six super-classy forwards. Donegal were the same. They all went on attack. Derry were a little different, but still played good football. As a result of those three counties doing so well, there was a serious inquisition in Tyrone, who wondered why they couldn't do the same.

'Then, of course, you had the advent of Peter Canavan. Any team he had been involved with were champions: Errigal Ciarán were Ulster champions, and he had won minor and under-21 All-Irelands with Tyrone. Suddenly he found himself in his mid-20s wondering what was going on. In his first four years as a Tyrone senior, they didn't win a single match in the Ulster Championship. They set up "Club Tyrone" and put in an infrastructure that was state of the art – way beyond anything we had ever seen before. You have no idea of the integration between schools, clubs, parishes and outreach programmes. They set about it like a military campaign because they were a fanatical football county who had never won an All-Ireland before, and they were sick, sick, sick about that. In 2003, they had great young players like Eoin Mulligan and so on arriving on the scene.

'All that was needed was a manager, and then Mickey Harte came along. He had managed the minor team for seven years, so nobody had a better overview of Tyrone football. Of course, that was all part of Tyrone's master plan, to have a minor manager for a long time, who would progress to the under-21 and senior teams. He's obviously a genius, a tactical master – which has been recognised. He innovated a new style of football that nobody had seen before, and that's what brought the house down on their heads. I think in '03 they just wanted to win an All-Ireland. They didn't care whether it was pretty or not, and that's why they used the swarm defence. They played against a great Kerry team and nobody will ever forget the image of Darragh Ó Sé with five Tyrone men around him. Kerry were caught on the hop. Armagh had won the All-Ireland the previous year playing a defensive brand of football, but there was something to admire about it, something heroic about it. Even Armagh couldn't cope that year with Tyrone's play. In Tyrone, the individual was anonymous. Peter Canavan was able to play in that final kicking on only one leg. People started to ask: "Is that football at all?" But Tyrone won their All-Ireland.'

Pat Spillane sees the primary cause of Tyrone's triumph in a somewhat different light.

THE GAA

'I have heard many compelling arguments for the reasons why Tyrone finally reached football's promised land in 2003. There was the deployment of their brilliant two-man full-forward line, their use of the blanket defence and Brian Dooher's role as a link-man. I believe, however, that Tyrone's trump card was Cormac McAnallen's performances at full-back. The decision of Mickey Harte to switch the star midfielder to the edge of the square after the team leaked four goals in the drawn Ulster final was the final piece of the jigsaw. From that moment on, Tyrone never looked back. Who could have thought that less than a year later McAnallen would have died?

'Cormac McAnallen was an icon of modern-day Gaelic football. A tremendous athlete, he was blessed with a great engine. He was an outstanding fielder and a versatile performer. But it was another quality that meant he stood out from all his colleagues. He was blessed with a maturity that stretched way beyond his tender years.

'In his tragically short time on earth, Cormac achieved more than most will ever manage in a lifetime. He captained Tyrone to victory in the All-Ireland minor and under-21 championships, won an All-Ireland senior medal, was a former Young Player of the Year and a current All-Star, and he represented Ireland with distinction in the 2003 Compromise Rules Series. And they're just the high points.'

Joe Brolly believes Tyrone's second All-Ireland was a very different affair.

'In '05, Mickey Harte had been working on the team for three years and had a harmonious blend between defence and attack. Although Kerry got off to a great start, Tyrone wiped the floor with them and humiliated them, playing beautiful football and showing they had some great players. At the same time, there was still the stigma of defence attached to Ulster football. I was invited to speak at the presentation ceremony when they got their medals and I said that particular team could win four or five All-Irelands, but that they were cursed by injuries – finally, they justified my prophecy in '08.

'What Tyrone did in '03, lesser counties imitated. Managers like Malachy O'Rourke in Fermanagh saw that the defensive system works. So did Westmeath. The attitude was that "we'll soak up the pressure and in that way we can compete". Derry, with a stellar team, were beaten three years in a row in Ulster semi-finals by mediocre teams: Donegal, Monaghan and Fermanagh. Kerry have been at the pin of their collar two years in a row, in '07 and '08, to beat a mediocre Monaghan team. It's ugly and it makes people angry, but it works.'

SEEING THE WOODS FROM THE TREES

In recent years, one of the ongoing controversies about the *Sunday Game* pundits is the perception that the most high profile among their number have an anti-Ulster bias. One of their critics in this context is Ireland's finest sportswriter, the acclaimed documentary-maker Peter Woods. The Monaghan native explains his passion for football in the following terms.

'Why I love Gaelic football – all of life compressed into those 70 minutes . . . everything except death. Well, almost everything, because Ulster is different. So perhaps I shouldn't be surprised when football pundits cast Joe Kernan and Mickey Harte as twin Voldemorts, bent on raiding south and razing those citadels of fair play and champagne football in Kerry and Dublin, their only real opposition those pundits, arraigned behind Pat Spillane, cast as Mad-Eye Moody, and an uneasy Colm O'Rourke – given Meath's record – as Severus Snape, a foot in one camp and a toe in the genetic pool of the other. And there's Joe Brolly, one of our own, severely conflicted, glasses glinting like Harry Potter.'

The main problem for the pundits is the way the top Ulster teams use the zone defence. After Tyrone triumphed over Kerry in the 2005 All-Ireland, the pundits bemoaned the fact that Kerry were badly served by the opposition they faced on the way to their final. Peter's solution to this problem was certainly original.

'The logic of all this is overwhelming . . . For Kerry to compete against an Ulster team, they must play in Ulster. Look on the upside: the Ulster Council's policy of appeasement, of moving the Ulster final to Dublin, has failed; we're still not liked down here. The Monaghan County Board want to redevelop Clones. With Kerry in Ulster, there could be more games for the pundits to travel to north of Ardee. More rainy days in Clones, the chip wrappings fluttering about their ankles, traffic backed up on every road out of the town. Hell, even AA Roadwatch would have to take notice. But the clincher is . . . just imagine what a boost Kerry would give to the "Love Ulster" campaign.'

Pat Spillane, though, has had a Lazarus experience.

'Before Tyrone played Dublin in the All-Ireland quarter-final in 2008 I was ready to write their obituary, but they produced the performance of the year and came out and totally demolished the much-hyped Dubs. They played with composure, class, total commitment, teamwork, flair and skill. They put up a great score in the most atrocious conditions. I know many people will be surprised to hear me saying this, but, in short, they played football the way it should be played. Even my beloved Kerry could learn from them on that performance, and they would prove that when they beat the Kingdom in the final that year.'

13

THE RIVERDANCE OF SPORT

WITH APOLOGIES TO PAUL SIMON, IN THE 1990S THE NATION turned its lonely eyes to hurling. Former GAA president Nickey Brennan was ideally placed to see why.

'A lot of things happened. We made a number of structural changes; probably the most significant was introducing the "back door" system in the championship – which I was involved in myself. The purpose of the back door is that we give every county a minimum of two games. Naturally enough, if you gave the stronger counties, like my own county, Kilkenny, a second chance, you might live to regret it. That remains the reality in both football and hurling – that the strong counties may not get caught a second time in the one year – but I think it is serving us well. It has given us more games and better games, and the profile of the hurling has increased enormously. The emergence of Clare and Wexford enlivened hurling.'

THE MAN FROM CLARE

Some Roman warriors who knew they were about to lose a battle killed themselves rather than face defeat: *damnata iam luce ferox* ('furious by daylight, having been condemned'). This intense desire to win was replicated by Ger Loughnane – a man born under the sign of contradiction.

When you meet him for the first time, you have preconceptions because you've been watching him for years walking up and down the sideline and his fist is clenched and he has that look on his face that says: 'You mess me with me and I'll split your head open.' When I was a boy, Neil Diamond had a song called 'Beautiful Noise'. In recent years, my favourite sound has become Ger's big, hearty, belly laugh. He's a man who laughs hard and laughs often. It is a shock to find how relaxed he can be, and there are times when you think that behind it all he's just a pussycat; but in his time as manager of Clare and then Galway, Ger had a 'few scrapes', and as soon as he starts to talk about them – the lion roars again. In fact, there were many stories Ger told me that had the hairs standing up on the back of my neck. But the biggest shock I got was to discover that this man was once – an altar boy. Is it any wonder the Catholic Church has had so many problems in recent years?

'The scenes when we won the Munster final in 1995 were something to treasure. Although there weren't that many Clare people there, they were absolutely fanatical. "Overjoyed" is too tame a word to describe them. It was a feeling of surprise mixed with elation that there hasn't been a word invented for it yet.

'Before the team went out on the pitch, I did something I'd never done before. I held up a Clare jersey before the players. I reminded them of all the disappointments of those who had worn the Clare jersey down the years and all the heartbreak the Clare fans had experienced – but that those would be cast away by five o'clock that evening.

'We were out on the pitch first, but when Limerick came onto the pitch you could feel the whole place shaking. It was as loud a cheer as I ever heard. I was standing at the end of the tunnel, and as Limerick's Steve McDonagh was coming out, something inside me said, "Will I flatten him?" It would have been an absolutely crazy thing to do. I wanted something to show them that although they had all the noise from the supporters, by God, we were going to take them on that day.

'When the final whistle blew, it was such a relief. The hoodoo had been broken. It had nothing to do with beating Limerick. We were incredulous. It only really struck home when Dalo said in his victory speech, "We'll go to Croke Park in our thousands." I thought, "Jesus, we're going to Croke Park." This was fantasy stuff. We had talked a lot about winning the Munster final, but when it happened we couldn't actually believe it. Even when we saw the cup, we were wondering if we were dreaming and whether it would be gone when we woke up in the morning. There wasn't a huge sense of excitement because we just weren't prepared for it. Although we had won the match, the significance of the occasion hadn't sunk in.'

Seánie McMahon echoes this sentiment.

'Personally, the memory that will stand out for me was when we won the Munster final. I never dreamed of All-Irelands, just the Munster final, and I remember when we won I just went down on my knees and said, "Thank you, God." It was such a relief. There were lots of tears shed – but, for once, Clare people were crying tears of joy. It brought a huge uplift to Clare people.'

Clare's full-back Brian Lohan is the greatest full-back of all time. Loughnane's summation of him is just three words: 'Simply the best.' Does Lohan reciprocate the compliment?

'Loughnane on the training field was a brute. He just dictated everything that you had to do, and you did it or else you stood outside and watched other people doing it. So it was very simple – his way or no way. Nobody would have dared question it. Loughnane constantly did things that were to the benefit of the players, and everything was for the benefit of the team. He was brutal, but he was very honest. He didn't allow you to have feelings for him. You did what he asked you to do because of pure respect for him. When we did what he asked us to do, we were winning matches – so that's why we kept doing what he said.'

DALY TASKS

During a game, communication between managers and players is almost impossible because of the noise. Loughnane had to rely on his players for leadership on the field. Anthony Daly was the natural choice to be the team's spokesman and captain. As a player, he deserved all the plaudits heaped upon him with a string of performances as captivating as the sport can offer. Daly had to be what he was: an excellent craftsman with a superb fighting spirit and the stamina of body and mind to cope with the long haul. While his famous speeches and innate media skills might have seemed to be his obvious credentials, Loughnane chose him for his ability in the dressing-room, given his flair to help players cope with frustration and disappointment. 'Dalo' was adept at deflecting any anger by giving his teammates a chance to air their complaints.

'I think that after the league final in 1995, 90 per cent of Clare followers felt, "That is it: we can't take any more trouncings." You couldn't blame them. Although we hadn't been trounced on the scoreboard, in hurling terms we were. Coming out after the game, one supporter said, "Kilkenny were a different class." This massacre came on the back of major defeats in the two previous years in Munster finals. When Ger Loughnane spoke about us winning the Munster final, none of the fans believed him.

'There were fewer than 15,000 fans at our first game in the championship, and most of them were from Cork. Even when we beat Cork and the Munster final was jammed, it was mostly filled with Limerick people.'

Never was Daly's role as captain more clearly illustrated than the Munster final in '95.

'Everybody in Clare was convinced that we had no chance of winning that game because two weeks before, we had played Galway in a challenge match in Shannon and we bombed. On the day of the final, we stopped in the hotel in Cashel for a cup of tea. We were on the way into Thurles and just when we came to the bridge, the place was crowded with supporters wearing the Limerick colours. A few of them shouted at us, "What a waste of time." They were sure they were going back to the All-Ireland final. Straight away I said, "We'll show ye whether it's a waste of time or not." A small thing like that can make a big difference. Some of the lads afterwards said it made a difference. I'm not so sure.

'Bringing home the cup was absolutely incredible. There was a wonderful feeling of achievement and togetherness. We came over the bridge in Limerick and that was fantastic, but we were on our own because there wasn't a Clare person in sight. We thought it would be just a bit of a celebration in Ennis.

'When we got to Cratloe, we couldn't get through the crowds. It was such a scene of celebration and sporting hysteria. We couldn't even get to Shannon because we were a mile late getting to Ennis, but they had bonfires for us and everything. Clare FM was well established, and it was putting out bulletins on our progress so everybody knew where we were.

'In 1992, the Clare footballers had won the Munster title and that generated great celebrations, but hurling was the game that had produced all the disappointments. This was a real breakaway from all that. You have to remember that when people talked about winning in Clare, all they meant was winning the Munster final. The All-Ireland final wasn't even contemplated because the Munster final had always been such a stumbling block.

'For myself personally, it was about winning the Munster final and the satisfaction I got out of that. The boys often talk about how unprepared the Clare people were for our win. We got back to Clarecastle and there was no podium. I had to stand on the top of the bus. My mother was an avid bingo goer on Sunday nights, and all I said was it must be a very special night when my mother wasn't gone to bingo.'

THE HILLS ARE ALIVE

Clare's 1995 triumph was hurling equivalent's of the ugly duckling who matured into a swan. To gain an insight into the inner secrets of this transformation, I trekked up the famous hill of Shannon in the company of ace forward Jamesie O'Connor.

'On a typical Tuesday or Thursday night, we would meet in Wolfe Tones. Mike McNamara would do some upper-body exercises with us, like sit-ups. Then we would don the woolly hats and head to the hill. We would park in front of the school where the two Lohans went. Generally, you would approach the session with a sense of absolute dread. You could sense the lethargy and you would troop from the cars practically crying. Everybody felt the same way. Mike Mac would then break your heart by saying, "Right lads – we've 40 to do," and you would sink even deeper into your boots. I was one of the guys that would be in reasonably good shape, and I was better equipped to run up the hill than Sparrow (Ger O'Loughlin) or Liam Doyle or fellas that dreaded physical training. Mike was psychologically trying to break you even before the session started by telling you how many you had to do. Mike was on top of the hill with the whistle, Tony Considine was standing in the middle and Ger was on the bottom starting us off. When we reached the top of the hill, you would be gasping for oxygen. I don't know what altitude training is like, but at the top of the hill, the air always seemed to be that bit thinner. It was a mental thing and a physical thing. By the last four or five rounds there would be water on top of the hill, but you would be unable to take it. On some occasions, you would be literally incapable of starting the car. Your head would be spinning and your mind was gone. That training was very important to us, particularly coming into the last ten or fifteen minutes of big games, when most matches are won.

'We set out to take the league seriously, and won our first five games and qualified for the league semi-final. We went for a weekend down to Killarney for a kind of bonding session, and I think that might have been the making of us. We had a really great weekend, and I remember at three or four in the morning lying awake talking to Brian Lohan and asking him: "Did you ever think you'd be like Cyril Lyons and play for ten years and win nothing?" His response was: "Jesus, we'll win something," and I remember rolling over thinking, "He's dead right."

'People were in euphoria after we won the Munster final. Sixty-three years was a long wait. People couldn't believe it was actually happening. I remember towards the end of the game, as people started climbing in towards the pitch, thinking, "Jesus, get off the pitch or the ref'll abandon it." I thought some catastrophe was in store for us.

'With that win, a massive weight was lifted off the county. Clare people had travelled to so many Munster finals – minor, under-21 and senior – and always come home with their tail between their legs. I had the cup the next week and I brought it to Don Ryan, who lived just around the corner from my parents' shop in Ennis and was a diehard Clare fan; he'd been the first fan to every match for years and years. I said that he might like to take a look at that. He just broke down in tears, and I said: "I will call back later." That's what it meant to the guy.'

So how important does Jamesie feel Loughnane was to Clare's success?

'He was looking for a particular type of player – a player who wouldn't roll over. If a guy was going to roll over here in Shannon, he wouldn't survive in Croke Park. Much of the training was psychological. They were testing you and looking for a certain reaction. They were looking for a type of guy who would bite his lip and grit his teeth and say: "I'll prove you wrong." Ger would say tough things to me. The guy who used to mark me in training was Christy 'Rusty' Chaplain, and I would have awful battles with him. I remember one wet evening he was cleaning me out and Loughnane would let out this roar: "Good man, Christy, you have him cleaned." I'm saying under my breath, "You bollix," but at the same time gritting my teeth to win the next ball. That's what he was doing. If you sunk down in your boots, you were going to be no good to him in Croke Park. That was part of his psychological approach.

'I used to live in Galway, and ten days before the All-Ireland final we went down to a summer camp in Woodford. One of the men running it was Paddy Kirwan from Offaly. Paddy is a fierce hurling man, but I just got a sense from him that he didn't rate us. Ger said to us a week before the game that if we made a battle out of it, nobody was going to beat us, and I remember thinking: "He's dead right."

'Another thing that was crucial to Ger's contribution was in driving us on to get the hunger back two years later to win the second All-Ireland. I always think that first one was for the county. The second one was for the team.'

Anthony Daly identifies one moment when Loughnane's contribution was particularly significant.

'No one will ever forget the night the training was bad and Stephen McNamara had complained of a stomach bug, and Loughnane brought us all back into the dressing-room because we were so lethargic in training. He gave a tyranny of a speech and began with me: "It starts with the captain." He lambasted me and then everybody else, and eventually he came around to Stephen Mac and he hit him a kind of belt in the stomach and said: "Sick, Mac? Sick is coming out of Croke Park beaten." I think that was a turning point because we weren't going to settle for winning Munster – we were going to go all the way.'

RAISING THE BANNER

Although it was only one step in the long climb that the team had to make if there was any chance of surviving among the best in the country, Clare's Munster final victory was more feverishly acclaimed than any other in recent decades. Even when the small hairs stood up on the back of his neck and the war whoops of victory echoed all around him, Anthony Daly never imagined the attendant fanfare that might accompany it. It quickly became evident, though, that they had to forget about that game if they were to capture the All-Ireland title from the current holders, Offaly.

'We were different people and there was a swagger in our steps going into work, and thus we were nearly like new men.

'The Sparrow and myself went for a swim the day before the final, and I asked him what did he think, and he said he thought we were going to win. I said I felt the same. I had bought into the theory that it was our year. There was a bit of magic in the air in Croke Park that day. It just seemed the way that things fell into place. I just felt that on the day Offaly got two fortunate goals, but we never dropped our heads. We came out and hurled away and got the break with the goal two minutes from the end. Offaly got the goal just before half-time, and everyone says that's a great time to get a goal, but it is probably a better time to get one with two minutes to go.

'When the All-Ireland started, everything was going grand. Seánie McMahon scored two great points to set us off. We were doing everything we planned. It was a war of attrition. We were blocking them and hooking them.

'Then, just before half-time, disaster struck. Michael Duignan came along under the Cusack Stand and he seemed to try and lob the ball over the bar, but it fell short. Fitzie [Clare's goalie Davy Fitzgerald] tried to control the ball with his hurley, which was unusual for him, but the sliotar skidded off his hurley into the net. It looked like the classic sucker-punch that could destroy us. If there was any fragile area in our make-up, that would undo us.'

His gifted team were suddenly buzzing, and Clare were on their way to victory.

Croke Park takes you like no other place, but add in Anthony Daly's famous victory speech to the emotional mix and it's a recipe for emotional release: 'There's been a missing person in Clare for 81 long years. Well, today that person has been found alive, and that person's name is Liam McCarthy.'

Daly saw how much it meant to Clare people.

'I will never forget the colour the Clare fans brought to the game. That's when it all really took off. Donegal had brought it first in 1992, but in '95 it really took off. We take it for granted now.

'It was great going to the schools just to witness the magic, the awe and the wonder, but to me, the most special part was meeting the older people. I remember meeting my brother's father-in-law crying in Thurles after we won. He could remember back to '55 and all the catalogue of Clare's heartbreaks. At the time, I was so wound up and drained from games that I didn't fully appreciate it till later.'

Ger Loughnane saw Clare's victory in 1995 in spiritual terms.

'The win was for all those who wore the saffron and blue with pride down through 81 barren years, who gave their best for Clare with no reward in terms of medals, but who passed on the torch that lit the flame that burned so brightly on 3 September 1995.

'Every now and again, something happens that brings the memories of '95 flooding back: memories of the colour, joy and excitement the Clare supporters brought, especially with the flags hanging out of the windows on the way home after victories in Croke Park. When I think back, it was seeing in their eyes how much it meant for Clare to win, and in latter years it was hearing people talk about those who had passed on that they were glad they were there to see Clare winning an All-Ireland. That was the great thrill of it and worth more than any medals. That was what brought such great contentment – that I think will last a lifetime. It showed to everybody that hurling was more than a game. It was a movement of people, a liberation of people in Clare.

'To misquote William Wordsworth, I would sum it up like this:

> For oft, when on my couch I lie
> In vacant or in pensive mood,
> They flash upon that inward eye
> Which is the bliss of solitude;
> And then my heart with pleasure fills,
> And dances with the Croke Park thrills.'

THE SEARCH FOR GREATNESS

If a week is a long time in politics, 11 years is a long time in hurling, and in 2006, a bizarre series of events involving an overheard phone conversation and a complaint to the guards created a virtual civil war in Clare hurling that entered the vernacular as 'Claregate'. At its core was a row between Loughnane and what he terms 'the Clare hurling establishment'. How does Loughnane reflect on the bitter controversy?

'I believe there is an element in charge of hurling in Clare who want to rewrite the history of what happened in '95 and '97 because they want to keep things in their own hands. Essentially, they were bypassed in our glory years and they don't want that situation to be repeated – even if it means we are not successful as a county.'

The controversy reheated itself in '07 when Loughnane weighed in to back his old friend Tony Considine, who was experiencing a turbulent time as Clare manager. What raised most eyebrows was the timing of his comments – shortly before his Galway team were playing Clare in a crunch game. Loughnane was bemused by the hullabaloo: 'I threw a pebble and everyone thought it was an earthquake.'

Loughnane sparked an even bigger controversy that summer when he complained that Kilkenny's tactics did cross the line on occasions.

'Christ, I got such criticism, some of it for words I never actually used, that I thought at one stage I was going to be blamed for global warming! I sometimes laugh when I turn on the radio and listen to sports shows and find they are talking about something I said as if it was more newsworthy than the Gettysburg Address! What makes it all the more laughable is that they invite journalists on to interpret what I have said and they talk about "Ger" as if they know me well. Some of these guys are people I have rarely, if ever, spoken with in any meaningful way, and often they know as much about me as I know about synchronised swimming.'

DANCING AT THE CROSSROADS

The joy in Clare in 1995 was replicated by Wexford fans in 1996. After he retired from playing, Martin Quigley immediately took charge of piloting Wexford's fortunes. His new role was no bed of roses.

'Managing is not nearly as enjoyable as playing. When you are playing, you only have to worry about your own job, but when you're the manager, you have to worry about everybody else. There are so many things outside your control as a manager, from players getting injured to bad referees' decisions that can cost you a game. Once I retired as a player, I missed the buzz of it, and I got involved in managing Wexford almost immediately. With the benefit of hindsight, I should have taken a break from the game and turned to management later, but while hindsight is great, it's not any good when you have to make a decision. I should have given myself a bit of distance between the switch from playing to managing. It's hard to have a clear perspective when emotionally you're too close to the centre of things.'

How would he assess his own term in charge of Wexford?

'I'm not the best person to judge. Ultimately, a manager is judged by results. In my three years in charge, we got to two league finals but we won nothing. I suppose, though, any manager is only as good as the players he has at his disposal.'

Quigley was replaced as Wexford manager by Christy Keogh. Among Keogh's innovations was enlisting the services of Cyril Farrell to assist the team in their preparations for the Leinster Championship, particularly the clash with old rivals Kilkenny. The move did not have the desired impact as Kilkenny inflicted a heavy defeat on the Slaneysiders. How does Quigley react to the criticism that was aired at the time: that instead of rallying Wexford, Farrell's mere presence inspired Kilkenny?

'I wouldn't pay any heed to that sort of talk. Anyone who thinks that Kilkenny need Cyril Farrell's involvement to be fully motivated to beat Wexford in the championship knows nothing about hurling, and Kilkenny hurling in particular. Kilkenny had a strong team and beat us badly. I don't think it would have made much difference who was managing us that particular year. The one thing that Cyril's involvement did achieve was to dramatically heighten the expectations within the county. Not for the first time, though, they were to be cruelly dashed.'

In 1996, Wexford became the home of the Riverdance of sport and the story of paradise regained. Why did they win the All-Ireland that year and not earlier?

'Expectations were low in 1996 because we had been beaten in the league semi-final. To me, the key match in 1996 was not the All-Ireland final but beating Offaly in the Leinster final. That really set them up as a team of winners. I think the supporters played a huge part in Wexford's win – almost as much as the team itself. It was fascinating to see the way the support snowballed in the county throughout the championship. It was said there were 8,000 Wexford fans at the Kilkenny match, but there were 40,000 there for the final.

'I think there were two crucial factors to explain why Wexford won that year. First, there was Liam Griffin and the passion, motivation, organisation and leadership he gave to the team. Second, there was Damien Fitzhenry. I don't want to cast any aspersions on anybody, but Wexford had been waiting for a long time for a goalie up to that standard. He's the best goalie in Ireland, in my opinion. If I had to pinpoint one player on the pitch who meant the difference between victory and defeat in 1996, it would be him.'

WHO FEARS TO SPEAK OF '98?

Nineteen ninety-eight was dominated by Ger Loughnane and the many controversies that dogged his team: the clashes with officialdom and the rows with referees, as well as the unprecedented media attention. Things really ignited after the Munster final replay against Waterford, where the intense aggression began even before the match started. The man at the centre of the storm was referee Willie Barrett.

'The criticism of my performance did get to me, and I wasn't appointed to any other intercounty games that year. I got letters from people who were very angry. I stopped answering the phone for a while; my wife started taking the calls and she got the brunt of it. Someone said to me once that it was nice to have your picture in the paper, but I saw my picture every day for 12 or 13 days in a row and it didn't add to me, I can assure you. It did affect me, and I didn't know at that stage if I would have the confidence to referee a big game again. My daughter was in France at the time and I felt under siege so I brought the family to France until things settled down a bit.'

Clare's All-Ireland semi-final replay against Offaly spawned a new controversy when referee Jimmy Cooney blew up the match early.

'After I blew the final whistle, I saw my umpire and he had his hand out with his five fingers up. I thought to myself, "Oh, Jesus." All the photographers were nearly pushing themselves out of the way to get a picture of me. The umpires told me afterwards that I didn't tog in for two hours. I don't remember it, but I remember my wife eventually coming into the dressing-room and she was crying, of course. We went to the Aisling Hotel and 'twas news time and I was flashed across the screen. The waitress looked at the screen, then looked at me and before she said anything, I said: "That's me." I just wanted to get home. We had a young family, and I knew there could be phone calls.

'There were lots of calls. If one of the girls answered, they were asked if their daddy was a referee. When they said yes, they were told that their daddy was going to be killed and their house was going to be burned down and if they didn't pass on the message, they would be killed as well. When I got to the phone and offered to meet the callers face to face, they hung up quickly. It would have lasted till Christmas and after that.'

After Offaly lost the Leinster final in '98 to Kilkenny, Babs Keating controversially described the Offaly players as 'sheep in a heap'. Babs met with the county board and decided to stay, but the next morning he resigned because he was 'shocked' by an interview in a newspaper with Offaly's star midfielder Johnny Pilkington, who had questioned his record with the county, stated that Babs had abandoned Offaly's tradition of ground hurling and questioned the tactics against Kilkenny. Pilkington is not someone to hide his feelings.

'It really got to me. Babs was manager of Offaly. We had some very bad wides on the day and we conceded two soft goals in the last fifteen minutes. It just seemed he was passing the buck. Maybe it was the players' fault, but he was the manager and he could have come down on Tuesday night and said what he had to say in the dressing-room. He always referred to Offaly as "them" – never as "us". It was a case of "they" were poor out there and "they" did things wrong.

'Michael Bond came on the scene after about a week. He just said he liked Offaly hurling and off we went training. Nobody knew who he was. Nobody knew his hurling credentials or anything. We knew he was a teacher. Someone told us he was a principal. He spoke Irish and some of his instructions were in Irish. The training sessions upped significantly. We were a group of lads who were down at the bottom of the barrel. We were after speaking out against the manager. It wasn't anyone else's responsibility to pick it up – only the 30 lads who were there. After Bond came in, there was a great buzz in training and we were thinking we were great lads again. We played Kilkenny in a challenge match, though, and they gave us an even bigger beating than they had in the Leinster final! So where did that leave us?

'Loughnane took his eye off the ball before we played Clare in the All-Ireland semi-final. If they had been playing Kilkenny or Galway, it would have been a different story. He took Offaly for granted.'

Not surprisingly, Babs Keating's reading of the events of '98 differs sharply from Pilkington's.

'Johnny Pilkington took great exception to my remark, but one of my biggest battles at the time was to get Pilkington to train.'

Broadcaster Peter Woods offers an interesting perspective on

Offaly's revived fortunes under Michael Bond: 'You could lead them with a thread, but you can't drive them with an iron bar.'

Hubert Ringey, the Offaly captain, in his victory speech after Offaly beat Kilkenny in the All-Ireland final, said: 'We might have come in the back door, but we're going out the front door.' Offaly came through the back door, having voted against it, and Offaly, true to form, voted against the back door the following year.

THE PRINCE OF HURLING

One player dominated the 1990s. For many hurling fans, D.J. Carey has somehow been transformed from a great athlete to a sports deity. It might be unfair to say that a Kilkenny forward line without D.J. was like *Hamlet* without the prince, but if that is the case, it is a marginal call.

'Hurling is a team game. I've never won a match on my own. No player can. I would be nothing without the other 14 players. It's a bit unfair that I got so much of the praise when everybody else worked as hard as I did. Winning games is not just about who can swing the hurley the best. A lot of the time, it is about who has the right attitude and who wants to win the most. A lot of people think we do what we do for the medals and the glory. It's not about that. It's about fun and pride in one's parish and county.'

Yet in every life some rain must fall. D.J. has had some dark moments of his own. There was a lot of controversy before the 2000 All-Ireland final when he was not selected on the Team of the Millennium. But that same year, like a beleaguered army greeting the hero who brings relief, D.J. answered his critics in the most emphatic way possible with a five-star performance in the All-Ireland final. Offaly on that day found themselves confronted by the sort of talent that knows few boundaries. D.J.'s goals and classy performance ensured that Kilkenny won back the All-Ireland crown their fans almost consider their birthright.

Nickey Brennan has had the opportunity to see D.J.'s progression up close and personal.

'I was asked first to get involved with the management of the

Kilkenny football team, which was far from the most glamorous role in the GAA. I managed the Kilkenny under-21 team to an All-Ireland success. I then became a selector for two years – at a time when I was county chairman. I have to say, I did have some hesitation about going in to manage the Kilkenny senior team. When I look back at all my time in the GAA, my time as senior manager was probably the least happy time. When I took over, it was probably a bit of a rebuilding phase. I always felt that some of the lads I brought through would make their real impact in my successor's time, which turned out to be true. As a player, you get the opportunity to put your own stamp on things. I was manager in the mid-'90s, and since then, the pressure on managers has become more severe.

'I have a long association with D.J. I was coaching him at under-21s. I was a selector in his early years on the senior team, and then I was coaching him in the two years I was in charge of the senior team. You always ask the inevitable question – who was the greatest: Ring, Keher or Carey? It's very hard to say. I never saw Ring play, myself. I have no reason to doubt that those who saw Ring play and claim he was the greatest of all time are speaking with authority. I played with Keher and would say he was an exceptionally dedicated individual. His attention to detail was incredible; for example, the way he practised his frees. No player I have ever seen could match him in that respect, though Noel Skehan was also very, very dedicated. I think Carey's primary strength was that no player could turn a game as quickly as he could. He could be quiet for much of the game, but then he could explode and turn in maybe two minutes what was a fairly hopeless case for Kilkenny. He had every skill in the book and his pace was electric. He was a different type of player. Keher played in an era where the physical exchanges were, let's say, a "bit rawer" than today. Don't get me wrong: the physical exchanges today are still an important part of hurling, but you don't have the level of physical exchanges you had then. Whenever people talk about the greatest hurler of all time, Carey has to be one of two or three names you mention, but it's the same as asking, "Was Ali the greatest-ever boxer?" It's a good topic for a pub on a cold winter's night, but it is impossible to give a definitive answer. The one thing I will say is that when you talk about the top three hurlers of all time, you have to talk about both Keher and Carey, and I was very privileged to be so close to both of them.'

Ger Loughnane offers an appraisal of Carey's career.

'Look back over D.J.'s record, and you'll see the difference between him and everybody else is the wonderful collection of goals he's got. What people underestimate about him is his courage. Down the years, he has collected many injuries. Yet his nerve has remained as good as ever. His one instinct was to go for goal no matter what kind of punishment he was going to be subjected to. Under every category of defining a great player, he is without doubt the finest player of his generation, if not ever.'

Nicky English also shares in the plaudits for D.J.

'It is hard to compare players. D.J. was one of the best I've ever seen. He had such skill, great hunger, could get inspirational scores, but above all, he had blinding pace and no defender could handle him at his best. In a different way, Henry Shefflin is also an outstanding player and one of the greats. For such a big man, he has such skill. I was close to him in the stand when he hit the first ball against Waterford from close to the sideline in the 2008 All-Ireland final. I knew from the sound of the ball hitting the hurley that he had caught it sweetly, and I didn't even have to look to know it was going over the bar. The only other time I've heard that sound was Tommy Dunne's first ball in the 2001 All-Ireland final. Again, I didn't need to look. It was going to take an exceptional player to come out of D.J.'s shadow, and Henry has done that.'

IN THE HOT SEAT

In the late '90s, Nicky English would take on the job of managing Tipperary. At the time, though, the omens did not seem favourable.

'When I was approached to take on the job as manager, I got lots of advice not to take it, because the belief was that the players were not in the county at the time to match Clare or whoever. To be honest, everybody told me not to take it, but I couldn't stop myself.

'I think we were unlucky in 1999. I feel that the referee made a bad decision to give a penalty to Clare at the end of the match, which

THE GAA

Davy Fitzgerald scored. We had a young team and our lads thought it was easy after that game, because although Clare were still a great team, we had more than matched them. That Clare team had some of the greatest players in the history of the game, like Seánie McMahon, Brian Lohan and Jamesie O'Connor, and in the replay, they really upped their performance and blew us away. I've heard Loughnane and some of the Clare lads saying since that that was their best-ever performance. I learned from my own mistakes during that game. I had left Declan Ryan on the bench with a view to getting the Tipp crowd going when we brought him on. We sprung him after 20 minutes, but the match was lost at that stage. I was talking with Seán Boylan shortly after the game and he said he had made the same mistake once leaving Gerry McEntee on the bench. That day taught me that you play your best players from the start. We made it to the Munster final the next year, but a lot of our lads got distracted by sideshows like the crowd and getting tickets for the game, and we lost to Cork. I knew that in 2001 we had a great chance of winning the All-Ireland if we could get over Clare in the Munster Championship. By then, we were a battle-hardened team and were ready to make the big breakthrough, especially with Eoin Kelly arriving on the scene.

'People talk a lot of nonsense about motivation. I think motivation is a really simple concept. It's about getting a player to give his best, but also to do what is best for the team. Before the final, I told the players to go out there and make as many mistakes as they could. I wanted to free them up. The last thing you want is players closing in on themselves. People talk about the importance of having a great leader, but the best leaders are not always the best players. We had great leaders on that team, like Tommy Dunne, Eddie Enright, Paul Ormond and Declan Ryan.

'My abiding memory of that All-Ireland is that the referee played four minutes of injury time. That was sheer agony because we were just two points up at that stage and if Galway got a goal, we were beaten. I couldn't wait for Pat O'Connor to blow the whistle. It wasn't like winning the All-Ireland as a player. What I felt was sheer relief. There is so much pressure on the manager because you are expected to know on a Saturday what everybody knows on Monday.'

THE RIVERDANCE OF SPORT

English's delight would bring crushing disappointment for his opposite number on the Galway sideline, Noel Lane.

IN THE FAST LANE

Lane controversially became manager of the Galway senior team having served his apprenticeship at club level and with the county minors and under-21s. It is quickly evident that he still feels aggrieved by the manner of his treatment by the county board. Yet things began promisingly for Lane when Galway beat Kilkenny in the 2001 All-Ireland semi-final.

'I succeeded Mattie Murphy whether it was right or wrong. He was doing a good job, but was only given two years. I believe that Galway should have won one or two All-Irelands in the last ten years because the team was good enough, but there was a lack of continuity at management level. The players were the ones to suffer.

'Beating Kilkenny was a win against the head and one of the highs in my life because I had prepared a team to beat the best. But I knew that the knives were out for me at the county board level even when we won, for reasons unknown to me. It was fed back indirectly to me that the county board was not supporting me. Things had deteriorated after a league match in Tipperary. It was blatantly obvious that I was not acting as they wanted. I was doing things that I felt would help us to win, like flying the team to Croke Park for games. As manager, I had taken control of the team and I don't think that pleased them. I brought in Mike McNamara from Clare. He was a great trainer and was very good on mental toughness and mental preparation.

'The lack of support from the county board took its toll on me in the lead-up to the All-Ireland final against Tipperary. I had a huge management job outside the players, with media commitments and everything else. If I got the chance again, I would do things differently and put more focus on the players alone. By contrast, Nicky English, the Tipp manager, had been in the job for four or five years so he had that experience to call on. The referee made some astonishing decisions that day that I felt cost us. As the co-operation from the county board wasn't there, I had to take on all the organisational details myself. I was emotionally and physically drained from the whole management of the weekend, which I think meant that I didn't react sharply enough to events on the sideline during the game, and in that respect, I feel I let down the players. I lost five All-Irelands as a player, but losing as a manager was worse because I felt responsible for thirty people in the squad and the back-room team. I knew straight away that the knives were out again.

'The next year, we beat Cork in the quarter-final in Thurles so I must have been doing something right. We played Clare in the semi-final in a very tight and intense game. Clare sucked us in and played the game on their terms. Colin Lynch floated a typical point to snatch the victory for them. That was when I knew that the show was over. The press knew. There were wide smiles on many of the county board. I felt I was just growing into the job and would have benefited from another year or two, but it was very hurtful to effectively be sacked.'

THE SPOKEN ENGLISH

Having reached the summit in 2001, Nicky English would have a less happy time in '02.

'Kilkenny beat us in the All-Ireland semi-final the next year, and I heard Henry Shefflin saying recently that was one of their greatest-ever performances. That was the end of the road for me. Whenever I have been approached since about returning to management, my instinct is always to say "yes", but because of work and my young son, it is not feasible at the moment. Sometime, though, I plan to return to it because I just love the involvement in the game.

'I am still confident about the hurling future. I want to see great players. I had heard all the hype about Joe Canning, and I wasn't sure the first time I saw him playing for Galway minors whether it was all justified. Then I saw him scoring line balls for fun in the Fitzgibbon Cup and I began to reassess him. For me, the turning point was the 2008 league final. He had excelled for Portumna in the club championship and had just come onto the Galway panel, and I couldn't believe the way he was able to run through the Tipperary defence. It changed the way I viewed him. I thought to myself, "This guy can become anything." I was lucky enough to see him play against Cork that summer. It was incredible to watch him almost pushing his own players out of his way because he was so confident he was going to get the scores. In the second half, especially, he was a one-man show, and it was just incredible to see three of the finest players we have seen in recent times – John Gardiner, Ronan Curran and Seán Óg Ó hAilpín – just in a panic because they had absolutely no idea how to handle him. After that game, I felt that "This is a guy who has the potential to become one of the all-time greats."'

THE SECOND COMING

In 1999, after a young Cork side defeated the hot favourites Kilkenny in the All-Ireland hurling final, Jimmy Barry-Murphy stated that Brian Corcoran was the greatest Cork hurler of his generation. Barry-Murphy is not a man given to wild statements or hyperbole, so it was not a remark to be taken lightly. The hurling pundits nodded sagely in agreement.

Corcoran exploded onto the Gaelic games scene in 1992. A series of masterful performances in the Cork colours saw him crowned as hurler of that year. In 1999, he reclaimed that honour. That same year, Corcoran was a key player on the Cork football team that lost to Meath in the All-Ireland final. Not long after that, the cumulative wear and tear of unending training sessions and games took its toll. Corcoran retired prematurely from intercounty football and hurling.

The arrival of a young family also played a major factor in his decision to quit at the top of his game.

'To be honest, hurling had become a chore. I'd be on my way home from work and all I wanted to do was play with the baby, and instead I was being dragged away to do something that I didn't want to do. By the time I came home from training, she was asleep. It got to the stage where I was getting up in the morning and saying, "Oh no, I've got training tonight."'

Initially, he did not miss the game. For a time, it seemed as if Cork could get on without him, too, and it seemed as if Cork hurlers were more interested in off-the-pitch activities than on-the-pitch stuff, such as when they famously went on strike to get better facilities and conditions from the county board.

In 2003, in the course of Cork's triumphant march to the All-Ireland final, a new sporting icon was launched on Leeside. Setanta Ó hAilpín thrilled the Cork public in the way that Jimmy Barry-Murphy had inspired Cork to All-Ireland final glory at 19 years of age in 1973. Cork fans were bitterly disappointed losing the final to Kilkenny. Their sense of misery was compounded when they heard that Setanta had gone Down Under to carve out a new career for himself as an Aussie Rules player. After his departure, only another legend could fill the void. The time was right for Corcoran's second coming, not least because the expectation of a success-starved county awaiting retrieval of its oldest sporting prize demanded another All-Ireland.

'It was a big gamble to come out of retirement. I could have fallen flat on my face and Cork could have struggled. Some people told me that I had twice been hurler of the year and I had nothing to prove. But you make decisions and you live by them. To be honest, I was half-afraid of going back. I wasn't sure if the lads would be welcoming me back with me having been out for so long.'

A Hollywood scriptwriter could not have written such a fairy tale for Corcoran's championship story in 2004. It began and ended with him on his knees. On his return in his opening match of the Munster Championship against Limerick, he scored a wonder point while still on his knees. In the dying seconds of the All-Ireland final, he sprinted onto the ball, rode a tackle, turned on his left, shot and scored the insurance score. He fell on his knees just as the final whistle went and roared in triumph. It was nice to be back. Yet there had been a few anxious moments on the way.

'In 2003 in the Munster Championship, after getting over the grievances with the county board, with a new management team, Cork were all out to prove that they were right to strike and the only way to do that was to win something. We won the Munster title. In 2004, the story going into the Munster final was a very different one. Setanta Ó hAilpín had departed to Australia, and after a relatively unconvincing league campaign, Cork struggled to beat Limerick in our semi-final.

In marked contrast, Waterford were the form team in the Munster Championship and had had an excellent league campaign, apart from the final, when they flopped against Galway. They beat us in the final, but I hadn't come back to the game to win a Munster medal. I came back to win an All-Ireland, and after that game, we put things right and achieved our goal.'

Corcoran found himself unexpectedly embroiled in controversy before the All-Ireland quarter-final. The Antrim manager, Dinny Cahill, adopted an unusual strategy before the match when he publicly rubbished Cork's chances. Corcoran was singled out for special criticism: 'Cork have to have a problem when they recall Brian Corcoran. They have to have problems. They have a dreadful inside-forward line all season, couldn't get the scores, they had to recall a man who finished playing. Well, he will be finished after Sunday, there's no doubt about that. If you look at their games, they had a dreadful centre-forward, but got away with it. We have a class centre-back; we know how to stop that man from hurling. We are going to win the All-Ireland this year. We can win the All-Ireland. After getting over this game, anything can happen.'

Corcoran responded in the best way possible and scored the two goals that obliterated Antrim's chances. In 2005, he was at the centre of two of the most important moments of the championship. The first came with his wonder goal against Waterford in the All-Ireland quarter-final. He remembers that magic moment with characteristic modesty.

'A hit-and-hope high ball was brilliantly rescued by Joe Deane on the endline and he sent it back to me. I took two steps back while turning, dropped the ball and let it bounce, held my backswing in case I was hooked and skimmed the sliotar off the top of the ground – and it ended up in the net.'

The hand of fate is especially fickle when it comes to sport. Accordingly, after a single victory or defeat, the hurlers on the pitch can change their colours faster than Manchester United. For all the benefits of leading a confident and unchanged side, Cork really struggled in the semi-final against Clare. With the minutes slipping away, it seemed that Cork were on their way out. Resignation was actually what the Cork fans in the stands had in common, even if none of them had a language that could express it. The 2005 All-Ireland semi-final brings mixed memories for Corcoran.

'Even the Cork fans felt sorry for Clare. They were arguably the better team; they just didn't take their chances. With twenty minutes to go, we were six points behind and hadn't raised a single flag in the second half. Clare had scored points and were rampant. Brian Lohan was giving one of his greatest-ever displays at full-back and was "cleaning" me. Clare's Tony Carmody was on fire and causing us untold damage in the centre half-forward position.

'Something had to be done. John Allen courageously took off myself and Ronan Curran, two All Stars the previous year, and sent on Wayne Sherlock and Neil Ronan. Wayne went to wing-back and John Gardiner moved to the centre. Neither Carmody nor Lohan exercised the same dominance again. Neil scored a crucial point.

'John Allen rightly said afterwards, "We had to make the call. We would have been lacerated if we hadn't. We were five points down and the game was slipping from us. We have 29 people on our panel. I mean, it was a case of what do we do here? Do we throw in the towel or do we try and stem the tide?" We scored seven of the game's closing nine points to sneak a one-point win, and then won the All-Ireland against Galway with more comfort.'

WATERFORD'S WINNING STREAK

Cork's supremacy in Munster in the noughties was threatened with the re-emergence of Waterford as a major power. Yet the Liam McCarthy Cup would prove elusive. Babs Keating has a firm view on the reasons for Waterford's failure to go all the way.

'I would say the Waterford team of recent years was very unlucky. Waterford had three massive players: Tony Browne, Ken McGrath and Paul Flynn. On the crucial days, they never got the three of them to play well on the one day. If you take 2004, Paul Flynn got 13 points in the All-Ireland semi-final against Kilkenny. If he had got any help at all, they would have won, but neither Browne nor McGrath backed him up properly. Ken McGrath let them down badly against Cork in '06 in my opinion. That was the team's undoing. They were so dependent on those three. They were like the Waterford team of the late '50s and early '60s. They were just short of two or three players.'

Although best known as a twice world cross-country champion and for his silver medal in the marathon at the 1984 Olympics, Waterford's John Treacy was inculcated into the culture of the games at an early age.

'Growing up in Villerstown, we played football and hurling on the Commons. I went to many a club match where there was skin and hair flying. A number of the games never finished!'

How does he react to the view that Waterford's attempt at the start of 2008 to physically intimidate Kilkenny belonged to an earlier era? And does he think that the game has moved on since then?

'One of the greatest lessons I learned in sport is never piss off your opponents. I remember when I was in my prime in Providence College, myself and Gerry Deegan were running against a guy from Holy Cross College in Massachusetts. We put on a bit of a spurt at one stage, but the guy stayed with us and said in a very arrogant way: "You're not going to drop me that easily." We didn't like the way he said that, so we dropped him by half a mile in the space of a mile!

'Waterford hadn't learned that lesson going in to that final. You never piss off Kilkenny. The only chance you have is to cosy up to them and tell them that you are delighted to be in their company. It was incredible to watch the game to see how much it has changed from my youth because there is so much speed and skill. I think of Henry Shefflin scoring with consummate ease from an almost impossible angle. Nothing adorns the game like a player of his skill, just like the way players like Brian Mullins and Jack O'Shea lit up Gaelic games in the 1970s and '80s. In a different way, D.J. Carey had lit up the game with his speed and artistry. I marvelled at him because he was fantastic. What really stood out for me attending the 2008 All-Ireland final was Kilkenny's half-back line. They were awesome. Nothing but nothing could get past them. I think of Brian Cody as the Alex Ferguson of Irish sport. He is an incredible manager. He sets the bar very high, and demands and gets the highest standards from his players. If you don't reach them, you have no future as a Kilkenny hurler, no matter how much skill you have. He knows everything about every promising player in every corner of the county. He is always looking for ways to improve the team. He leaves nothing to chance, and everything about his preparations is always well thought through.'

Treacy had something of an insider's view on the fortunes of the hurling team.

'I really admire many of the players, like Tony Browne, Paul Flynn, Dan Shanahan and John Mullane. Justin McCarthy called me a number of times when he was coach and brought me down to speak to the team. He got Seán Kelly in as well. Justin did a lot for Waterford hurling, and let's just say the manner in which he was forced to leave the job left a lot to be desired. When I spoke to the team, I tried to instil in them something of the culture of discipline, sacrifice and wanting to win more than anybody else that is essential to success in athletics and, indeed, all sports.

'The only GAA player I have seen to bring the culture of an individual sport to a team sport like hurling or Gaelic football was Kieran McGeeney. As he worked with us for a while in the Sports Council, I had the opportunity to see him at close quarters. I would compare his mindset as similar to my own because of his discipline, focus and self-sacrifice. I saw how hard he worked. He brought it to another level and left no stone unturned and brought the culture of individual sports to the GAA. You didn't see him downing pints. What he also brought to football was leadership. You knew he would be a manager's dream. If I was ever in charge of a team, the two people I would want playing for me would be Kieran and Roy Keane. I met Roy once before a match at Lansdowne Road. I went over to him and introduced myself. He said he knew who I was, and immediately he wanted to know about the way I trained because he was looking for anything that might give him a little further edge. That's the kind of focus you need to reach the top. You also need a team effort, and the best example of this in recent times for me in Gaelic football was Tyrone's performance against Kerry in 2008. They kept coming back, and the way they fought for each other was something to behold.'

KING HENRY

Henry Shefflin has taken over from D.J. Carey as the undisputed king of hurling, as Babs Keating acknowledges.

'When you talk about the complete player, you have to talk about them in relation to the position they play in. You are talking today about Mick Kavanagh, Noel Hickey and Tommy Walsh – apart from the odd mistake, which he is cutting down on. J.J. Delaney is the complete left-back. You can't compare Henry Shefflin with D.J. Carey because they played in different positions, though you could have played D.J. full-forward, depending on who was full-back. D.J. went through an All-Ireland final without scoring, but I don't think Shefflin would do that. The scores that D.J. got were spectacular. I don't want to make comparisons. Henry Shefflin is perfect.'

In 1997, Shefflin had tasted defeat in a minor All-Ireland final to Clare. His memories of that game are still vivid.

'A few of us didn't perform that day. I hit a few frees and missed a good few of them. There was a breeze blowing in the second half and I went out to hit a few 65s, right into the Clare crowd. All I could see were these lads waving behind the goal – the Clare hurlers as well as umpires. It was a tough and lonely place. When you're a minor, you'll always remember those kinds of days, you'll take it to heart. You heap some of the blame on yourself when you're hitting the frees. It was a day I wouldn't like to go back to again.'

He lost his first senior All-Ireland title in 1999, when hot favourites Kilkenny lost to Cork. He is still pained by the memory.

'They came back, and to see point after point flowing from Cork was a sickening thing. I know Seánie McGrath got a few points, but I just remember it slipping from us. It just went. I remember standing in the rain, listening to "The Banks of the Lee" roaring out over the speakers. You're there on your own and you have your thoughts. You could have done this; you could have done that. To think you have it, and then it's just snatched from you.

'We were kind of in shock. I remember walking out of Croke Park and there were still Kilkenny people around, coming over congratulating us, saying "well done" and all this. It just rubbed it in more. To think you have to go home and face these people the following night. They come out clapping you, and you're after losing an All-Ireland. It's gut-wrenching. I took it badly. It upset me a lot.'

In 2000, he won his first senior All-Ireland against Offaly. The next year, though, Shefflin was to experience the bitter taste of defeat again when Kilkenny were sensationally beaten by Galway in the All-Ireland semi-final.

'After winning the All-Ireland in 2000, there was great hype about us. We thought we were great lads, and a small bit of that seeped through to our hurling. We probably didn't think we'd have to put in the hard work and we definitely didn't put in the hard work. Training was very poor, and you could feel in training that it wasn't going well.

'It was a turning point for some of us, that we had to cop on. It was a wake-up call. I didn't hurl well all year. I think I was a small bit gone away from the game concentrating on maybe other things, certainly not focused on the game and the things you have to do. And doing the simple things instead of doing the great things.

'Against Galway, we were horsed out of it, simple as that. We weren't hungry enough. We weren't able for the physical battle. Hopefully, it was a turning point for myself. I went looking for protection that day: I went on to the referee and the umpire and the linesman. You don't do that. Hurling is a man's game. Rather than look for protection, you have to drive out and try to win the next ball and horse on.'

Later that summer, Shefflin and two friends went to New York. He played a match on the Sunday. Two days later, the twin towers of the World Trade Center were attacked.

'I don't know how many blocks we were from it, but it was a crazy feeling. Unbelievable. Unbelievable. We didn't know what had hit us. Three Irish lads over in the fastest city in the world. We didn't even have any experience of going to New York. We ended up staying for about a week. Couldn't get out of there. We walked down to Times Square and we were looking at the big screen. It was only that night that we sat down and watched telly for days, the same as everyone else did.

'We rang home and our parents were saying, "Are ye all right, are ye all right?"

'"Ah, we're grand."'

Despite his status within the game, Henry has not had his head turned by success. He refuses to take the credit for Kilkenny's great performances in recent times.

'We never depend on one or two individuals to produce the goods. If I am having an off-day, the likes of Eddie Brennan can produce a big performance. We are very much a team. Brian Cody does not want to see anyone come off the field happy after a defeat. There was no point in saying I played well, but the others let me down. We won as a team and we lost as a team. We used defeats to motivate us to achieve even more success.'

Henry is keen to pay tribute to his coach with Kilkenny, Brian Cody.

'It is vital to a team to have a coach who thinks about the game, especially ways to improve it, and to have a manager who can read a game and can keep his composure and turn things around when things are going badly. Brian gives inspired leadership.'

Shefflin's high opinion of Cody is shared by Nicky English.

'I don't believe in the cult of a manager. The way I see it is, a bad manager will stop you from winning an All-Ireland, but a decent manager will win the All-Ireland for you if he has the players, and that's the key. It is players who win the All-Ireland, not managers. The one exception I would make is that I rate Brian Cody very highly. He has achieved so much over such a long period, but above all he has changed the tradition of Kilkenny hurling. He has brought in a new system and a way of playing that has become part of the hurling culture now in Kilkenny.'

Nickey Brennan joins the chorus of approval for Cody.

'The whole science of training has developed a lot and managers today have a lot more support staff, from physios to dieticians to people who look after the stats and all kinds of medical people. Kevin Fennelly succeeded me as Kilkenny boss; he had a relatively short term and then Brian Cody took over. The funny thing about Cody is that he didn't have a very impressive record in club management when he took the job, but the one thing he brought to the job was a fierce passion for hurling, and he was a great thinker of the game. It maybe took him a while to fully get his feet into the management game, which is understandable, but he's a quick learner. The style of Kilkenny play has definitely changed under his management. He is fortunate in that he inherited a great assembly line of talent, and for that, great credit must be given to people down the line in Kilkenny – and I know that Brian would be the first to acknowledge that. While he has honed their skills, the Kilkenny player of today tends to be a strong, physical player, and even those who may be small of stature, in a few cases, tend to be well able to handle themselves physically on the field. The type of play brings a strong physical dimension to the game, and it must be said that they have an exceptional level of skill. Some teams have opted for a very physical approach in the past, but they don't have the skill levels. Kilkenny bring both elements to the table. Cody also has a great capacity to get players to take personal responsibility for their part of the pitch, but equally to group together and fight the cause as a team. If you're an attacker, you have to take on responsibility as a defender to stop your opponent from clearing the ball under the defensive system he has brought in and vice versa. He has made very good hurlers into extraordinarily good hurlers. He's got people to believe in a system. They are single-minded when they play for Kilkenny. Nothing fazes them. Nothing gets in their way. They are not distracted by what they might gain out of the game. They are, of course, very well looked after by the Kilkenny County Board, but they are not allowed to have anything else interfere with their play. I think apart from the skills and the tactics, that attitude is as important to Cody's success. If any other football or hurling county was to take anything out of the Cody era, it would be to adhere to the coach's code without any question because that's why ultimately other counties fail. OK, many of them may not have the same skill levels, but if you have the single-mindness and camaraderie that Cody has instilled, then you are on the road to success. That philosophy has made Kilkenny the success it is today.

'As a player, I was going for the three-in-a-row in 1984; as a selector I was going for the three-in-a-row in 1994; but we failed both times. As president, I presented the cup in '06 and '07: you can imagine how nervous I was in '08 that I would put the hex on Kilkenny's three-in-a-row! Thankfully, I didn't deprive Brian Cody of his glory!'

THE RETURN OF BABS

While Kilkenny brought hurling to another level in the noughties, many managers perished in other counties as they failed to reach the same dizzy heights. Among the casualties was Babs Keating in his second incarnation as Tipperary manager.

'The first time I was Tipp manager, I never heard of any player having any grievance. It was a huge culture shock for me when I went back the second time to see the lack of commitment I was getting from some of the players wearing the Tipperary jersey. I was also shocked that the advice I was giving to the Tipperary players who were supposed to be well educated went in one ear and out the other. I saw myself as a counsellor because these players were the same age as my own son, and I wanted to treat them the way I would treat my own son. My basic job, as I saw it, was to serve the people who were paying their money to travel around the country to support the team because these are the people who make the GAA and fill Croke Park. I always recalled my father, a small farmer, taking us in his van to matches on a Sunday when there was very little money around.

'I couldn't get the message through to the current Tipperary team. I know Brian Cody can get the message through to the Kilkenny team. In '08, we saw that Justin McCarthy wasn't the problem in Waterford, nor was John Meyler the problem in Wexford. Likewise, Gerald McCarthy was not the problem in Cork. The problems are more with the present generation, who have an exaggerated opinion of their own importance. I think it would have been better if the likes of Dónal Óg Cusack, Seán Óg Ó hAilpín, Ronan Curran or Eoin Kelly had the approach of J.J. Delaney, Tommy Walsh and Henry Shefflin, or Mick Harte's Tyrone, because they are focused. I think it's time many of our players stopped looking for what others can do for them and started asking what they could do for the game.

'The basic thing was that when I went in the first time, a fella like Nicky English was an established top performer. I basically had very little advice for Nicky, but I had plenty of advice for the fellas around him so that I could make Nicky a better player. The discipline we had in the '60s was that nobody struck a ball without a reason for it. That message was driven into us in training. If a player ever came to me and asked me for advice about how to play the game and I couldn't give him an answer, I would consider that I've failed him as a coach. My discipline was still the same when I went back a second time, but there was too much carelessness and too much of an "it will be all right on the night" kind of attitude. It was a huge attitude problem, and unfortunately for us, we had too many with that attitude problem.'

There were two major controversies in '07. The first was the failure to start star forward Eoin Kelly in big matches.

'We took it easy with Eoin preparing him for the championship in '07 and wanted him to have a gradual build-up. Towards the end of March that year, the three of us on the management team made the decision that Eoin Kelly was probably one of the most skilful players in the game, but in the present game skill wasn't sufficient, so we called him in and sat him down and he agreed with us. We made a different decision in relation to Eoin from the rest of the team. We decided we didn't want him to come into training with the rest of the team; what we wanted him to do was to get out of his bed each morning and run six miles and return to training with about two weeks to go before the Limerick game, when he felt he was ready to come in. He rang me earlier than that to say he was ready to return. I replied: "No. Keep doing what you're doing – if you are doing it."

'He said: "Why do you say that?"

'I responded: "I've good reason to believe, Eoin, that you are playing games with us."

'I had been sickened about what I heard about his lack of application when he was supposed to be preparing for playing for Tipperary in the championship. Basically, we never had him fit. We had a running exercise in training. The fastest did it in ten minutes. Eoin Kelly was up to two minutes behind the fastest. He hasn't improved in that respect since my departure.

'We put him in for 54 minutes against Wexford, and the records will show it was a mistake to put him in. There were a few specific things that I asked him to do that he didn't, but I'm not going to hang him on them in public. I did say to him: "I've seen several guys like you down the years, and, Eoin, hurling will pass you by." He has abused a great talent in my opinion. He didn't get an All-Star in '08. Unless he comes to his senses, he will never fulfil his potential and his career will be shorter than it should be. He's not the only one with an attitude problem. I could name the hurlers Tipperary will never win an All-Ireland with.'

THE BRENDAN VOYAGE

The second controversy facing Babs in 2007 arose with the sensational decision to drop star goalkeeper Brendan Cummins.

'This was a very difficult decision for me as we come from the same parish. We couldn't get him to direct the puck out the way we wanted him to do. We tried everything. I mean everything. The day against Limerick was the final nail in the coffin before we dropped him. I told him at half-time: "Brendan, this is serious. You have to come on board with us." After a time, maybe ten minutes, he pucked a ball out where he was told not to puck it out. I sent John Leahy up to the goal because John was our "runner", and I said: "John, tell him: do what you are told." John was walking back, and Brendan had a puck out and he did it even worse. He pucked out over the sideline, the side he was told not to go to. John was about 50 yards from me when I roared at him: "Did you tell him at all?" He said: "I told him. Tell him yourself, but I won't be telling him again." The third member of our management team is Tom Barry. He is "Mr Perfect". He is the nicest man you could ever meet. Tom said, "We have to do something. We can't keep taking this." That's why Brendan Cummins lost his place. In training, there was no competition. If we had to pick a team based on training, Gerry Kennedy was far superior.

'It hasn't got any of the press attention that the Cork situation has, but there's a clique of players who ended Michael Doyle's reign, who ended Ken Hogan's reign, and who essentially ended my reign.

'Looking back on my two years with Tipperary, there's no decision I made that I wouldn't make again. I knew the knives were out. The county board took the easy option. They did what the Wexford and Waterford county boards did in '08 and didn't stand up to the players.

THE GAA

'When I was interviewed for the Offaly job, 90 per cent of the interview was devoted to discipline. I had a similar interview for the Tipperary job. The people who interviewed me didn't stand behind me. If Tipperary are to be successful in the future, they've got to go back to the old values, which are Brian Cody's values.

'I was having sleepless nights. I developed a rash all over my chest and stomach and had to get medical care for it. My whole nervous system was suffering. I am not sure I could have survived it for much longer. I've never given a county board the opportunity to sack me so I stepped down. I was so disillusioned with what went on that I basically put hurling out of my head.'

14

WHERE DO WE GO FROM HERE?

IF YOU PRAISE THE SUNSHINE IN SOME PARTS OF IRELAND, YOU'LL be told 'it'll never last'. Yet, despite the cold chill of economic recession, there is ample reason for optimism about the ongoing health of the GAA. As chief executive of the Irish Sports Council, John Treacy is ideally equipped to offer a dispassionate appraisal of the role of the GAA in Irish life.

'I think there's a danger that we take Gaelic games for granted. A number of years ago, we hosted a gathering for all the top sports officials in the EU. We showed them a hurling match and they were watching it with their mouths open. They couldn't believe that amateur players could produce a game of such skill and speed. All through the day, they kept asking about it.

'The GAA showed real leadership in revoking Rule 42 and opening up Croke Park to rugby and soccer. Nobody will ever forget the atmosphere and the sense of history in 2007 when Ireland beat England in Croke Park. It was a defining moment for many people, and it meant so much to everybody in the country.

THE GAA

'For an amateur organisation, it is a staggering achievement to have created an incredible stadium like Croke Park, especially in the middle of Dublin. It has shown incredible leadership. The GAA has adapted to the changing times. It is keenly aware of the need to bring modern marketing methods into Gaelic games. I think a critical step came in the 1990s with the decision to introduce live coverage of a large number of games on the TV. Young people get their heroes from television. If you go down to Kilkenny, you will see almost every young boy with a hurley because they want to be like their heroes. In recent times, you can see some young lads with hurleys walking on the streets of Dublin. You would hardly ever have seen that 20 years ago. That has not happened by accident and shows the forward-thinking approach the GAA has taken.

'It has shown great creativity in the way it has managed to defy the tide and ensure that so many people continue to volunteer. The Economic and Social Research Institute produced a report on the social capital aspect of sport, and it is basically 90 pages of a glowing tribute to the GAA and the way it has harnessed the voluntary capacity. Instead of saying to people, as in the past, give us all your time, the GAA now says, give us two evenings and a Saturday morning to train a juvenile team or whatever. We can't put a price on the kind of social value the organisation brings.

'To me, the question is: "Where would Ireland be without the GAA?" My wife's family is from Monaghan and it dominates all aspects of life in a place like that. Every Sunday and Monday morning, throughout the summer especially, the topic of conversation is the GAA. It just pervades Irish life. Ireland owes the GAA a great debt of gratitude.'

SHE WAS LOVELY AND FAIR LIKE THE ROSE OF THE SUMMER

A major boost for the GAA is its increasing appeal for women. Ireland's fastest-growing sport is ladies' football. One of ladies' football's biggest champions is the 2008 Rose of Tralee, Tipperary's Aoife Kelly. Aoife has made her own mark in the game.

'I went to San Francisco for a summer. I discovered there was a clique of Irish people there, and decided that sport was a good way of meeting some of them. I wasn't sure which sport to choose, but I met a girl who persuaded me to play Gaelic football. I had never taken a football in my hand in my life. I decided I would try it for the craic, and joined the Clan na Gael club there. I had the best time. We lost the All-American final in Boston in 2004. When I went back to university in Scotland, I decided to get involved playing Gaelic football there and we won the five-a-side championships. In the five-a-sides I played midfield, but otherwise I played wing-forward. My problem is that I have weak ankles – which become a serious problem when the opposition get to know about it! I definitely want to go back to it. I have a good friend, Fiona May, who plays for Sligo, and she is kind of my idol because she is so fanatical and so dedicated. When I came back to Ireland to work in Dublin in the National Rehab Hospital as an occupational therapist, I had planned to get involved in a club, but then the Rose of Tralee intervened.

'During the Rose of Tralee competition, we were brought up to see the ladies' football final in Croke Park. We had the best time. My fiancé Leon, who is from South Africa, had seen many hurling games, but had never seen a Gaelic football match before, and he thought it was wonderful.

'The great thing about playing I found is that it is great for character building – because you have to learn to win and lose. It's not just about the winning. It's about the experience. I am obviously Tipperary biased and I think Eoin Kelly is unbelievably skilful, but I don't like singling out individuals because Gaelic games are team-based and it is teams who win and lose matches, and being part of a team appeals to me. There's also a great community involvement behind it. I think the GAA is so important when you are away from home. I have lived in San Francisco, and the one time the community gathers, whether it's three or five in the morning because of the time difference, is to watch a match. It is then you really see how important the GAA is for our identity of being Irish. It brings people together.

'In my travels, I have never met anybody who doesn't love the Irish, and the one thing I would like to see happening is for the GAA to reach out more to other nationalities. In terms of ladies' football, the one thing I would like to see is a greater emphasis on it in the schools. In the school I went to, the emphasis was on basketball and we had zero exposure to ladies' football in either primary or secondary school. I don't think women get the same recognition as the men. I think people think men are tougher, but I think women withstand a belt from an opponent much better, whereas men will fall down and look for a free! Women have a higher pain threshold, which is reflected on the field. So I would like to see more media exposure for ladies' football and camogie.'

MAGIC MOMENTS

It is often said, usually by Tipperary people, that Tipperary is the home of hurling. On the basis of recent All-Ireland titles, it is much easier to claim that it is now the home of camogie. One of the stars of their multi-All-Ireland-winning team was centre half-back Ciara Gaynor. For Ciara, the fascination with camogie arrived like talking, too early to remember.

'I can't recall when I actually started playing camogie. Back home, my sisters and I would be playing around the yard. My interest developed further when I got to primary school. Our principal, Albert Williams, won an All-Ireland club hurling medal in 1986 and he was a big influence. I went to St Mary's secondary school in Nenagh. We had great success winning junior and senior All-Irelands.'

No camogie player of the present day has more right to distorting vanities but has never showed less trace of them than Ciara Gaynor. Being cursed by neither arrogance nor pride, she is selfless in pursuit of the remedy and never above seeking advice. From the outset, though, there was one voice whose whisper was worth more than the shouts of most other critics. No one is more attuned to the nuances of the game than her father, Len Gaynor. He won three All-Ireland senior hurling medals, trained both the Clare and Tipperary senior teams and took Tipp to the All-Ireland senior final in 1997.

'When I was young, Dad was still playing at interfirms level. When he got into management, with Clare and Tipperary, we'd all head off with him when he was going to training or to matches. As a result, hurling was always talked about back home, and I suppose that was part of the reason why I became so passionate about camogie.'

There is one jewel of memory from the sport's greatest theatre that outshines all others for Ciara. She launches into nostalgia about a victory that has left bubbles of pleasure that will never disappear.

'The highlight of my career was winning my first All-Ireland in Croke Park. The buzz was great in winning each of the All-Irelands, but the first one was really special.

'I suppose it was all a bit of a fairy tale, really. We had only been playing at senior level for four years and we'd won three All-Irelands. The team had been building for many years. A lot of us played together at minor and junior level in the '90s. The junior team won an All-Ireland in '92. The talent was there, and it was just a question of getting the blend right. Then Michael Cleary, who had been a great hurler with Tipperary, got involved in training us, and he was the biggest influence of all. He put the emphasis on the skills.'

In autumn 2001, a major controversy developed when it emerged that a huge sum of money had been provided to enable the Tipperary hurlers and their partners to take a two-week holiday in South Africa. Meanwhile, the camogie players were not getting any tangible reward, even though they had just won a historic three-in-a-row. Is Ciara annoyed by the obvious inequality?

'It doesn't bother me at all. I was at the hurling All-Ireland like all the Tipperary camogie players, and we were delighted to see the hurlers win. I think it's great that they went to South Africa and that their wives and girlfriends went with them, because they made a lot of sacrifices too. After our second All-Ireland, we got a week's holiday in Lanzarote. It was great, but in all honesty I'd prefer if we got the basic things like a cup of tea and a sandwich after training and proper travelling expenses for training and matches rather than a holiday.

'I think the biggest compliment we got is that in Tipperary now camogie is very strong with young girls, and a lot of them are now swinging hurleys for the first time. We know that whatever happens to the team, the future of camogie in the county is secure.'

THE GAA

The president of the Camogie Association, Miriam O'Callaghan, described Máirín McAleenan as 'one of the finest ambassadors that the game has ever had'. Máirín's immersion into the game began at an early age.

'My earliest memory of camogie is torturing my brother, John, to make me a stick, so that I too could join in the bone-crushing, shin-bruising five-a-side matches that my eight brothers and sister, Brid, engaged in religiously every evening in life on our front street. Having just turned five, I had come of age, you see, and although my brother Ciaran was but a *tachrán* of three years, he got the same call-up on the very same evening. I consoled myself with the fact that it was only to make up the numbers. I was duly measured up, and such important details as the distance from the ground to my hinch-bone were noted. After what seemed like a lifetime, I was finally presented with a rectangular plank of wood, about a foot and a half in length, which narrowed abruptly at one end – this, I was told, was the handle. Splinters in both hands were testament to the countless hours of practice after school and long into the darkness.

'From these family battles, I progressed to striking stray balls to the hurlers at their training sessions. At around eight years of age, I started formal training sessions with Liatroim Fontenoys. Since then, I have been very honoured and very "Proud to be a Liatroim Fontenoy . . ."'

Although Máirín has won a proliferation of honours, she is particularly concerned that the future generation of camogie players be adequately nurtured.

'I would envisage 15-a-side camogie as a well-marketed sport gaining in spectator popularity, regularly played in conjunction with major GAA games, resulting in a heightening of its profile. I would expect the Association to be moving towards the purchase of its own central ground in each county. The appointment of full-time camogie coaches at school level in all counties is also important, as is the organisation of Comórtas na nGaelscoileanna, which would grow in concurrence with An Ghaeilge at primary-school level. It would also be pleasing to see camogie being played widely enough at school and underage level.'

STICK WORK

Hurling is woven into Irish history. The roar of the crowds, the whirr of the flying sliotar and the unmistakable and unique sound of ash against ash have enthralled sports fans for decades. However, in recent years, hurling has spawned a fast-growing game in the world of disabled sports: wheelchair hurling. The man behind this new game is Tim Maher.

'As principal of the school attached to St Mary's Hospital in Baldoyle, I have introduced wheelchair hurling as part of the PE programme here for the past few years. I got the idea when I saw the students playing a lot of games with a ball and rackets. I decided it would be worth experimenting to see what would happen if we substituted hurleys for rackets. When I first suggested the idea, a number of people thought I was going a bit soft in the head, but I was determined to give it a go. Obviously, I was keen to modify the game slightly so that there was no safety risk to the students.

'The game took off and is going from strength to strength. We started it off just in the school here, but then the idea spread and we started interschool competitions. We held a blitz that featured six schools: Ballinteer Community School; ourselves; CRC Clontarf; Enable Ireland, Sandymount; Marino School, Bray and Scoil Mochua, Clondalkin. Both boys and girls play the game as equals.

'I think D.J. Carey himself would be impressed by the skills evident in this game. It is also noticeable that it is great for developing the students' co-ordination.

'There are so many benefits to the game. The most obvious one is that the pupils get great fun and enjoyment out of it. They also learn a lot about teamwork. Now that there is a competitive outlet to the game, they also learn about winning and, equally importantly, about losing.

'I am a great evangelist for the game and see an immense future for it. I think it has great potential. Although the game is only in its early stages, I have a dream. I would love to see it taking off in the international arena. Why not?'

THE GAA

Many concerned voices, though, are raised about the future of Ireland's national treasure. One of them is Babs Keating.

'I think there can be too much talk of tradition because both Offaly and Galway have proved that it is not essential for success. When I drive to Kilkenny and see hurlers everywhere, I refuse to believe that when I travel a few miles up the road in Carlow there are no hurlers. I just believe it is a question of working hard. I once was at a coaching conference, and one of the speakers was the late Irish rugby coach Mick Doyle. He said: "I'm here to contradict the old cliché that practice makes perfect – but I will say that perfect practice makes perfect." I don't think people are really serious about hurling in most counties. I'm worried about how the game will be in 25 years' time. Galway last won an All-Ireland in 1988, Offaly in '98; whether it was a freak or not, they haven't threatened anybody since at senior or minor level. Laois, I know and respect more than a lot of counties because I think there are great hurling people in Laois, but I don't think they are getting enough help.

'Kilkenny have set the standards. Cork did set standards, but not since they won their All-Irelands. A big worry in Cork for me is that when I went to see their minor and under-21 teams last year, the Cork city clubs were not represented. In the same way, I worry about Limerick. City clubs are not really represented. In the old days, these were the backbone of Limerick hurling.

'We hear words but not enough action. There's too much lip-service and not enough effort. I'm not sure that we should be depending on the private sector to guarantee there's a hurley in every young fella's hand. I would have thought we should have our own factory that produces its own hurleys, which go into every child's hand for the good of the game. I don't think it's on any more that we have a situation in which we are depending on people in the Far East to make hurley balls for us.'

Nickey Brennan is more optimistic.

'We are waiting for a new county to come on the scene. Maybe that could be Waterford. If Waterford were to win an All-Ireland, there is no doubt that would lift hurling in the same way Clare's victory did in

1995. We need a new county to come out and give new life to hurling again. Hopefully it will happen sooner rather than later.'

Whatever his worries for the Wexford team in the immediate term, Martin Quigley is more perturbed about the future impact of major sociological changes in Ireland on the structure of the club.

'In rural places especially, I've seen big changes insofar as the traditional loyalty to the club is weakening. There's a lot more young fellas going to third-level education now, and they are emigrating for the summer and playing hurling in America or somewhere and not in their local club. There's a lot more mobility now in the workplace, and guys are moving around from place to place, but are generally not willing to travel back to their parish for training every evening so they are switching to clubs in Dublin or wherever. In the club-versus-county stakes, the county is winning. Each of these changes on its own is not that significant, but when you add them altogether they become very significant, and they are decimating some of the clubs, especially in the rural areas. I have to say, I'm very worried the old-style club may be in danger.'

PRIDE OF THE PARISH

Joe Brolly's assessment of the future of the club is more upbeat.

'In the mid- to late '90s, my concentration became focused on Dungiven. It is very hard when your dream in a county like Derry is to win an All-Ireland and you actually do not just simply think, "Well, it's done." I don't subscribe to the view that you have to win two All-Irelands to be a great team. I don't even know what that means. As you get older, you start to appreciate the real power of the GAA: the sense of togetherness and community and the importance of the club. In '97, Dungiven won the Derry Championship for the first time in six years, which was a long time for that team. We trounced Peter Canavan's Errigal Ciarán in the Ulster final – the Tyrone dogs they are! It was like waking from a dream and realising it was real. The downside was that I got injured late in the game and was not really fit for the All-Ireland semi-final. We had a man sent off early in the game, which we lost by a point. It was a crushing disappointment.

THE GAA

'I gave up playing with Dungiven when I was 36 because it was a 130-mile round trip, and I transferred to St Brigid's in Belfast. I've got five kids so that eats into your time. It has given me a new lease of life. The club is based on the Malone Road. Bob McCartney, the controversial Unionist politician, made a great comment on the changing demographic about the Malone Road (which used to be home to the Protestant aristocracy but now belongs to the Catholic nouveau riche). He said: '*Tiocfaidh ar lá* has given way to *Tiocfaidh our la-di-da!*' I am heavily involved in underage training in the club, and you see all the Bentleys in the car park. We are now in the first division, but I started playing in the fourth division. It was hairy enough there, particularly as you get punched in the back of the head as you are hearing: "I'll give you a f***ing All-Star."'

Peter Woods captures the power of the club and parish with typical economy: 'The parish is not just the DNA. It is the DNA.'

WHAT'S THE NAME OF THE GAME?

Joe Brolly is one of the few players who turned down the opportunity to get involved in the International Rules Series: 'I was asked about it a few times and I couldn't run away from it fast enough. I'm too much of a coward!'

International Rules football, sometimes called 'Compromise Rules', is a hybrid code of football that was developed to facilitate international representative matches between Australian Rules footballers and Gaelic footballers.

The first games played were test matches between Australia and a touring Meath Gaelic football team that took place in late 1967, after Meath had won that year's All-Ireland Senior Football Championship. Following intermittent international tests between Australia and an All-Ireland team, which began in the Centenary year of the GAA in 1984, the International Rules Series really entered the popular consciousness in 1986 following a major controversy. One of the Irish players on that tour was Pat Spillane. What are his memories of that tour?

'There was hullabaloo before we went to Australia when the Dublin coach, Kevin Heffernan, was appointed as tour manager ahead of

Mick O'Dwyer. Micko is the most successful Gaelic football coach of all time and he has never managed the International Rules team, which is extraordinary.

'However, what really made the tour come alive was when the manager of the Australian team, John Todd, described the touring side as "wimps" following complaints about the "excessively robust play" of the Australian players. His remarks provoked a storm of outrage not just among the Irish team but back at home in Ireland, too. It was a huge story throughout the country. It wasn't quite as big as Roy Keane and Mick McCarthy in Saipan, but it was pretty close. Todd's comments were taken as a slur on the Irish character, and as a result, people who had no interest in the game back home in Ireland became fascinated by the series. It became a matter of national pride for us to beat the Aussies. Thankfully, the fighting Irish provided the most effective rebuttal possible to Todd's comments when we won the series.

'Although people talk a lot about violence on the pitch, a lot of people love watching the games because of the physical contact. Yet the controversies the violence generated brought the games to everyone's attention, and I guarantee you that when there is massive interest in the series, it is because people are wondering if there will be more violence.

'From my point of view, it was a tremendous honour to be invited to play for my country and I was delighted with the chance to be part of the experiment to give an international outlet to Gaelic football. Of course, it did come as a shock when you were on the ball that an Aussie player could come up and knock you to the ground by any means necessary and keep you pinned down. I do think we could learn from them. There is a very high emphasis on the basic skills, but as Kerry showed in 2004 in their defeat of Armagh, there is still a major place for "catch and kick" in Gaelic football.

'It is great for players from so-called "weaker counties" in particular to get the chance to play alongside the cream of the GAA talent and to get a chance to showcase their talents to the nation. Take a player like Westmeath's Spike Fagan, who could really show the country how good a player he was on live television when he played for Ireland.

THE GAA

'I wonder, though, is it possible to play a Compromise game between the two codes. For example, I think asking the Australians to play a game without a tackle is like asking the Irish soccer team to play a game without heading. I sometimes wonder if it would be better if we went out there to take them on at their game and they came to play us at ours.'

Paul Earley, who spent two years playing Australian Rules football, is ideally placed to comment on the future of the series.

'I went on a sporting scholarship to Melbourne, Australia, in 1982 as an 18 year old, having played championship football for Roscommon earlier that year. Effectively, I was a semi-professional – training and studying accountancy in college at the same time. Everything was much better organised over there, and facilities are so much better too. There is a very high emphasis on the basic skills on both sides of the body because they believe that you shouldn't make elementary mistakes in a match. Here, elementary mistakes are made in every match. If you were to introduce back-to-basics training sessions with senior teams in Ireland, you would be laughed at. When I came home, I was a lot stronger because of the emphasis on weight training. My catching had improved. I was more athletic and had more endurance. The only skill I hadn't developed was my kicking because I had been using an oval ball. To my mind, Anthony Tohill was the key player in Derry's success in the 1990s because of his skill and power. I suspect that he benefited enormously from his time in Australia.'

IT'S ONLY WORDS?

While the aggression of the International Rules Series has always been an integral part of Gaelic games, former Wexford manager Liam Griffin is more concerned about a more recent development in Gaelic games that is arguably more invidious.

'A lot of fellas have started to try and wind up opponents during the match, especially if they think they can be riled up. I think that has crept into the game in recent years. People see incidents that shouldn't happen in football, like Paul Galvin knocking the notebook out of the referee's hand in the 2008 Munster Championship against Clare.

Of course, he shouldn't have done it, but people often don't realise the verbal provocation, not to mind the physical, that a player may endure. The other thing that I don't like is players diving. Think of the way Aidan O'Mahony went down after he got a little slap in the 2008 All-Ireland semi-final against Cork. That is not the Kerry way. These are two things we don't want in our games, and I would like to see them addressed. I think Gaelic games are one of the few places left where the Corinthian spirit survives, where fellas are playing for the love of the game. Sledging or trying to get a fellow player sent off are not parts of our wonderful tradition, and we must ensure that they are not allowed to bring discredit to our games. Players are role models. What they do, young kids imitate – the good and the bad. Coaches have a big role to play in this. I always believe it's no good just mentioning things to players. You have to repeat things to them. I believe in the power of twice.'

Enda McNulty is less concerned.

'My most direct experience of sledging was in a Dublin Championship match. I got a barrage of verbal abuse from my opponent. It was so bad I wouldn't even repeat it to my closest friend. Playing county football, I've never really had sledging. You do get a bit of it in club football in Dublin. You can be called "Nordy bastard" or "Queen-loving f***er". Sledging is part of the game, but any coach who encourages sledging has their focus in the wrong place. Their time should be spent developing the technical and tactical capacities of the players rather than focusing on something negative.'

Pat Spillane, though, is not happy with all the new coaching ideas.

'I am still not convinced by all these new methods teams are going in for today. To take one example, it is now accepted orthodoxy in the GAA world that the night before big games, teams use a "buddy system" in the hotel: in other words, a senior player rooms with one of the more junior players on the panel. The idea is that the senior player helps the younger man to settle and handle his nerves better. I do not go along with that at all. I think you should room with the player you want to room with rather than finding yourself rooming with someone you have nothing in common with. In 1991, the night before the All-Ireland semi-final I found myself rooming with a young sub on the

Kerry team. I always liked to relax the night before a match by staying up late and watching television. My roommate, though, wanted to go to bed early, and I felt obliged to do so also for his sake. The problem was that because I was deviating from my normal routine, I could not sleep at all, and therefore it was very hard to be at my best playing a huge match the next day.'

IT SAYS IN THE PAPERS

Every rose has its thorns. One of the downsides of the higher profile of players has been the increased interest in their private lives, with a consequent increase in rumours and malicious gossip about their off-the-field activities. The wife of an All-Ireland winning captain in the 1990s was sitting at home one evening when she got a call from a woman who purported to be her 'close friend'. The woman told the player's wife that her husband was at that moment in the company of another woman with whom he was supposed to be having a clandestine affair, and proceeded to describe in great detail what 'his mistress' looked like and told her where they would be spending the night. The player's wife was too shocked to speak. She hung up and turned to her husband, who was actually sitting beside her on the couch watching television.

Nicky Brennan is concerned about the increased pressures on players and managers.

'The media spotlight has changed dramatically. There is certainly a fair bit of negativity in the media coverage. What particularly annoys me is what I consider the blight of radio phone-ins. It creates a much more difficult environment for players and managers to operate in. You have to remember these players are amateurs, but often people under the cloak of anonymity ring in and often make very personalised comments about them. We can all have a view on a pundit's comments on TV, but at least they're putting their name to their comments. I don't have any time, though, for radio stations that give credence to comments from callers who have not the guts to put their names to their opinions. And, of course, on the Internet you can say absolutely anything and sometimes these comments can be very destructive.'

Nicky English sees the new media attention as a mixed blessing.

'I rejoice in the high media profile that hurling and the GAA enjoy now. I see the benefits of it all the time. It helped me get a very good job. It opens doors for players in their careers. What they do when they get in the door is a different matter. When I joined AIB and started in investment banking, nobody in that world was interested in hurling. Some of them would have seen it as backward. Now a good many of them have a real interest in it. Hurling has become sexy and the media has to take some of the credit for it. When I started playing, the only live matches that were on television were the All-Ireland semi-finals and finals, and live coverage of games has brought a new audience. When I was playing, there were relatively few journalists covering the games, but because of local radio stations and the tabloid newspapers and more local papers when I managed the Tipp team, I entered the era of having multiple microphones stuck in your face. Competition between the media is intense now and that pushes out the boundaries of what is acceptable. One example is that people are allowed to get a lot off their chests and often make very harsh and often very ill-informed comments about players and managers. There is no question that all this extra media puts more scrutiny on players and managers, and this brings a lot of extra pressure. That takes its toll on people. I don't think it's going to get any better. In fact, I'm pretty sure it's going to get worse.'

English famously said after missing a series of chances in the Munster final in 1991: 'If I had ducks, they'd drown.' He has no problem with criticism per se, but feels there ought to be limits.

'I had many bad days as a player myself and I made a lot of mistakes. A player knows when he has made a mistake and doesn't need a pundit to tell him. As a pundit now, I understand that. I do think we should draw a line, that a player should only have his performances discussed. His private life should be out of bounds. I personally try and make constructive criticism, and I don't like it when people go over the top or when criticism is too personalised.'

English has more reasons than most to be circumspect about the role of the media. In 1993, a magazine alleged that he had been involved in a relationship with the former Miss Ireland Olivia Treacy.

THE GAA

'I had never met Olivia Treacy. In fact, after the case was eventually settled I saw her walking up to me, but she walked right on by because she didn't know me from Adam. I knew the day before that the story was going to break in a major way. I was away with the Tipperary team for a match against Down, and I rang my wife, Anne, to warn her. She laughed at the idea because it was so ridiculous, but when she actually read the story the next day she found it extremely upsetting, as did her parents. It's a very surreal experience opening a magazine and reading a totally fabricated story about your private life, especially when you know that the people closest to you will be hurt in the process. People believe what they read in the newspapers. I had to go into work the next day not knowing how many people had read it. You don't know whether to comment on it or not. I didn't say anything to the Tipperary players at first, and for a while nobody said anything to me about it, until one of them eventually asked me straight out if the story was true or not. I went through the difficult process of going to the High Court to have the story exposed as a lie, but you do feel aggrieved that you have to go to the High Court to get your good name back when you have done nothing wrong. I did get money, but it's not about the money, and anyway, money does not compensate you for the pain and trauma that is caused.'

D.J. Carey, too, has received many plaudits in the media, but his private life has also been the subject of tabloid speculation.

'If you have young children, you really don't want people talking about the state of your marriage in the newspapers. I am in the public eye, but it is not fair that my kids should be.'

UNDER PRESSURE

Fans, too, have become increasingly belligerent. In March 2009, Gerald McCarthy stepped down as Cork manager after receiving death threats from disgruntled supporters. In his second incarnation as Tipperary manager, Babs Keating experienced the pressures on managers today at first hand.

'The main hardship was the constant phone calls and text messages in the middle of the night. I gave the name of one of the main people involved to the guards and they said they would take it from there. The calls and texts were from so-called fans – friends of the players. The most upsetting came at 2.28 a.m. from a guy high on drugs or drink. It was horrible, horrible stuff. I was staying with my daughter that night and one of her little girls was awakened by the call and could sense that it was nasty. That was very distressing for her and it made it even harder for me to see her crying because of that. It was pure intimidation. I gave the guards the caller's name. I knew the house he lived in. The guards called on him and gave him a warning. Although my phone was off, the calls and texts would come during matches. Typical messages would be: "Do you know what you're doing? You f***ing idiot." And they were just the nice ones! The whole thing left a very bad taste.

'Everyone in Tipperary knows who was behind it. The county board were slicker in Tipperary than many other places because they ran with the flow.

'The players have enough to do with going out and playing, rather than worrying about who is going to be manager. If you look back to the row in Cork in '08 – Gerald McCarthy has forgotten more about hurling than those lads will ever learn. It certainly hurt me intensely when I heard there were 27 players who came out against Gerald. When I was down to see Cork play Tipp that year, there were only seven players I could see performing in the day, so I don't know where the twenty-seven came from. Would Waterford have been any worse in the All-Ireland final in '08 if Justin had still been in charge?

'The other thing that drove me from Tipperary was the dirt and sh*t some of the media wrote about me. These journalists were driven by the players who they were friendly with. One of the crazy stories that appeared in a paper was that there wasn't room on the team bus to Croke Park for the Wexford match for all the players because my family and I were taking up too many places. In actual fact, owing to a family wedding, I wasn't even on the bus myself – not to mind any of my family.'

THE GAA

MONEY, MONEY, MONEY

Mick O'Dwyer claims: 'When I played we got a piece of orange at half-time, and if you were very quick you might get two.' Those days are long gone.

As manager of Roscommon in 1993, Dermot Earley saw a more mercenary attitude from some players.

'Just before the Connacht final in 1993, our county secretary, Paddy Francis Dwyer, God rest his soul, had purchased a new set of jerseys for the team. The first two jerseys he took out had no numbers on them. For a moment, there was panic. What would we do without numbered jerseys? Then we discovered the unnumbered jerseys were just spares. Things got back to normal. Shortly afterwards, I noticed that one of the players was trying to sneak an unnumbered jersey into his kit bag and that another player was trying to act as a screen for him. I found myself in a dilemma: should I intervene and risk the players going out to play a Connacht final in a state of disharmony or do nothing? I opted for the latter. The loss of two jerseys was insignificant in itself, but looking back now, it speaks volumes about the players' focus and commitment less than half an hour before playing in a Connacht final.'

Hell is a lesson learned too late. Although amateurism in rugby apparently ended abruptly, the reality was that the cracks had been there for years and widened every season. The big question that will inevitably threaten the GAA's core philosophy is, "Can the amateur ethos be sustained?" Gaelic games remain the last bastions of amateurism among the major sports in Ireland. It does not take a prophet to appreciate that the GAA's unique position will come under serious attack in the coming years.

As major sponsorship deals continue to fill the GAA's coffers, the question of pay-for-play will inevitably present itself with ever increasing urgency. A defining moment in the history of the GAA occurred in 2000. For years, there had been rumblings about moves to professionalism in Gaelic games. Then it seemed that the genie was out of the bottle with the groundbreaking announcement that the Gaelic Players Association had secured a major sponsorship deal with the Marlborough Group for ten prominent players. Is this a seismic shift and the first step towards pay-for-play? Or is it, as its critics have claimed, an elitist deal that will only benefit a privileged few and do nothing for the impoverished many?

Rumours continue to abound about under-the-counter payments to managers. Babs Keating readily admits he was once offered big money to train a county team.

'One August evening in '95, I was out cutting the grass when a car pulled up outside my gate. A man got out and started to chat to me, making small talk. All of a sudden, he said: "I want you to train Laois."

'"What do you mean?"

'"Look, I will give you fifty thousand pounds over three years to do it or fifteen thousand a year."

'I naturally thought about it. I accepted the job after meeting the county chairman and key officials. Only for an internal row involving one of our star players, Declan Conroy [who withdrew from the team because of a dispute he had with the county board], we would have made significant breakthrough. As it was, Offaly only beat us by a point when we could have qualified for an All-Ireland quarter-final.

'Naturally, I never saw the money. Much later, I met my "benefactor" again. He asked: "What do you need?"

'My reply was: "F*** off."'

GONE TOO SOON

ON THE 125TH ANNIVERSARY OF THE GAA, I WANTED TO TRY TO pick one player who best encapsulated what the essence of the Association is. I was spoiled for choice, but in the end the decision was very clear for me. I felt it could only be the late Lulu Carroll, who died so prematurely on 26 August 2007 at the tender age of 35. With this in mind, I sought the help of the person who knew her best as a player, her teammate and great friend Sue Ramsbottom.

'It was her persistence and nagging of our teacher, Mr Sayers, that led the way for girls to play on a boys' national school team. Lulu got a great kick out of saving penalties on the boys and would taunt them with: "Ah, you couldn't score a goal on a girl." Lulu dreamed of playing in Croke Park on All-Ireland final day – which she did in 1988 against Kerry.

'Lulu played in the forwards, midfields, backs and goals. Many people have done this before and many will do this in the future, but the difference is that Lulu was brilliant in all these positions, with All-Stars to prove it. We had a wonderful time together on that journey to get an All-Ireland medal. Girls came and went, but Lulu's steely determination, focus and energy made sure her dream was realised.

THE GAA

'The year 1996 was a great year for Lulu as the sports commentators remarked that she was "the Liam McHale of ladies' football, with her long, tanned legs". It was also on the day of the final that Lulu got that marvellous equalising goal for Laois in the last seconds, so we could have another bite at the cherry.

'It was in 2001 that the Laois Ladies won that famous All-Ireland. Not many people remember that Lulu got Player of the Match in the 2001 Leinster final. This was the hardest game Laois faced and played en route to the All-Ireland in 2001. While all her teammates lay down, Lulu rose above everybody else that day and ensured the dream was kept alive. Lulu was a real hero, and if it weren't for her, there would be no All-Ireland medal in Laois.

'Lulu was a proud Timahoe and Laois woman and wore her jerseys with pride. When she finished playing for Timahoe, she enjoyed coaching and passing on her skills and knowledge to the new kids on the block. She had eight county medals to her credit. I know the last county medal she won the year she died meant so much to her. The Timahoe club owes a great deal of gratitude to Lulu as a player and a manager, helping it to the dizzy heights of reaching a club All-Ireland in 2000.

'Lulu was the epicentre and the heart and soul of every team she played on. We will all play again some day with Lulu in the great pitch called heaven. The best of things come in ones – one great friend, one Croke Park, one All-Ireland medal and one Lulu.'

Although I never had the good fortune to meet her, I was shocked to hear of Lulu's untimely death. It seemed that a light was extinguished when she passed on. The gap in the life of her husband Ozzie and her family is immeasurable. Few gave so much so often. If we want to see the true spirit of the GAA, her career captured its power, magic and heroism.